HEARTLAND
Serial Killers

HEARTLAND
Serial Killers

Belle Gunness,

Johann Hoch, and

Murder for Profit

in Gaslight Era

Chicago

Richard C. Lindberg

NORTHERN ILLINOIS UNIVERSITY PRESS / *DeKalb*

© 2011 by Northern Illinois University Press

Published by the Northern Illinois University Press, DeKalb, Illinois   60115

Manufactured in the United States using postconsumer-recycled, acid-free paper.

Design by Julia Fauci

Library of Congress Cataloging-in-Publication Data

Lindberg, Richard, 1953–

Heartland serial killers : Belle Gunness, Johann Hoch, and murder for profit in gaslight era Chicago / Richard C. Lindberg.

   p.   cm.

Summary: "The chilling true story of two turn-of-the-century serial killers, Belle Gunness and Johann Hoch"—Provided by publisher.

Includes bibliographical references and index.

ISBN 978-0-87580-436-1 (hardback)

1. Hoch, Johann, d.1906. 2. Serial murderers—Illinois—Chicago Metropolitan Area—Biography. 3. Gunness, Belle, 1859–1908. 4. Serial murderers—Indiana—La Porte—Biography. 5. Serial murder investigation—United States. 6. Murder—United States. I. Title.

HV6248.H4618L56 2011

364.152'32092277311—dc22

[B]   2010051206

For Dr. Bernard Brommel, Professor Emeritus

Northeastern Illinois University

---

my mentor and champion these many years.

"Every man expresses astonishment that I was able to win and marry some fifty-odd wives. Now that is just as easy for me as it is for a life insurance solicitor to sell fifty policies. He knows his business and so do I. However as far as I know, I am the only man who really knows the business of making love scientifically."

—Johann Hoch quoted in
"How I Married 50 Wives—and What Became of Them,"
American Magazine—Supplement to the *Chicago Sunday American,*
July 23, 1905

Contents

HEARTLAND
Serial Killers

Introduction

Serial killers are not a unique manifestation of our troubling, modern times. Examples of men and women who kill for profit, lust, or the sport of it dot the pages of world history; however, the phrase itself only dates back to the 1970s, when former FBI Special Agent Robert K. Ressler, a criminal profiler in the Behavioral Science Unit, categorized the repetitive killing pattern of certain violent offenders based upon the popular movie theater "serializations" he remembered from his youth and British law enforcement's common designation of "crimes committed in *series*."[1]

The compulsive killers whose names are most familiar to us today—Albert DeSalvo (the alleged Boston Strangler), the Zodiac Killer, Ted Bundy, Gary Ridgway (the Green River Killer), John Wayne Gacy, Jr., Henry Lee Lucas, Ottis Toole, Dean Arnold Corll, Richard Ramirez, Juan Corona, Jeffrey Dahmer, Dennis Rader (the BTK killer), and Eileen Wuornos—committed their crimes after 1960, suggesting that mass communications and an increasingly sophisticated police investigative technique account for a higher percentage of detection and apprehension of these individuals than a hundred years ago. Doubtless there was a criminal class akin to the modern serial killer throughout antiquity and in the Middle Ages, but the names and the details of their atrocious crimes are permanently lost.

The crimes of the fifteenth-century child murderer Gilles de Rais (1404–1440) stirred great public outrage, and the trial and execution of this terrifying figure inspired the original telling of "Bluebeard," the title character in *"La Barbe bleue,"* one of a collection of fairy tales included in *Les Contes de ma Mère l'Oie (Tales of Mother Goose)* by the French writer Charles Perrault and set down from old oral folk traditions. The book was first published in 1697 and gained popularity throughout Europe.[2] In the story, Bluebeard murdered six wives and hid them away in a secret chamber after each had disobeyed his command not to enter the forbidden, locked room. Bluebeard was himself slain before he could do away with the seventh wife.

The Bluebeard legend transcends generations—the familiar character was re-introduced time and time again in scores of theatrical productions, books, and movie adaptations down to the modern day. The Bluebeard killer, however, is distinguished from the ritualistic murderers whose deeds are characterized by blood lust, sexual deviance, mutilation, and other assorted grotesquerie. The Bluebeard who murders for greed and personal profit is both a serial killer and a comfort killer. A comfort killer's motivation is material gain, the desire for conspicuous consumption, and the attainment of a comfortable lifestyle. The victims are most often husbands, wives, and acquaintances who have been drawn into a lethal trap and done away with for their insurance money, personal assets, property, or jewels. Poison, most notably arsenic, is the preferred weapon of choice for the female comfort killer, who is also known as the black widow. Resourceful, and often more successful than her male counterpart, the female serial killer is active for eight years—sometimes longer—before she is detected by law enforcement or the murder spree is otherwise stopped.

Lydia Sherman (1824–1878) was a prolific Gaslight Era serial killer devoid of conscience. The term Gaslight Era, so named because street lamps were lit by gas jets, refers to the late Victorian Era, from the 1870s through the early 1900s. Sherman, an illiterate from Burlington, Vermont, killed her husband, Edward Struck, an unemployed former Yorkville, New York, police officer, with rat poison after twenty uneventful years of marriage because she could no longer cope with his despondency and depression following his unexpected discharge from the police department. Encouraged to commit her husband's murder by a male acquaintance, she purchased arsenic from a drugstore counter without any questions asked. Then she systematically disposed of all six of her children—three girls and three boys over a twelve-month period. Sherman later explained that she could not afford to provide for them without a husband, so she had decided to take their lives in the same gruesome manner that she had taken Edward's life.[3]

Then this thin-faced, rather gaunt-looking woman proceeded to murder two elderly widowers she had wedded. She also disposed of their children. Arrested in 1871 and sentenced to life in prison, Sherman died in the State Prison at Weathersfield, Connecticut, in May 1878 of natural causes—a consideration she never extended to her victims.

In the prairie land of Kansas between Fort Scott and Independence in the 1870s, America's first family of serial killers waylaid a dozen—maybe more—men heading west along the Osage Trail to their death through the allure of the fetching female psychopath Kate Bender, whose German immigrant father, John Bender, Sr., owned a roadside inn and grocery store ten miles west of Galesburg in Labette County. Kate's beauty and her mysterious reputation as a spiritual medium, not the grocery items and other provisions offered for sale, were a powerful lure, but murder for profit was the family business they all shared equally, and the young woman seemed to derive satisfaction from the act of killing.

The routine never varied, and the scheme of the family was an ingenious one. The prairie house was admirably and purposely arranged for robbery and murder. The parlor of the house would be divided by a cloth partition strung from end to end. The unsuspecting victim would be seated with his back to the curtain, expecting to be served a light supper or a glass of lager. Instead, Kate's brother John or her father, "Old Man" Bender, would emerge from behind the curtain and bludgeon the unsuspecting victim over the head.

Next, the unconscious man's throat was cut, and the body was dropped through a trapdoor into the cellar. At nightfall, the remains would be dragged out into the field by the men and buried in a shallow grave. To avoid suspicion, the Bender clan was careful not to prey on the local residents. They were only interested in itinerant wanderers carrying cash and valuables. But they slipped up after Dr. William H. York went missing in 1878. The victim's brother, Colonel Alexander M. York, a Kansas state senator, traced William as far as the Bender store. He made discreet inquiries and spoke with the eldest Bender for a long time and decided that the family was suspicious. Discovery came on May 4, 1878, when York and a party of investigators returned only to find the store cleaned out and the Benders gone. Eleven bodies were unearthed on the property, including the body of William York. The Bender clan had seemingly vanished into thin air and remained officially missing.

Around the time of the Belle Gunness investigation in 1908, George Evans Downer, an "old settler" living west of Chicago whose grandfather Pierce Downer lent the family name to the present-day bedroom suburb of Downer's Grove, made a startling deathbed confession. Shortly after the Benders fled their abode, he said he had joined up with a vigilante party of five men including a Deputy U.S. Marshal and a former associate of the legendary gunfighter and frontier sheriff "Wild Bill" Hickok. Together they hunted down the family near Cherryvale and administered old-fashioned frontier justice. According to the old man's recollections, Kate was shot through the forehead and buried with her father and brother in an unmarked, shallow grave. The tale was related in the *Chicago Tribune* on July 12, 1908, in which Downer received congratulations from well-wishers who sent in letters to the editor, but, lacking independent verification, it was quickly forgotten.[4] The legend of the wild-eyed but beautiful murderess Kate Bender escaping her pursuers spread across the country and a legend took root.

In the early years of the twentieth century, an epidemic of poisoners and comfort killers confounded law enforcement in Chicago, although none were quite as bloody and violent as the Bender clan. Cook County Coroner Peter M. Hoffman expressed the solemn belief that "many persons annually murdered are killed by poison and the murderers are never brought to justice."[5] Pathology as a science of modern criminal detection was in its infancy. Attending physicians often gave the excuse that they had been "deceived and misled" in cases of unnatural death, thereby hinting at the presence of poison as the leading cause. This was Hoffman's shocking conclusion after seventeen years of careful observation and monitoring of suspected homicide cases filtering through his office.

Hoffman was a professional politician; he had no actual medical training, and the coroner's office, as was so often the case in nearly every public agency in the Windy City at that time, was a trough of corruption run by incompetent spoilsmen there by the grace of the elected mayor and the whims of the party that happened to be in power. But in this instance, Hoffman was on to something.

Beginning in 1895, when the evil doings of Herman Webster Mudgett, aka "H.H. Holmes," Chicago's "Monster of 63rd Street," were first exposed, the city was forced to contend with a cast of killers experimenting with test tube poisons used on their targeted victims. Holmes's oddly constructed "castle," with its many trapdoors, secret vaults, deadfalls, and hidden passageways was the final destination for twenty-seven visitors to the 1893 World's Fair who sought affordable lodging and comfortable accommodations not far from the attractions of the Midway.

The *Chicago Tribune* commented: "The instinct of the remorseless brute, constantly nourished and ruthlessly obeyed, has won for Holmes the first place in the criminal history of the century."[6] Every state and large city could claim at least one such character fitting that profile.

One intriguing aspect of early serial killers was the level of media coverage each received in the local and national press. Traditional nineteenth-century newspaper coverage was presented to the public in a stilted, conventional "tombstone format," rows of text laid out in vertical columns—minus photographs and illustrations—that listed bare-bones information in bland, stilted prose, lacking modern sensationalism. Nontraditional journalism—that is, the ragged, voyeuristic, and often lurid accounts of crime and criminals—was first popularized in the pages of the *National Police Gazette*, a tabloid newspaper founded in 1845 by journalists Enoch E. Camp and George Wilkes as a means of presenting to adult male audiences titillating accounts of highwaymen and murderers along with sundry popular culture amusements of the day such as circuses, theater, and sporting events. The first true sports page in America actually debuted in the pages of the *National Police Gazette* tabloid.[7]

The *Gazette* was spiced with a blend of cartoons and crisp line drawings depicting crime scenes (if only from the illustrator's fertile imagination) and scantily clad showgirls and prostitutes. It followed that the scandal sheet was considered pornographic by the clergy and the upholders of virtue and decency—society's moral censors. The salacious publication reached its apex of popularity in the late nineteenth century and enjoyed strong circulation in large urban areas, but the reading public consisted mainly of unattached men loafing in saloons, barbershops, bawdy houses, and even in the more refined setting of membership clubs and smoking rooms.

Meanwhile, the mainstream press continued to present international events, news from the financial markets, and political matters above all else. Hard news always trumped the stories of street crime played up in the *Gazette*. But crime in and of itself could not be completely dismissed or ignored, so it was the custom to relegate this material to the interior pages, where crime accounts were presented with the rest of the day's city news. Rural newspapers feeding off of the wire services paid no special attention. (Rural papers rarely sent their own reporters on location to gather the facts independently, although they would often be provided with the original copy of the local paper near which the crime occurred.)

The names of many of the poisoners and serial killers might have simply faded into the abyss of history—as their crimes merited only a few paragraphs of mention in newspapers published well outside the local circulation territory in which they were first reported—if not for a fundamental change in the nature of American journalism wrought by the *National Police Gazette*. Beginning in the mid- to late 1890s, Joseph Pulitzer of New York and William Randolph Hearst, the publishing baron of San Simeon, California, imitated and embraced the fast and loose standards set forth by the *National Police Gazette* and elevated sensational crime coverage and dispatches plumbed from the "lower depths" of society into a new and emerging style of "yellow journalism" replete with lavish illustrations. Pulitzer, publisher of the popular *New York World*, and Hearst, who had many newspaper holdings, rearranged the priorities of what constituted "important news" versus the type of stories they believed the public really wanted to read.

At Hearst's flagship papers in New York and San Francisco, what is known in the business as hard news played second fiddle to sleazy, exploitive stories of violent street crime, suicides, society scandal, murder, embezzlement, fraud, and daring nocturnal burglaries. The change was slower to occur in Chicago. The city, dominated by reputable, gray, conservative Republican journals like the *Chicago Tribune* and *Chicago Inter-Ocean,* presented the news in characteristic tombstone format until the arrival of the Hearst team who inaugurated "yellow journalism" with the publication of the first issue of the *Chicago American* in 1900. Once established, the *American,* laced with purple prose, the liberal use of action verbs, and a tight writing style, offered up scintillating fare unlike anything that had ever gone before. With new technology available to Hearst, photographs could now be easily reproduced in the paper—not just ordinary landscape and portrait photos of athletes, statesmen, buildings, and battleships, but elaborate portraits of killers, crime scenes, victims, police, and corrupt politicians framed by screaming 48-point headlines in bloodred type.

The *American* missed out on the opportunity to sensationalize H.H. Holmes by six years. By 1900, he was a name from the past, and the *American* had to be content, for the short term at least, to play up New York society murders, the usual rap sheet of bank robbers, "bucket shop" (stock) swindlers, and heat-of-the-moment passion killers whose names were culled from the police blotter.

In December 1904, the crimes of Johann Hoch (pronounced Hock), a bold new "Bluebeard comfort killer" and serial bigamist believed responsible for at least ten murders and twenty more abandoned and embezzled wives across the U.S., came to the attention of the *American.* The story was fantastic and hardly required embellishments from the press: Hoch was a fascinating rogue with the gentlemanly flair of a Parisian roué. Soft, delicate, and possessing subtle wit and perfect manners, he swindled and scorned numerous middle-aged widows and spinsters during a twenty-year marital odyssey through the central United States, New York, and California. The *American* believed Hoch to be an apprentice of H.H. Holmes, and its reporters pushed their way into an ongoing police investigation to establish linkage—if only for the purpose of stimulating reader interest and boosting newsstand sales of the paper.

Sixty-three miles southeast of Chicago in LaPorte, a small city tucked into the fertile farmland of northwest Indiana, a matronly, rather unpleasant looking Norwegian immigrant woman named Belle Gunness was marrying and murdering Midwestern bachelors, dispensing with the artificial romantic charm in favor of a more direct approach: an appeal to economic necessity. She lured them to her domain, often from long distances, through matrimonial solicitations placed in the Scandinavian newspapers serving the Upper Midwest and Great Plains regions. Belle promised a safe and secure home and the prospect of marriage to a "good and kind" lady who would always look after her prospective suitor.

Belle Gunness fits the common profile of the nesting black widow that does her killing from a fixed location. Hoch was primarily based in Chicago, but he traveled the rails in search of new victims. At one point during his peripatetic career, his journeys took him into northwest Indiana, where he was operating within a scant twenty miles of the Gunness murder farm.

Times were hard. Middle-aged and elderly people without a family to look after them or means of support faced the daunting prospect of poverty in old age if they had not saved enough money to see themselves through until the end. Without the modern safety net of pensions and personal investment plans (working people in those days rarely played the stock market, and their assets were usually locked away in passbook savings accounts—or hidden inside a mattress), the last chance to maintain a comfortable lifestyle in old age was to "marry-up."

The hope was to connect with a man or woman of means, thus accounting for the widespread popularity of storefront matchmaking agencies and the daily listings of marital solicitations published in the classified sections of the newspapers. The foreign language print media enabled the schemes of Gunness and Hoch, but it was Hearst's *American* that influenced, and at times dictated, the tempo of law enforcement as big city and small town police sought to unravel the complex threads of two dynamic and unusual cases.

In an age of social upheaval and tremendous mobility that uprooted and transplanted immigrant populations from the old world to the new, Hoch and Gunness perfectly understood their victims' fears and apprehensions about living alone in this bewildering new social order. They ruthlessly exploited these concerns by choosing people of their own ethnicity—modestly successful working class individuals from the cities and farms who had shared the hardships of assimilation. German immigrant women were preferred by Hoch, and Norwegian men were targeted by Gunness. It was the custom in the nineteenth and early twentieth centuries to court and marry only within one's nationality.

More than a hundred years later, Johann Hoch, for all of his pretentious notions of savoir faire and a self-styled reputation as a sly but charming continental seducer of women, is a completely forgotten figure. However curious and ironic, the coarse and barbaric Belle Gunness, on the other hand, has been transformed into a folkloric legend of the Great Lakes region, and historians and psychologists must ponder the reasons why.

She was a serial killer without peer—smarter and more cunning than both her male counterparts of her time and the present day. The final tally of her victims exceeds that of John Wayne Gacy, but she is also a historical crime figure who has inspired pundits, humorists, and the composers of poetic verse and lyrics to weave her name into the lexicon of American popular culture in the same fashion as Lizzie Borden, the Fall River, Massachusetts, murderess.

To relate the story of Belle Gunness and the men she victimized to an audience of listeners in a public forum is likely to invite a nervous chuckle and an occasional cynical smile from the women. The unsettling reaction to the Belle Gunness tale suggests the paradigm of the oppressed rising up against the oppressor—a challenge to antiquated perceptions of gender in modern society and the chance to ventilate inwardly directed feelings of hostility by women against historic and "traditional" male-female roles, if only for a fleeting moment in a lecture hall or library community room.

In the decades following her arrival in LaPorte, Indiana, a sleepy little Midwestern hamlet was transformed in remarkable and bizarre ways by this one woman. Through the years, the Gunness story has summoned to LaPorte's main street scores of true crime buffs, authors, researchers, curiosity seekers, and documentary filmmakers from around the world. An episode of the Investigation Discovery cable television program *Deadly Women* encapsulated the essential facts of the Gunness story. And, more recently, a Hollywood motion picture company went into development with a highly fictionalized cinematic portrayal of a story that a percentage of LaPorte townspeople wish the world would forget.

The sensational coverage of these criminals during the time in which they lived was an early antecedent of what we have increasingly come to expect not only from the *National Enquirer*, *News of the World*, the *Star*, and the *Globe*, but also in the mainstream media of our own frenzied supermarket tabloid world—a world we have come to know all too well today.

Chapter One

The new year was barely three weeks old when Inspector George Shippy of the Chicago Police detective division announced that he was closing in on the trail of Johann Hoch, the nomadic serial bigamist, archfiend, and lady killer. "He is," in the purple prose of the *Chicago American*, "a modern bluebeard; a Svengali whose mysterious, unnamable powers reduced his middle-aged female victims to quivering compliance."

Who was this Hoch anyway? "A hypnotist of brain and nerve, that's all," Shippy dismissively informed Evelyn Campbell, the *American* reporter personally dispatched to the East Chicago Avenue station by William Randolph Hearst to unearth the facts (with the implied understanding that she was to embellish or invent them if necessary) and give the public what they craved most with their morning coffee and newspaper: blood and betrayal.[1] To add the ingredient of raw sensationalism, an editor would often scribble a note to the re-write man who had received the essential facts of the story from the street reporter. Through the 1940s and into the 1950s, street reporters typically did not write their own stories but phoned them in to the copy desk. If the essential facts of the story were bland, the editor would advise the re-write man in a scribbled note to "hype this up!" The aim, of course, was to hook the reading public—and thereby boost newspaper sales—with sensational accounts featuring sex, scandal, crime, corruption, adultery, and murder.

Evelyn Campbell was the nom de plume of Nana B. Springer, the paper's chief "sob sister" who lent a desired feminine angle to police reporting with sad but true human interest tales of abandoned mothers, lost children, and murdering gigolos. Campbell stood shoulder to shoulder with veteran plainclothes detectives scanning and reading aloud recent telegraph dispatches at morning roll call at the police station. Some of those dispatches provided a description of Hoch, a squat, balding German immigrant standing 5 feet 5 inches tall with soft blue eyes, a double chin, chestnut brown mustache, and penetrating stare. Campbell took copious notes as Shippy briefed his men. The veteran police inspector attached the highest priority to the capture of Hoch, and during the first snowstorm of 1905, he set out to follow the path of the elusive killer.

But just where was this man Hoch whom the papers were comparing to a sorcerer? No one could say with any degree of certainty. The last report had him heading east, and Shippy, delayed by blizzard conditions, caught an overnight train from the LaSalle Street station in Chicago; he was chasing down a rumor in the belief that he was just one train stop in back of the fugitive Hoch.

Andrew "Long Green" Lawrence, the *American*'s managing editor, saw in the Hoch story a chance to divert attention from a recent, messy scandal that had landed him and other members of the *American*'s editorial staff in the county jail, a public embarrassment that had dangerously compromised the standing of Hearst's flagship Chicago paper. The *American*, a late entrant in the brutally competitive world of Chicago journalism, was launched on the Fourth of July in the old Steuben County Wine Company building on Madison Street and incorporated on September 19, 1900. Charles Edward Russell, an avowed socialist and the winner of the 1928 Pulitzer Prize for a biography of Theodore Thomas, was the first publisher until Lawrence assumed his regular duties in 1903.

"Long Green" was a first-rate scoundrel but a scoundrel with a keen eye for news. He performed standard editorial responsibilities such as managing circulation, hiring the typographers, calculating advertising revenues, paying utilities, and overseeing business operations. His less traditional duties included cultivating street informants and wining and dining City Hall chieftains, police captains, and tough union bosses, whose willingness to cooperate with the paper provided Lawrence the grist he needed to produce the kind of sensational reports that the paper relied upon. Arthur James Pegler, a formidable news-getter and father of the nationally syndicated columnist Westbrook Pegler, was one of the original staff reporters. Hearst was particularly adept at attracting top-notch reporters like Pegler by elevating starting editorial salaries from $30 to $50 a week.

Launched by "concerned" Democrats to provide the party with a voice in the conservative Midwest in order to boost the chances of four-time presidential candidate and political idealist William Jennings

Bryan (1860–1931), the *American* aligned its interests with Mayor
Carter Harrison II (1860–1953). Harrison, a five-term mayor, presided
over a wide-open city in which segregated vice districts flourished with
minimal police interference on the South and West Sides and illegal
gambling proliferated in residential neighborhoods and the downtown
business district within the shadow of city hall. In 1904 Harrison was
mentioned as a possible vice-presidential candidate, but inter-party
rivalries doomed his chances. The paper gored the Republicans, mo-
nopolies (called trusts), and the judiciary while denouncing animal
vivisection with its rival newspapers with equal impunity.[2] The paper,
to its credit, wove higher principles into the standard fare of crime and
sex. Hearst was an anti-vivisectionist, fiercely opposed to "sadistic dog
torturers," as he labeled scientists conducting bio-medical research on
animals. His editors championed women's rights and boosted labor
unions in their struggles with trusts and corporations. Informants on
the coroner's payroll and others from city and county agencies kept
Lawrence and his team apprised of the goings-on in high places. When
unsubstantiated rumors were printed, libel suits were inevitable and
had to be defended.

In November 1901, Russell and Lawrence directed their editorial
vitriol against Judge Elbridge Hanecy, a candidate for mayor opposing
Mayor Carter Harrison II. Printed accusations that Hanecy was influenced to render a favorable decision for the People's Gas, Light & Coke
Company in an antitrust case resulted in temporary incarceration for
two newspaper staff members but not the editor, Lawrence, who had cut
a deal with Hearst to throw editorial support behind Harrison. From
California, Hearst issued a terse statement saying he knew nothing
about the editorials until they were published, and he retained former
Illinois Governor John Peter Altgeld (1847–1902), then in partnership
with famed criminal defense attorney and social reformer Clarence
Darrow (1857–1938), to represent the paper.

Altgeld and Darrow were relentless in their defense of the Hearst interests, and the publisher spared no expense in the matter. The former
governor, a stoop-shouldered, bitter, and disappointed old cynic, had
left office in 1896 after voters turned down his bid for re-election. After
four years of jousting with the entrenched powers and unable to push
through his agenda, Altgeld bore the body scars of the failed idealist. He
had entered private practice, took on this First Amendment issue with
Darrow, and essentially agreed with the prosecution that the standards
of journalistic decency had been breached. Nevertheless, Altgeld said:
"The publication of these articles was a foolish proceeding I will admit.

[But] . . . if we are to choose between a licentious press, if you will, using its power recklessly and viciously, and a muzzled press, subject to censorship and with writers subject to the orders of governmental agents, there is not a man who understands the theory of American institutions but who would unhesitatingly choose the former."[3]

Less than a month later, Judge Edward Dunne, a future Chicago mayor and Illinois governor who enjoyed the blessings and unflagging support of Hearst and the *American* throughout his career in public life, conveniently set aside the Hanecy ruling, freeing Lawrence and reporter H.S. Canfield from their holding cells in the interest of preserving the sanctity of a free and unfettered press. But Dunne curtly added: "Both of the articles, if not libelous were of such a character as to have a clear tendency to intimidate, coerce, frighten and terrorize the Judge." He continued, saying that "to slander or speak disparagingly of a judge was contempt of court under the common law—but not under the law of Illinois."[4]

Chastened, but undeterred in his mission to peddle scandal, sensation, and licentiousness, and call attention to police incompetence in order to ratchet up circulation, Lawrence shifted the focus ever so slightly away from the drama of city hall and the gang of prickly, litigious politicians and judges likely to trouble him in the future with similar lawsuits and directed his reporters toward the crime beat. Minute by minute coverage of fraud, deceit, con games, arson, assault, blackmail, and murder in a half-dozen daily editions was extensive and unrelenting. The paper was a throwback to the *National Police Gazette* and the more sordid gossip sheets circulating in the red light districts of the city.

The very suggestion of "MURDER!," the odd and ghoulish snippets of daily life from across the city and around the globe, and morbid incidents from foreign wars and great natural disasters as a stand-alone front page headline blazing across the *American* in red, 36-point type was a tantalizing invitation to the mildly curious to peek below the fold. This writing satisfied the latent curiosity of the reader on his or her way to the train station for the early evening ride home.

"Woman Sells Finger for $500! Surgeon Crafts it on Purchaser!"

"Queer New Facts about Wasps"

"Wild Bull Fights Thousands in Panic"

"Jew Slayers Burn City"

"Insane Heiress Kidnapped in Auto"

"Fear of Gallows Drives Woman Insane!"

"Girl Slayer Held as Ripper!"

"Chicago Woman is Tarred and Feathered"

"Scarlet Lies: A Mystery of Chicago"

"Girl Loses Pet Dog after he Sits for Picture"

"The Cruelest Man in Chicago!"[5]

Tabloid journalism in Chicago was christened by Hearst but put into practical use by Lawrence, a newsman often vilified as a scoundrel and blackguard by his fellow journalists. Colonel Robert Rutherford Mc-Cormick, publisher of the staid, conservative *Chicago Tribune,* branded Lawrence a "criminal blackmailer" for alleged schemes to extort advertising dollars from businessmen and wealthy individuals in return for promises to withhold salacious gossip or compromising information overheard in the streets by reporters.

The moniker "Long Green" stemmed from earlier, vicious shakedown attempts dating back to his San Francisco days when Lawrence had edited the *Examiner,* dictated police appointments to the Democratic Mayor James D. Phelan, and swaggered through Union Square with his bodyguard, Wyatt Earp (1848–1929), the famous western gunfighter and law enforcement officer in Arizona, Kansas, and the Dakota Territory.[6] In Chicago, even as Lawrence was hard at work censuring criminal malefactors on the editorial page, he employed a few head-knockers of his own. Moe and Max Annenberg, jackbooted thugs from the Near West Side, were hired on as "newspaper sluggers" in the paper's early days to pummel newsstand dealers and paperboys who refused to sell the *American* and its sister newspaper, the *Chicago Examiner,* from street corners. The newspaper circulation wars fought in the first decade of the twentieth century spawned some of Chicago's most violent and dangerous gunmen who emerged during World War I and the era of Prohibition.

For Long Green, the crime game paid rich dividends. Advertising revenues swelled, and the coercive methods of the Annenberg brothers guaranteed reliable and occasionally spectacular jumps in circulation. All that was left for Lawrence to do was supply the sensational story, and the rest would easily follow. In early January 1905, Lawrence and Moe Koenigsberg, Lawrence's young city editor, hit upon Johann Hoch and made him the only story worth telling.

The *American* established a local precedent in crime reporting by assigning Campbell to shadow Inspector Shippy and the detectives from the East Chicago Avenue Police Station as they hunted down fresh leads in the growing belief that "a more atrocious clique of professional marrying men is now known to exist in Chicago . . . and Hoch is known to be one of its chief votaries."[7] Andy Lawrence turned the investigation into a day-in, day-out cause celebre that trumped coverage of international news events, crises in financial markets, and the building of the Panama Canal. This kind of reporting was an eye-opener, and the memory of the *Times* and *Evening Post*, two earlier newspapers known to play up the notorious aspects of urban living to a lesser degree, paled in comparison.

Evelyn Campbell knew how to enthrall her readers and keep them coming back for more. Her stories were drawn from the streets and liberally spiced with a curious blend of anecdotal violence and sad descriptions of the pathos of slum living. In one such tale, she stirred her readers' sympathies with the sad plight of 14-year-old Lillie Roskosz, "girl thief and child swindler," whose young life was a "torrent of tears and a tissue of falsehoods." Evelyn laid bare the "Mystery [of] the Girl's Thieves Gang," publishing her findings and leading police to the den of female crooks Lillie had fallen in with. Now, for her next crusade, she prepared to match wits with a matrimonial swindler and bring him to justice with the passive help of the Chicago police.[8]

"I have arranged with Inspector Shippy to help in the solving of this problem," Campbell boasted to her readers on January 26, "the greatest criminal puzzle with which the police have had to deal for some time. Yesterday in my investigations, I stumbled upon a clew to this great mystery—a clew that promises to not only lead to the discovery of Hoch's whereabouts, but to the uncovering of enough evidence to convict him." In a flourish of melodramatic overkill not uncommon for the time, she vowed that: "Day after day I shall follow this clew through the labyrinths to which even my inexperienced eyes can see it may lead. What I find out I will tell to you each day, excepting of course any fact the publication of which will impede the development of the investigation."[9]

Between Hearst and his incessant demand for lurid headlines to sell his papers, Lawrence and his need to deflect persistent criticism of his questionable methods, the activities of heinous criminals, and with each new breathless dispatch from Evelyn Campbell, the stage was set to showcase the principal player in the drama—Johann Hoch. The newspaper follies were underway, and a fine sideshow it was.

Stepping back to October 20, 1904, just three months before Hoch was destined to emerge as a page-one criminal celebrity and the focus of Campbell's sleuthing in the yellow press, the bigamist (who was at that time going by his birth name, Jacob Schmidt) was betrothed to Caroline Streicker of 3043 W. Stiles Street, Philadelphia, by the good Reverend Albrecht in a modest civil ceremony in the Quaker City. Caroline, like so many other desperate, malleable women, had answered a newspaper advertisement from a quiet, home-loving German mechanic who declared that he "would like to obtain board with a respectable German widow with no children."[10] After one week of courtship they were married in the presence of Edward Gorman, the best man, who, ironically, happened to be a Philadelphia police detective.

Eleven days later Hoch slipped away from the marital homestead with $1,800 of the widow's nest egg, never to return. Mrs. Streicker-Hoch reported the crime to Captain Donaghy and Detective Edward Ledmer of the Philadelphia Police Department. She fell ill shortly thereafter.

By then Hoch had retreated to his home in Chicago, where he presented himself to Johanna Reichel, one of his former wives living at 458 Milwaukee Avenue on the city's Northwest Side. With an imploring look on his face, he asked the woman if he might be permitted to spend the night. "I am working in the machine shops at Pullman," he lied. In his proposals of marriage to a score of Chicago women who concluded that he was a responsible, hardworking, and marriageable man who might support them in the twilight of their lives, Hoch frequently passed himself off as a well-regarded supervisor of the Pullman Palace Car Company.

The next day he appeared on the doorstep of a rooming house kept by one Katie Bowers, a married woman, at 674 W. 63rd Street in Chicago's South Side Englewood community. "I am a foreman at the Pullman Company presently enjoying a two week vacation," he said, "and would very much like to spend some time here to relax and unwind."[11] Mrs. Bowers studied the appearance of Hoch and concluded that he was all that he seemed—a pleasant, exceptionally well-mannered businessman employed by a respectable firm and doing important things. She agreed to rent him a room for the next ten days—just long enough for Hoch to locate his next victim to marry and murder.

He spent the next few days canvassing the South Side for a suitable rental property, a house preferably, that he might present to a prospective widow as his own dwelling. He found an ideal little cottage at 6430 S. Union Avenue. A sign in the window said it was the property of a Mr. Edwin E. Vail, and it was for rent with inquiries being taken at the Chicago

City Bank, 6225 S. Halsted. Proper introductions were made between Mr. Vail and Hoch, who was informed that the monthly rental would be $21.50, with proper references accepted of course. Hoch declared that he was the plant foreman at Armour & Company meatpackers, and was responsible for 25–30 men employed in the canning department. It was an important job, he said, and his responsibilities were many.

"I am drawing a salary of $125.00 a month, and you can call upon Mr. Armour at any time to verify this!" he said with an indignant air. As further proof, Hoch turned up the palm of his hands to Vail—calloused and worn from years of hard physical labor. This seemed to satisfy the property owner, who did not bother to check his references with Armour & Company or with the landlords at 646 East 63rd Street or 674 East 63rd Street, where Hoch claimed prior residence.

Hoch made a cash down payment covering his rent through January, then furnished the dwelling with tables, chairs, and sofas supplied by the Spiegel House Furnishing Company at 369 State Street. To the Spiegel salesman, H.E. Stringer, Hoch explained that he had been living as a widower at 6430 S. Union for the previous four years and that he was the recorded owner of the building and several surrounding vacant lots. "I am contemplating getting married again," he confided to the salesman as he handed over a $50 bill to seal the agreement. "For one such as me, the comforts of a home cannot be underestimated or denied."

With his rooms richly appointed with the new furniture and the woodstove casting a warm glow, Hoch sat down to pen a "lonely hearts" advertisement for placement in the *Abendpost* (*Evening Post*), a widely circulated German-language evening newspaper published in Chicago from 1889 to 1950.[12] Hoch delivered the ad to the newspaper office and paid the clerk, Mrs. Hedwig Milken, the advertisement cost. It read: "Matrimonial—Widow without children, under the 30s's, German, own home, acquaintance of a lady, object—matrimony. Address: M422 *Abendpost* Respectfully J. Hoch, 6430 Union Avenue, City."

He did not have long to wait for a favorable reply. Marie Schippnik Walcker, a 45-year-old matron divorced after 19 years of marriage, had frugally saved every penny earned from washing and drying other people's laundry until she could afford to buy a little candy store at N. 12 Willow Street, on the corner of Larrabee, on the North Side of the city. She possessed $270.00—the sum of her life savings gathering interest in a passbook account, with an additional $80.00 hidden under the mattress in the back room of the candy store for sudden emergencies.

Intrigued by the letter, and imagining herself about to be safely cared and provided for by a sympathetic man of her own age with common, shared experiences, Marie prevailed upon her sister Bertha Sohn to reply favorably to Mr. J. Hoch. She wrote: "Dear Sir: In answer to your honorable advertisement, I hereby inform you that I am a lady standing alone. I am forty-five years of age. I have a small business, also a few hundred dollars—a little fortune—a few hundred dollars. If you are in earnest I tell you I shall be. I may be spoken or seen at any time during the day. Address No. 12 Willow Street.—Marie Walcker."

Hoch answered the letter and proceeded by streetcar north to Willow Street, where, with hat in hand, and bowing ever so politely to Walcker's business partner, Bertha Knipple, he was ushered into the back sleeping room to meet Mrs. Walcker, a modestly attractive working woman who had suffered the toils of a lifetime of drudgery and unhappiness to achieve this modest station in life. She had sailed to the U.S. from Hamburg on September 12, 1891 in the hope of improving her station in life after a bitter divorce, but no bed of roses awaited her in Chicago.

Romance was incidental between the criminal and his victim for what they were about to conclude; future happiness subordinated to economic survival and the chance at prosperity in the twilight years of life. The deadly fear of reaching old age drove thousands of sentimental widows, divorcees, and aging spinsters from across the country into the clutches of shady "matrimonial agencies"—thinly veiled shell games operated by unscrupulous confidence men who would induce the victim to send a "registration fee" to a blind postal box or in some instances contrive a much more elaborate ruse to lure the woman into the city, where she would be met at the train station by a "handsome young man."

The woman would be escorted to the supposed marriage bureau and asked to put up all her money. Once the vows were exchanged in the presence of a sham "minister," the couple would repair to the man's flat or hotel room until such time when an excited and out-of-breath telegraph messenger would deliver an "urgent dispatch" to the husband, informing him of an important business meeting or some personal emergency requiring his immediate attention. The husband would put on his coat, promise his new bride that he would return before long, then hurry off—never to return.

In a variation of the same corrupt scheme, the conman would compose tender missives of love from imagined suitors with fictitious addresses and send them off via the U.S. mail to the unsuspecting victims once the required fee had been paid.[13] A more sinister trap involved criminal panderers running Chicago's entrenched white slavery racket. Posing as a wealthy Chicago bond broker or commission agent, the pimp would advertise for a bride in rural country towns of Wisconsin, Indiana, Kansas, Iowa, Utah, Missouri, Mississippi, and points west and south, hoping to bring the smitten victim into the city and force her into a white slavery arrangement in the South Side "Levee" segregated vice district.

The widely publicized matrimonial swindles drew the ire of Illinois State Representative William L. Martin, a Republican from the South Side 5th District who introduced a bill to the 40th General Assembly in March 1899 to permanently outlaw the bureaus and "the publishing or advertising of, for, or by men or women for purposes of marriage or courting or other purposes against the good morals of the community."[14] Sadly for many future victims of this painful, but familiar, fraud the bill never came up for a vote. "There are today in the United States no less than 50,000 women who have been married, robbed, and deserted by professional bigamists," estimated Charlotte Smith, president of the Woman's International Rescue League, an early women's advocacy group based on the East Coast and often derided and ridiculed by the national press.[15]

The presumably "safer alternative" for the lovelorn man or woman suspicious of conducting business with a matrimonial bureau was to place a discreet personal inquiry in city and rural newspapers advertising for a "life companion." Mrs. Walcker, who studied the *Abendpost* personals lest she be taken in by a cad, required assurances of Mr. Hoch's good intentions—and proof of the blessings of his prosperity. He said that he was a rich man with a secure $8,000 nest egg in the bank and a nice home on a big lot. Marie asked to look over the property just to be sure. Hoch spun a fantastic tale of tragedy and fortitude. He said he had emigrated from Germany with his four children in 1880, but they had all died. He said his wife had been an invalid for eighteen years before God called her away, and his old and infirm father of eighty-five years would be leaving him a $15,000 inheritance any day now.

"Well, if what you say is true, it is all right," Marie replied as Bertha refilled their coffee cups. She told him of her early life in Breason, West Prussia, and coming to America. They had in common.

"Do you like me?" Hoch asked timidly.

"Why, Mr. Hoch, of course I do."

"Well, you like me and I like you, so we can get married, eh?"

The next afternoon, December 7, 1904, Hoch took Marie out to Union Avenue in Englewood to inspect the home. He escorted his new companion in a rented carriage, a handsome brougham, pointing out all of the local buildings and land parcels he pretended to own. Hoch spoke of his faith in the Almighty, how his father was a man of the cloth, and the supreme wisdom of his blessed mother inspired his earliest devotions. He said he had delivered a series of religious speeches while in New York, but his listeners were either too stupid or too listless to fully comprehend his spiritual message. But now God in all his wisdom—and the bank—had provided the necessary funds for him to fix the place up. And, finally, with the work complete, all that was missing from his life was the companionship of a loving, tender wife to share his good fortune.

Marie Walcker decided at that moment that it must be all true—at last the chance had come to be free from the daily struggles! The sun had burst through the clouds! At this point in her life, practical considerations outweighed silly girlish romantic notions and the rituals of courtship. There would be no need for a long engagement—for by now she was convinced of his sincerity as well as the truthfulness of the riches in his bank account.

Three days later Marie and Johann were married by a justice of the peace in a private ceremony at Bertha Sohn's residence. The bride surrendered $80.00 of her mattress money to Hoch, sold the store for the trifling sum of $75.00, and drew out the $270.00 of laundry money from her account at the Home Savings Bank and gave it to Hoch. Later that joyous day, after everyone had pleasantly settled in to enjoy the afternoon tea, Hoch was furnished with additional details of his new wife's family circumstances.

Marie told him that she had a younger sister—a plain-looking, inconspicuous widow woman who owned a rather modest boardinghouse at 133 Wells Street in the parish of St. Michael's. Marie explained that her sister, Mrs. Amelia Fischer, was a horrible person who had been married to a carpenter named George Fischer for twenty-one years, but after the poor man died in October 1903, she had abandoned nine of her children in Germany and had taken 1,000 Deutschmarks to Chicago along with her eldest daughter. "She is a *raven* mother!" exclaimed the disgusted Marie, invoking an unkind, insulting German phrase for an unnatural kind of woman.

Hoch furrowed his brow. This was certainly an unexpected and odd development. He probably thought, "Well, you should be reconciled to her after all these years. Although she must be an ungrateful mother, I will admit, but I must encourage you to repair these bruised feelings

Marie, by all means." Johann contemplated the sister-in-law's money pile, the risk involved with prying loose her money while still married to Marie, his expenses, and the future possibilities.

That night, after he had retired for the evening, Hoch opened his daybook and calculated the anticipated costs of "separating" from his new wife.

Funeral Expenses

Coffin #45
Shroud $7
Carriages (3) $15
Hearse $7

Total $94
Gravedigger
Hat $5[16]

Chapter Two

Awakened from a dark and disturbing dream in the wee hours of the morning in late April 1908, Anton O. Olsen, who was living in a rented flat on Chicago's South Side, was not a man prone to superstition—but this fearful dream on this night gave him pause. He did not put much stock in ghosts, séances, or portents of evil. Olsen was an engineer at the Munger Laundry Company and a practical thinking man. He had known hard times and had suffered the loss of his beloved wife twelve years earlier. Olsen enjoyed the company of his two grown daughters who lived in the Chicago area. They gave comfort in times of loneliness and travail, and they reminded him of his youngest daughter, Jennie Eugenia—the eight-month-old girl he had given up for adoption after his wife died of typhoid fever on December 31, years ago. Olsen had not seen Jennie in nearly five years as she had gone off to live with Belle, but he was looking forward to a reunion with his long-lost daughter on her eighteenth birthday, which was fast approaching on May 5th. She was nearly a grown woman, and her father could only imagine what she must look like now.

In his haunted theater of the mind, Olsen witnessed a horrifying vision of his youngest daughter lying dead in a shallow, unmarked grave—a grave located on a farm just outside LaPorte, Indiana, belonging to Belle Sorensen Gunness (nee Brynhild Poulsdatter Størset), widow of the late Mads Ditlev Sorensen, a night watchman for the Mandel Brothers Department Store and Anton Olsen's closest friend. Nearly eighteen years earlier, Sorensen had agreed to care for the girl after Olsen's wife passed away and provide for her as his foster daughter.

Olsen could not care for an infant in diapers on his own, not without a woman in the house to help him provide a proper upbringing, but he knew Mads Sorensen to be a good and decent man who had journeyed to America from his birthplace in Drammen, a city located 40 miles from Oslo in Buskered County, Norway.[1] Sorensen gave assurance that his wife, Belle, was the "right kind of mother" who would raise Jennie in a loving home.

Olsen was only vaguely familiar with the character of this woman. But he knew that his old friend Mads was joined in marriage with Belle, an immigrant from Selbu, Norway, when she was only twenty-four years old. The union was solemnized in Chicago in 1883, and the couple began their married life in Austin, then a quiet, 280-acre, tree-lined subdivision west of Chicago bordering the village of Oak Park.[2] John Larsen, a nephew of Belle Sorensen, remembered that she had a "weakness for adopting children, "but was a queer woman and there was estrangement in the family with her for fifteen years. When first she met people she was cordial. Later she would appear indifferent to them."[3]

Belle Sorensen was prone to fits of violent rage followed by a quiet calm, her manner suddenly self-contained. Everyone who knew her was in agreement on this point. "Nellie" Larsen, John's mother and Belle's sister, was a reserved, dignified woman with soft, delicate features and a round face. She remembered that, even as a little girl, Belle caused problems in the family. "When she first came from the old country we noticed there was something strange about her. She seemed to be wild and flighty in her speech. Often she would mutter to herself and when we asked her what she said, she only laughed. My husband disliked her from the start and that also did much to keep us apart."[4]

As Jennie Olsen's mother lay dying, a Lutheran minister drew up the papers of adoption on December 10, 1890, defining the terms of the agreement between the Sorensens and the Olsens. Anton Olsen, imbued with the terrible guilt of a father's failed obligation, wanted it understood that Jennie would legally remain his daughter and that she would eventually reunite with him when he remarried.

Olsen personally knew Mads Sorensen from the Wicker Park Chapter No. 121 of the Independent Order of Mutual Aid, a fraternal lodge associated with the trade union he belonged to that sold life insurance policies to its members.[5] Around the same time, Mads had purchased a small confectionary and notions store at 318 Grand Avenue, near Elizabeth Street, from Charles Christiansen and ran the neighborhood business while Belle looked after children other people did not want or could not care for. The business was heavily insured, and relations between Belle and her husband were becoming strained.

In 1897, after nearly thirteen years of marriage, Sorensen considered leaving his quarrelsome wife for a life of adventure in the Alaskan Skagway as an employee of the Yukon Mining and Trust Company. Gold had been discovered in the Klondike River near Dawson City, Yukon, in August 1896, sparking a stampede of fortune hunters and adventurers from all over the U.S. and Canada to Skagway and Dyea. However, Mads decided it was best not to leave Chicago: his demanding wife refused to allow such an impetuous action. Sorensen was a compliant, easygoing man who bent to his wife's stronger will. This time the unfortunate decision cost him his life.

A year after Mads considered leaving for Alaska, a fire consumed the store. Belle was alone with her children in the store at the time. She led them to the safety of the front sidewalk, rousing the neighborhood by screaming "Fire!" at the top of her lungs. A kerosene lamp had exploded, she told insurance adjustors, but no trace of the lamp or the kerosene could be found. The interior of the store was completely destroyed, but amid the gossip of the Austin neighbors that the fire was an arson job and Belle was responsible, the company paid the premium on the Sorensens' reported loss. After they received the insurance money, the charred and gutted building was sold back to the Christiansens.

It was after the checks were cashed that Belle and Mads moved their family into a musty, spired Victorian home at 620 Alma Street, between Chicago Avenue and Ohio Street in Austin, for the upscale and well-to-do. The couple realized extra income by renting office space on the upper floor to a physician.[6] It was a spacious three-story wood-frame home with a large fenced-in backyard—presumably an ideal setting for young children to play and run around in; however, a neighbor girl who came by to see Jennie described a peculiar air of mystery surrounding the home. She was frightened by the "strange actions" of Mrs. Sorensen, the woman who lived there. "It was a cold, dreary place," the unnamed girl remembered. "It made me shiver to go into it. I always was afraid. It seemed so mysterious. Now I feel like something terrible happened there."[7]

Trouble continued to shadow the Sorensens. A second fire of mysterious origin broke out in the Alma Street house not long after, and the flames spread to adjoining properties. Belle blamed it on a careless neighbor and denied that she lit the spark that caused so much property damage.

In 1900, Mads' health was in decline—a heart ailment was the learned opinion of the doctors, but Mrs. Larsen had her own suspicions about the sudden deterioration of Mr. Sorensen. "I do remember that the children were sitting on the porch and that Sorensen had been complaining of illness. Then she went into the house to prepare supper and later called her husband. She said he refused to eat and went upstairs to lie down on the bed. After a while my sister went upstairs to see how he was and then she told me she found him dying," Larsen said. "Some of the neighbors had said Mrs. Sorensen had given her husband poison and murdered him. And I heard there was talk of exhuming the body, but my husband and I never mixed in the affair and I know little about it. . . ." She added: "It seemed she would do anything for money. I never saw such a money-mad person in my life."[8]

The family doctor had been treating Mads for an enlarged heart, and his diagnosis was accepted despite the contradictory opinion of Dr. Charles E. Jones, who insisted that the patient exhibited all the symptoms of Prussic acid poisoning. Arriving at the Sorensen home after the man's death, Jones was convinced that the death was suspicious. "The appearance of Sorensen's body was very unusual. I could hardly convince myself he was dead. There was a fresh pink color about his cheeks and I was reminded of a patient of mine a short time before who was victim of a trance. This man was apparently dead for many hours but was revived and is alive in Austin today. The pupils in Sorensen's eyes were not contracted as we would suspect in morphine poisoning. If he was poisoned only prussic acid could have produced the effects I saw."[9]

Mads Sorensen passed away on July 30, 1900—just one day before his $2,000 life insurance policy with the Independent Order of the Mutual Aid was scheduled to elapse. A few days earlier Sorensen had notified the lodge that he intended to let his old policy lapse and would cease to make payments. "I remember the circumstances because the widow appealed to me to as a neighbor to help her collect the insurance money," store owner A.B. Christensen of 719 53rd Avenue told police. "She got it without much trouble."[10]

A court order for an autopsy was secured by the deceased's suspicious relatives on August 30th from Judge Marcus A. Kavanaugh of the Superior Court of Cook County. The body was exhumed, but the postmortem was superficial because the intestines were not examined. No one, least of all Belle Sorensen, intended to pay the added cost of a thorough medical inquiry that might shed light on the mystery.

Relatives and neighbors paid their respects, and the dead man was laid to rest at nearby Forest Home Cemetery. Enlargement of the heart was listed as the official cause of death, but such a condition is also a symptom of arsenic poisoning. What was her motive, and where did the poison come from? By the time Chicago police finally launched a second investigation into the suspicious death of Mads Sorensen, the enormously influential Assistant Chief Herman Schuettler, one of the gamest and most highly regarded members of the Chicago Police cadre, recounted some of the tell-tale signs of a potential homicide.[11] "There are many things that point to the woman's murder of her first husband," he said. "She did not call a physician promptly. She did not act like a bereaved woman beyond the first hysterical outburst which probably was nothing but clever acting."[12]

Belle cashed in Mads' $8,000 life insurance policy and kept up appearances in the Austin community for another year. She did not seek out male companionship at this juncture of her life nor did she advertise her availability through matrimonial bureaus and the newspaper personals as she was wont to do just a few years later in LaPorte. Her sole concern, at least superficially, seemed to be the well-being of the children—as they were being singled out for ridicule and torment by cruel and thoughtless schoolmates who taunted Jennie with the vicious accusation that her mama had killed her daddy. "It is known that such taunts were made and what [is] more natural under the circumstances [than] that this woman should wish to remove from the scene of the crime?" Schuettler wondered.[13]

The Sorensen woman was a study in contrast. To some she was an arsonist and poisoner—the Black Widow of the West Side, a plain, corpulent, masculine looking woman possessed by the devil. How could any sane-thinking, hardworking man suffer such an evil, overbearing wife as that? The children of Austin listened to the ugly whispers of their parents and took the gossip with them to the schoolyard to mercilessly torment Belle's youngsters. Their cruelty knew no limits.

But Mrs. Josephine Burkland, an Austin resident and close friend, saw a kinder, gentler side to Belle—or "Bella," because she signed all of her written correspondence that way—than the commonly held image of her as the man-hating, neighborhood battle-axe. "Years ago, when Jennie was burned in the fire at 813 Grand Avenue, Mrs. Sorensen nursed her night and day. She displayed the same affectionate interest in her daughter Myrtle when the child was ill. She always had a pleasant smile for everybody," said Mrs. Burkland.[14] Neighbors recalled a large, gala house reception that Belle held for the teachers and principal of the nearby Julia Ward Howe School at Laurel Avenue and West Superior Street. She received her guests with a warm, engaging smile and pleasant handshake. Everyone admired the elegance of her table and the lavish preparations. All agreed that she was a devoted parent.

Others were not so sure about that. They noted a subtle change in her attitude, especially toward Jennie, once Mads was lowered into the ground and she was now the head of the household. She became increasingly cold and aloof to the child and was often critical and impatient. Meanwhile, Anton Olsen had remarried and signaled his intention to take Jennie to his South Side home to begin family life anew. He was in for a surprise.

"I asked Mrs. Sorensen, as she then had children of her own, to give Jennie up to me," Olsen related. "She said she would but did not like to quite then. A second time, when I asked her to give Jennie up to me, she said she would not. I told her I still had something to say about Jennie but she said she had me beat on that. Another time I spoke with her about the matter and her answer was that if I would I could go into court with it. She was then living in Austin. Soon after that I went out to Austin again to see her, but she had left. I did not know where she had gone. I did not locate her again for about two years."[15]

Belle effected a property swap with Arthur F. Williams, president of the Trade Circular Advertising Company, at 125 Clark Street on the North Side of Chicago. In exchange for the house in Austin, the Sorensen widow acquired the title to Williams's sixty-acre farm just outside the business district of LaPorte, Indiana, on McClung Road. The deal was brokered by M.E. Cole, a real estate agent. Cole and Williams met with the widow frequently. "I remember her quite well," Williams said later. "And she appeared to be sharp and well-versed in business methods."[16]

Sorensen delayed her move to LaPorte. Uppermost in her mind was the need for a man to help her work the land. She was intuitive enough to understand that money—and a strong man to perform the demanding physical labor—were necessary in order for her plans to succeed. The bitter cold of a LaPorte winter and the heat of summer were sure to take their toll. What chance did a woman living with small children have in such a place? Brynhild Sorensen was becoming accustomed to having a man around for the heavy lifting tasks.

With the children at her side, she set off for Janesville, Wisconsin, to begin her husband-hunting expedition. In that small Wisconsin city north of the Illinois state line, Belle attempted to induce Peter Frederickson to sell his home, increase his life insurance, and run away with her to LaPorte. She had placed her first matrimonial advertisement in a local paper and, at first, Frederickson responded with enthusiasm.

His home, Belle discovered, was free of encumbrances and worth $1,500. "So you must come with me to Indiana where it is much nicer and there is so much to do," Belle urged him, but for the moment Frederickson demurred. A wedding supper was planned, but no one on his side of the family agreed to attend. The man was told by his relatives to think twice about marrying Belle Sorensen, and he took the advice to heart and called off the nuptials.

Belle left Janesville disappointed but unflinchingly determined in her efforts to forge a matrimonial bond. She arrived in west-central Minnesota for an extended visit to a cousin living on a dairy farm in Otter Tail County, near Fergus Falls. In this heavily Norwegian and German enclave divided along strict religious lines between Lutherans of the high church, who favored theological traditions and a hierarchial structure, and the low church, those who advocated reforms and liberality in religious doctrine, Belle renewed a friendship with widower Peter S. Gunness, a restless seeker of romance and marriage who had lived under her roof in Chicago and paid rent to her while Mads Sorensen was still alive.

Gunness had immigrated to America in 1885 from Kongsberg, Sandsvaer, in the Numedal Valley lying in the heart of southern Norway between Oslo and Bergen in Buskerud fylke. After a short period of time in Chicago, he settled in Janesville with his two uncles before continuing north to Minneapolis, a major settlement for Norwegian and Swedish immigrants. There he married Sophia Murch (Mørk), who bore him a daughter, Swanhilda. The couple lived at 3024 Hennepin Avenue, and he was employed as an order man for a grocer. After Sophia died, Gunness found himself in the same unenviable predicament as Anton Olsen—struggling to provide a home for a motherless child.

The tight-knit Nordic immigrant communities coalesced in the fertile plains of Minnesota, northern Wisconsin, and North and South Dakota through the mid-to-late nineteenth century, whereas the immigrants whose livelihoods were not directly tied to farming the land often made their way to the big cities. Chicago was a hub of Scandinavian immigration and men engaged in the building trades. Large Norwegian and Swedish neighborhoods, sealed off from other immigrant groups, formed west and north of the central business district.

The Swedes moved north up Clark Street and west of the Chicago lakefront. The Norwegians settled further west into Wicker Park and the adjoining Logan Square area and later Austin. There was little interaction between the Northern European immigrants and the people from Southern, Eastern, and Western Europe. Such was the balkanized, highly segregated nature of big city living for new arrivals from other lands in the closing decades of the nineteenth century. For many of the rural Scandinavians living on the sun-scorched prairies and grasslands of the Dakotas and Minnesota, Chicago was seen as a daunting, crime-ridden, and diseased hellhole that ground up poor people in the factories, machine shops, and slaughterhouses.

Within these insulated communities where English was rarely spoken, the foreign language press thrived. Anton B. Lange's weekly *Chicago Scandia*, published at 2818 W. North Avenue, and the *Scandinaven*, the largest circulating Norwegian-Swedish-Danish newspaper in the U.S., connected rural and urban immigrants separated by vast distances. As was true within the close-knit German communities, the widely circulated foreign language press made it possible for men and women to socially interact with one another and broker marriages through the placement of personal notices.[17] It was also the vehicle of opportunity for Belle Gunness and Johann Hoch.

Already there were objections to the coming nuptials from the Gunness relatives. "We were all opposed to his second marriage," his brother Carl said and sighed. "We knew he was afraid of the woman and we thought her influence over him was too great for us to prevail."[18]

Together Mrs. Sorensen and Mr. Gunness went to LaPorte, Indiana. (La Porte is French for "the door.") Tucked into the heart of mid-America, its commercial main street was built up along an old Indian trail connecting Detroit to Chicago, a well-beaten path once traversed by the native Potawatomi.

LaPorte was laid out and surveyed in 1833, and its first permanent residents were Aaron Stanton and Adam Polke. Stanton settled two miles north of the eastern boundary of the city of LaPorte on March 28, 1830.[19] Lured by cheap government land, others soon followed. Walter Wilson, Hiram Todd, John Walker, James Andrew, and Abram P. Andrew, Jr. (the "original" old settlers) purchased 400 acres of land at the Michigan Road land sale in Logansport in 1831. This event put LaPorte on the map.

Less than a year later, in May 1832, LaPorte County was incorporated, and the infant town became the county seat, although at the time there were only three families living there. The government offices, of course, became prime movers spurring local employment. The sylvan beauty of its forests, the surrounding prairies, and the sixteen passenger trains belonging to both the Michigan Southern as well as the Indianapolis, Peru and Chicago railroads arriving daily from points east and west brought yeoman farmers, mechanics, and professional men into the community. The pivotal year for development was 1852, when the Michigan Southern and Northern Indiana Railroad linked LaPorte to Chicago.

Newly arriving settlers building their homes on the south and west ends found broad reaches of fertile prairie land with outcroppings of beautiful bur oak groves. The north part of the township was heavily timbered. Within this cornucopia of woodlands and prairies in LaPorte County were many sparkling lakes, the loveliest of which lay nearest the location of Belle Sorensen's future home. Industry, commerce, and the abundant harvest of the farms fueled strong residential growth during and after the Civil War—by 1863 there were 8,000 residents—although the town was eclipsed in prominence by its larger neighbor thirteen miles to the north, Michigan City. Nevertheless, unabashed civic boosters proclaimed: "Taken altogether, LaPorte is unquestionably the handsomest city in Northern Indiana, if not in the state. Its wide and well shaded streets, its long rows of dark green maples, its groves and lakes and charming drives present attractions which are seldom equaled."[20]

The arrival of Belle Sorensen cast a gloomy pall on the optimistic notion that this tranquil woodland world far removed from the clamor, the noise, and the perceived horrors of Chicago living was somehow immune from the big city's attending evils. There was also something inherently ominous about the property Belle had acquired. Josiah Cheney wrote in *The La Porte Argus-Bulletin*:

> On the rising slope between those two lakes back from the road, sheltered under the friendly protection of the great Pines and beautiful shade trees stood a house homelike and attractive to look upon—an ideal home for the one who loved to read the messages of nature; a large two-story brick mansion surrounding thrifty barns and outhouses, whose condition bespoke for the owner a prosperity surpassing that of the neighborhood's proudest farms. Nearest the City of La Porte lies Clear Lake, surrounded on the south by the city and on the north by an undulating plain. A half-mile north of Clear Lake are the serene waters of Fish Trap Lake. The shores of this lake pass by McClung Road . . . a bypath. From time to time [there were] whispers through the community concerning its inhabitants.[21]

There is a lingering dispute among the townspeople about the odd history of Brookside Farm that the roundly despised Belle purchased out on McClung Road near the shoreline of Fish Trap Lake. Also in dispute is who actually built it. That some places are cursed by their very nature the residents of LaPorte would surely agree when reviewing the unseemly history of the property.

Residents, folklorists, and local historians debate the early history of the property, which is listed as Section 26, Township 37, North Range, 3 West, of LaPorte County. Adam G. Polke, the first white man in the region, likely bought the land from the government sometime in November 1831. He sold his interests to S. Treat, a cattle buyer, in 1842.

Treat, in turn, transferred the land to his brother George, who then sold the land to Dr. B.R. Car, a homeopathic physician, who constructed a sturdy log cabin home in 1857 from which he greeted patients and conducted his medical practice—with a section of the nearby property converted to a private cemetery littered with unmarked graves.

In this peaceful spot north of the town where the fish were always jumping and the water of Fish Trap Lake was pure and crystal clear, Dr. Car's practice was ruined when his son G. Hile Car, leader of a gang of Midwestern holdup men and desperadoes, utilized the surrounding property and the cabin his father had built as a rendezvous point.

Jerry Draper and Charles Tibets were lieutenants in the gang. From the stories told, the peaceful farm evolved into the "terror spot" of Northwest Indiana. Illegal gambling and lawlessness were everyday occurrences up and down McClung Road during the reign of G. Hile Car until the young man moved west to Denver, where he was killed in a shootout. Tibets was stabbed in a South Bend poolroom, and Draper was shot and killed by a policeman during a home burglary. "Young Car was a tough customer," recalled James "Jack" Haverly, famed Chicago showman and theater owner who made the acquaintance of the desperado. "But that was due to the spirit of those days in some measure. He stabbed a man and both he and his principal pals were killed at different places when the gang dispersed."[22] Dr. Car, by now trying to make a go of it in the coal and lumber business, moved away from LaPorte in 1875 in disgrace, leaving behind a stack of unpaid bills.

The August Drebing family replaced the log cabin in 1877 with a solid brick home, though in another version that is most often accepted as fact, it was reported that it was John Walker, one of the region's "old settlers," not Drebing, who built the home for his daughter Harriet Holcomb and her husband, John. Bricks were a costly commodity to transport from distant factories in the days before paved roads. All agreed, however, that Walker intended to erect the finest looking and most luxurious home in all LaPorte County—but still managed to fail in his objective.[23] The house on McClung Road was sinister in its appearance and repute. "When it was finished it was an unpleasant looking building in spite of all the money and skill that had been lavished upon it. It was heavy and gloomy and forbidding with glowering windows and shutters that were always closed, and odd overhanging gables. It was depressing merely to put one's feet in the door. It seemed that nothing could brighten it up not even the laughter of children. Even the sunlight seemed to lose its brilliancy when it streamed through those narrow, forbidding windows," a LaPorte old-timer recalled.[24]

The Holcombs abandoned the cursed property and eerie landscape and moved to King's County, New York, supposedly because they were southern sympathizers, or Copperheads, during the Civil War. In 1888, ownership of the property passed from the Drebings to farmer Grosvenor Goss, who transferred it to his wife, Sarah. In 1890, C.M. Eddy, a Chicago streetcar conductor, went to LaPorte as a speculator and bought the entire lot from Mrs. Goss, who was anxious to be rid of the evil place after her son committed suicide by hanging himself earlier that same year. Eddy's hope for a quiet life in the country was dashed when his wife died in the house.[75] In 1892, he too decided it was probably best to dispose of the place. Eddy sold the house to Mattie Altic, a Chicago woman with a checkered past, who moved her brothel business from the Custom House Place vice district in Chicago's South Loop down to LaPorte. Her presence in the community amounted to a terrible scandal. The decent church ladies were forced to avert their gaze each time they traveled down McClung Road, the "sin spot of old LaPorte," perched atop the family buckboard.

Mattie, tall, striking in appearance and imbued with big city ways, was unconcerned about gossiping biddies and the opinions of the wives of some of her most loyal clients. She cleaned the place up and threw open the doors of her first class "resort." She spent the illicit revenue lavishly and added a jetty boathouse and a carriage house and installed new furniture, marble trim, wainscoting, a dance floor, and commodious bed chambers for her patrons once the evening's revelry reached an end. A visit to Mattie's brothel was much more than a "twenty-minute, two-dollar trick." It was "Chicago Southeast," a big-time, no-holds-barred adult frolic. Each night, the sound of popping champagne corks and dance music filled the house as the prosperous merchant men sashayed across the floor and made merry with Mattie's perfumed harlots. LaPorte, a quiet, religious town, was aghast by the woman's brazen effrontery.

Mattie suffered a heart attack in the doorway of her house following a night of revelry; the official coroner's verdict blamed her sudden passing on heart disease. It was widely known that Mattie had been jilted by a suitor, and there were whispers that the LaPorte madame had committed suicide. Old friends came down from Chicago to pay their respects. Her funeral in Michigan City was a lavish affair: an immense procession of the scarlet demimonde, friends from Chicago, and LaPorte patrons accompanied the hearse to the Pine Lake Cemetery for the burial.

By this time analogies of the McClung Road manse were inevitably drawn to Edgar Allan Poe's "Fall of the House of Usher." The place was weird and unnatural by everyone's estimation.

Thomas Doyle acquired the entire farm in foreclosure proceedings in 1894 and sold it to Arthur Williams in 1898. Williams moved his father-in-law, M.D. Train, into the house while he ran his business concern back in Chicago. Belle Sorensen finalized her property transfer with Williams and his wife on November 9, 1901. Five months later on April 1st, Belle and Peter Gunness were married by Reverend George C. Moor of the Baptist Church in LaPorte. The newlyweds settled into their honeymoon cottage at Brookside Farm to begin life anew.

Hearing of Belle's marriage to Peter Gunness from a neighbor woman on Francisco Avenue back in Chicago, Anton Olsen once again contacted her and demanded that Jennie be allowed to return home. By now Olsen had remarried and was living at 737 Evans Avenue and was prepared to resume his fatherly duties. "So Mrs. Gunness let Jennie come and stay at my house about a month, the understanding being that Jennie could choose where she wanted to live," Olsen related. He enrolled his daughter in the Cornell School at 75th Street and Drexel Boulevard on Chicago's South Side, and the girl seemed to be adapting nicely to her new family situation.

"Then Mrs. Gunness came to Chicago, to the school where Jennie was. She told me Jennie did not have food or clothes at my home and she was going to take her back. I persuaded her to let Jennie stay so I could talk to her. From that time on she was unwilling to remain at my house saying that there were no fruit trees growing there or places to play."[26] Olsen abided by his daughter's startling wishes and reluctantly conveyed her to the train station. Jennie had made it clear to him that she wanted to leave the city and return to Belle's care on the LaPorte farm.

As the train pulled away from the station, Anton Olsen, his heart full of remorse, stood sadly on the platform watching his daughter disappear into the Pullman car. It was his last glimpse of the lonely, blonde-haired girl who was dreading a move forward into the urbanized, mechanized world of Chicago, a girl who wanted nothing more than to retreat into peaceful country surroundings with orchards, room to run, and the smell of Belle's famous home cooking emanating from a sturdy brick house overlooking a lake.

Later, after the spring rains and the shovels and pickaxes of grim-faced men sluicing the muck and mire of the hog pens and backyard of the Gunness farmhouse for the grisly discovery of human remains, Olsen sadly reflected on his prophetic dream and the bitter irony of Belle's last spoken words to him: "I am a Christian woman with a passion for God."

Chapter Three

The early travails of Johann Hoch, the most common nom de guerre (among many aliases he employed) of the murdering Chicago bigamist, are recorded in the legends and folklore of the Rhine Valley of Germany and the picturesque region lying between Düsseldorf and Mainz where the Nahe and Rhine rivers meet. The family home was situated in Horrweiler, near *Bingen am Rhein* (or Bingen on the Rhine). The river port and railroad junction of Bingen is located in an ancient region renowned for its vineyards and fine wines and was once inhabited by Celts and Romans in the first century B.C.

The Romans built a wooden bridge across the Nahe and fortified the city, then known as Bingium. In the wake of conquering armies, forgotten kings, and the landmarks of the Roman past, the spirit and memory of Bertha of Bingen (*Heilige Berta*), the eighth century patron of the poor, the sick, and the downtrodden, was recorded and handed down to generations of Rhine schoolchildren by the writer and composer St. Hildegard (1098–1179), known as "Sybil of the Rhine" and canonized by the Vatican. Bertha, children learned at an early age, founded hospices for the poor. After a visit to Rome, Bertha and her devoted son Rupert gave away their earthly possessions and became hermits near Bingen. Rupert died when he was barely twenty years old, and the grieving mother spent the remaining twenty-five years of her life serving the poor and suffering until her death in 757 A.D. Thereafter a feast day honoring Bertha was celebrated every May 15th.

In this particular milieu, where the religious traditions of the past were honored and held sacred, Hoch was born to Adam and Anna Elizabeth Schmidt (nee Weber) and christened Jacob Schmidt on November 10, 1854, in nearby Horrweiler, a municipality in the Mainz-Bingen district of the Rhineland Palatinate, although various published accounts state that Schmidt first saw the light of day in 1860 or 1862 and that his parents were well-to-do. "My people belonged to the best element in the town where I was born and raised," he once boasted.[1]

The night that Anna Elizabeth Schmidt gave birth to her son, she had a terrible nightmare. In this weird and disturbing dream, she saw the devil standing beside the bed, pointing at the infant and laughing. "This child is cursed!" the demonic presence uttered. Jacob Schmidt was told about the story when he was old enough to understand, and it stuck with him throughout his life. "I think he [the devil] was right," he said. "I have had no end of hard luck."[2]

Adam was a man of the cloth—a devout, scholarly Lutheran minister but rather disdainful in his outlook and temperament and a firm disciplinarian with regard to the upbringing of his three young sons, two of whom were trained for the ministry. Jacob was a nimble-minded lad who showed early promise and, like his brothers, also seemed destined to stand behind the pulpit. He memorized the entire Lutheran catechism word for word, taking to heart the fourteenth chapter of the Gospel of St. John, which read in part, "Let not your hearts be troubled. He believes in you. Believe also in him."

Jacob was devoted to his mother, who encouraged his religious study, but Anna passed away when he was a lad of fourteen, and the last chance of a stabilizing anchor in his life was permanently lost. "She lived long enough to leave the impress of her noble character upon me, and young as I was when she died, I remember her well, and I can say this to all young men: love honor and respect your mother, for a man's best friend is his mother. She will never lead you astray with bad advice, and she will stick to you when all other friends fail," he sermonized.[3]

Shortly before her death, she presented Jacob with a Bible that he would carry with him throughout his lifetime. For all of his pretensions of piety and scripture quoting, however, Schmidt chose to ignore the most fundamental commandment of them all: "thou shall not kill."[4]

Jacob showed little interest in following his father and brothers into the religious life and cowered in fear of Adam's frequent tirades and physical discipline. Instead at an early age he discovered a secret world, a world of romantic voyeurism.

"My life history abundantly proves once again that happenings of real life are indeed stranger than fiction," he revealed in the only extended interview he granted to the press. As an adolescent, young Jacob Schmidt studied the art of seduction the way another youth might have devoted considerable time and energy to the pursuit of the law, medicine, or finance. Near the Rhine River, the eavesdropping Schmidt discovered a hidden recess in a rock formation—a secluded little spot where the young swains of Horrweiler and the adjoining villages would take their sweethearts to propose marriage. "I found a little place just above where I could hear and see everything that went on," he remembered. "And I watched some five or six hundred men blurt out the question with various degrees of clumsiness. It used to fascinate me to listen to these proposals and I willingly lay in wait hours at a time to hear one. The first mistake that they all make is to try to be a perfect gentleman when they propose. Now that is wrong. Love is a game of war, not politics. By the time I was of age, I had learned what apparently nobody else on earth knows—how to propose so that no woman would refuse."[5]

Johann Hoch was apprenticed as a metalworker by his father. But that kind of work was pure drudgery, so he joined up with the army and later boasted of his exemplary military service as an artillery man during the Franco-Prussian War. Yet if Jacob Schmidt was born in 1862, he would have been only eight years old when Chancellor Otto von Bismarck summoned his armies to war in 1870. The official record of Schmidt's birth is at odds with his sworn statements. He insisted that his true birthplace was Lutz in the province of Hessen in 1854—not 1862 as the city magistrate of Mainz reported to the American authorities. If so, Schmidt would have been sixteen when he joined Bismarck's invasion force and twenty-one when he received an honorable discharge from the service.

After Bismarck's forces seized Paris and crushed the whole of France in 1871, Jacob Schmidt resettled in Berlin and for two years was gainfully employed in a drugstore where he learned the rudimentary skills of his future murderous avocation. Working with medicines and chemicals was more to his liking than metallurgy. The newly found profession inspired his criminal fascination with mixing potions and poisons.

At the age of twenty-four, Schmidt entered the University of Heidelberg, where he attended classes through 1878, but he failed to complete work for his degree. The young man was mainly interested in the curiosities of science, the wonders of the natural world, mastering foreign languages—he spoke French, Yiddish, and passable Russian—and making the acquaintance of comely young women at tea dances and during late hours of beer hall merriment, while accumulating as much money as he could.[6] Money was his prime mover; contriving the ingenious ways and means of defrauding women of their money was his game.

Hoch had not yet resorted to murder. But he made his peace with being a criminal early in life, and the seeds of his violent, psychopathic behavior were already sewn. He had already experienced an alienation of affection from his father and was possessed of a cold, boastful arrogance disguised by a personable and outgoing nature, narcissism, and the great inability to distinguish between right and wrong.

Police and reporters digging into Hoch's early life found that he had left the university under a cloud of suspicion. "Oh, it was another woman," he recalled with characteristic flippancy. A Chicago police detective who interrogated Schmidt-Hoch at length likened him to the fictional Pickwick, who, like the Dickens character, uttered the simplest, but unpredictable remarks that inspired merriment among his listeners. "I was a gay young dog then—what you call a devil of a fellow," Hoch gloated. "This was just a college scrape and I had to get out—I don't believe I remember her name."[7]

Schmidt eventually revealed to the press that the girl's name was Anna Maltin, the daughter of a Viennese artist. He remembered her as a "pretty, dark-eyed girl who never talked much." Lacking the confidence born out of worldly experience, Jacob overcame his hesitations and set out to win the girl's hand in marriage. "Some malicious busybodies had spread a lot of stories around that I was a dissolute character. Her father said I had a bad eye and didn't approve of me."[8]

For the first time in his life, Jacob turned to deception and cunning in order to succeed in a "matrimonial investment." He invited Anna Maltin to join him for a moonlight ride out on the Jedlesee, a lake not far from Vienna, in a small rented rowboat. He told the impressionable girl that he was the pretender to the throne of Denmark. His act was convincing, but then it started to rain, and Anna asked him to turn back after he had proposed. Angered by her apparent rebuff, he demanded her hand in marriage—more forcefully this time. "I can never marry you[,] Jacob. I am afraid," she replied.

With chilling insight into the mind of the future serial killer, Schmidt rolled up his sleeves, collected his nerve, and prepared to throw her overboard for her insolent rejection. "Would you believe it? I really thought so much of that girl I was almost willing to lose her to avoid doing her any violence. But, knowing how happy I could make her afterward I felt it my duty to her and to myself to go through the ordeal. Well, I had to be pretty rough. I hate to think of it even now."[9]

With a menacing look, he asked her again if she would marry him, but Anna said no. "Then this is the end of your life and maybe mine," he declared just as he made a rush at her. The boat overturned in the struggle, and Anna disappeared under the surface of the water. She had stopped fighting, and Schmidt feared she was already dead. "Before I could say anything she found my hand and gave it a little squeeze that I shall never forget. I was at the point of admitting myself beaten and would have begged her to let me escape from town without arrest. She said 'You needn't drown me[,] Jacob[,] because I guess you really do love me.'"

Schmidt said he had "visions of tar and feathers" awaiting him on the shore if she revealed to her father what had really happened out on the lake. But Anna invented a plausible account of the accident to tell her father, and within the month they were married despite the disapproval of nearly everyone. "That was in 1881," he revealed. "Two years later her health began to fail. I did everything a devoted husband could do. Medicine seemed to do her rather more harm than good. I took her to New York hoping the change might benefit her. One day she drank some poison from my laboratory and I found her dead upon the bed."[10]

Schmidt admitted that he was bewildered as to why the New York Police would want to investigate what he considered to be an ailing wife's suicide as a potential murder. Detectives told him that after ingesting Prussic acid Anna would have collapsed to the floor instantly—and would not have been able to lay down on the bed and await death in quiet repose. "I was so much annoyed that I left town one night without letting anyone know where I went."[11]

Calling the police a bunch of witless bunglers, Schmidt fled New York to resettle in the Midwest, plying his trade in New Albany, Indiana, where he had married the widow Maggie Meuter. After she died a year later, he was betrothed to her sister, Matilda Fein. They lived together in the cornfields of the Hoosier State for eight months before Hoch eventually fled town with $6,000 of the sisters' life savings—and sailed back to Europe. He had discovered during his brief foray in the U.S. that the bigamy business paid handsome dividends, and the police seemed powerless to connect him with the crime of murder. He believed there was a place for him here and vowed to return.

Paris, with its many sublime and wicked attractions, was to be his next port of call. Exactly how many wives he married while in the French capital before returning to Germany is not known, but the boulevards in the City of Lights provided a romantic backdrop for his art of seduction, which entailed reciting poetry, strumming the zither (a German string instrument), and practicing his newfound hobby of hypnosis on his trusting female companions as they quietly sipped their sherry on the Left Bank. "I left a few wives behind in Paris," he admitted.[12]

Julia Lecierque, a pretty French widow who intrigued Schmidt, was initially coy. After resisting his continued advances, she finally agreed to become his second wife. Schmidt first attempted to propose to her while standing atop the Arc de Triomphe, but tourists interrupted his wooing. One night, when he thought she was alone, he crept inside her apartment like a phantom thief. "I began my romance with more confidence than before," he said. "I was a Russian nihilist this time and produced an imitation bomb made of iron fittings from harmless materials when the expected refusal came. The bomb did not frighten her much, and I had to resort to violence again. I squeezed her hands so hard that her rings cut her fingers and as that was not enough, I stepped on her bare toes. Even that was not enough. I had to choke her a little to make her stop shrieking and she gave in."[13]

According to Schmidt, Julia called him "the worst brute she ever knew" but consented to marry him nevertheless. "This darling wife of mine died six months after my marriage," he recalled. Complaining of stomach cramps consistent with the presence of arsenic in the system, Julia refused medical assistance. She said to Schmidt: "'You are an expert chemist and a good doctor. I would rather have you do something for me.' I did the best I could but she died. I could only hold her hand and weep."[14] His show of grief was of short duration after he pocketed 40,000 francs from her estate. The constable of the town made an inquiry and claimed to have found poison in the glass that she had drunk from, but Schmidt said it was not the same glass, and the gendarme accepted the straightforward reply and did not bother to press the matter any further.

Wilhelmina Scheidemantel of Dresden agreed to become wife number three not long after. Schmidt said he did not have to spin a "fairy tale" to win her affections. He said she was desperate for a man. Her late husband had left the widow with a nice bank account in Dresden, and the funds were transferred to Schmidt after the woman suffered a fatal accident on her honeymoon. Schmidt and Wilhelmina were hiking in the Tyrol when she fell over a precipice. "I was with her and was able to reach her side and kiss her goodbye before she closed her eyes," he said.

Thereafter Jacob Schmidt always adopted an alias in his pursuit and courtship of lonely widows. Among a bewildering collection of assorted odd, curious, and often amusing monikers during his games of seduction, he most often answered to the name of Johann Hoch.[15]

"He used to brag about his knowledge of chemistry," recalled William Brenck, a carpenter from Mecklenburg who met up with Hoch in Chicago some years later. "He said he could do things with drugs that would make my hair stand on end," he added. "And he would always boast about how inferior women are. He declared they believe everything they are told and are so dependent and confiding that they should be classified as domestic animals, not as human beings. Hoch was a bad man—he was crooked that I am sure, because one could see it in his face. I would not trust him as far as I could see him."[16]

As "inferior" as he imagined women to be, Johann Hoch could not resist their perfumed allure and powerful attraction. He was a compulsive romancer, and in modern day psychology, as we understand it, he was likely a sex addict. Hoch pursued the fairer sex with a rabid and obsessive energy. "My father used to tell me that women would be the ruin of me," the philanderer sighed. "I have such an affectionate nature and women are always—always what [do] you call it? Pulling the wool over my eyes. Yes, they take advantage of my nature."[17]

Suave and gentlemanly Jacob Schmidt assured these women that he was a man of sober, regular habits—a dependable businessman who did not drink whiskey, play cards, smoke cigars, visit racetracks, or keep company with bad associates. These points he impressed upon his female victims to demonstrate that he would be a dependable and loving husband. He said he enjoyed a glass of beer with his dinner but could not tell one playing card from another.

After settling the estate of Mrs. Scheidemantel of Dresden, the wandering bon vivant returned to his home in the Rhine Valley to court Christine Raub, a woman with a trusting nature who consented to his offer of marriage. They were betrothed on January 1, 1887; however, it does not appear that this was a marriage-for-profit arrangement. The union produced three sons, and for a brief spell Hoch lived cautiously under the same roof with his family as he carved out a living as a wholesale gem merchant.

In Gensingen, just 10 kilometers southeast of Bingen and 25 kilometers southwest of Mainz, winemaker John Graf struck up an acquaintance with Hoch and remembered that his friend was working as a jewelry speculator and diamond agent but had squandered a modest fortune. Facing a bankruptcy petition, criminal prosecution, and the unhappy prospect of child-rearing and the dull domestic routines of his lifeless marriage, Hoch fled from the family home in Horrweiler before the authorities could present him with a bill of particulars.[18]

Hoch was rumored to have escaped to distant Alritzin, Russia, where he embezzled 15,000 rubles from a woman he married. But when the German authorities and his jilted wife demanded that he return to the Rhine Valley, he continued on to England where he courted and married a widow named Mrs. Roddy. (He said he could not remember her first name.) Again he employed brute force to compel the Widow Roddy to marry him after his yarn about being a pirate who commanded a vessel in the South China Sea was rejected with ridicule and disbelief. "I was very much ashamed of myself when I found I had broken her left wrist," he recalled. "Of course I did not dare show any regrets. She forgave me and I really think felt greater admiration for me than any of my other wives."[19]

After six months of marriage, Mrs. Roddy decided that they should henceforth set sail to America for reasons that remain unclear. The couple set out from Bremen via Liverpool and Southampton, England, aboard the *Norddeutscher* (North German) Lloyd liner *Stuttgart*. The year of his final departure from the continent has been variously reported as occurring between 1888 and 1895. That his transatlantic crossing occurred prior to 1890 seems more certain, given the amount of time he would have needed to traverse the continental United States and Canada seducing and marrying so many women.

Schmidt registered as John Huff and crossed the ocean under this assumed name, although to one fellow passenger he answered to the name Hoch. "The voyage was a unique experience in my life. For the first and only time a woman frightened and fascinated me and forced me as I have done to so many of her own sex," Hoch remembered. "Her first name was Aida—never mind the rest. She was handsome and caught my eye as soon as we boarded the steamer. Almost before we were out of sight of land I had told her that I was married to a woman with some property and she adroitly wormed it out of me that I was *not* very much in love."[20] Aida, whom Hoch estimated to be of southern European or quite possibly Turkish descent, insisted on meeting Mrs. Roddy. "The last day before we sighted land, my wife disappeared mysteriously. I never knew what happened to her. In some way she got overboard. At the time I had no idea. Now I think Aida was responsible."[21]

The recollections of Frank Weninger, who settled into a job with the Columbus Brewery in Chicago after sailing with Hoch on the transatlantic steamer loaded with immigrants bound for New York and Baltimore and the hope of a new and brighter life but with more honest intentions, confirms the existence of Aida. Weninger attested to the date of the sailing: it was 1888. He vividly remembered his shipboard companion paying "marked attention" to a young servant girl bound for New York. "Hoch devoted much of his time to courting a pretty working girl who was bringing her savings to the United States and intended to seek employment as a domestic," said Weninger. "He won the girl and married her, the first thing after the ship touched the dock in New York. I lost track of the couple after the landing but six weeks later I met Hoch in the street. 'Hello[,] Hoch!' I said, 'How's your wife?' 'Oh,' said Hoch. 'My poor wife is dead.' I thought nothing of it at the time," Weninger continued. "But I think in the light of Hoch's career, it may mean one more murder added to the long line."[22]

In Hoch's version of events, his marriage to Aida never occurred on American soil. Upon arrival, the couple booked passage on the next steamer bound for England, agreeing to tie the knot and claim Mrs. Roddy's estate, although Hoch had a sense of foreboding about his new traveling companion. "All through the next two weeks, I was in fear of my life. She suggested my doing various things with my wife's property. In the end she got it all away from me." The pretty young domestic whom Hoch accused of pitching Mrs. Roddy into the Atlantic Ocean pressed a loaded pistol into the back of his cranium and demanded that he surrender the estate settlement in cash. The money was handed over, and Aida vanished from his life. For the first and only time in his life, Johann Hoch had, so he said, fallen victim to a duplicitous woman.

Hoch ruefully observed that "In Germany a cash bonus goes with every wife. No cash, no husband. Money is the only compensation for the disappointments of married life." It was to be his life's manifesto. With the remaining savings in hand, Johann Hoch sailed back to the U.S. to resume his bigamous stateside career.

The fastidious, scripture-quoting little Bluebeard possessing joviality and wit had not the slightest intention of reconciling with Christine Raub and the children he had abandoned in the Rhineland—not with so many eligible women in America he believed would become entranced by his smooth manner and hypnotic gaze. Others saw him differently. "Hoch is about as far from being handsome as mud is from being ice-cream," observed a *Journal* reporter after sizing up the full measure of the man. The reporter continued:

> He is a brown man with a high forehead like a cow's. He has a scrubby, almost kinky black hair extending back from the equator of his skull to the short thick neck. A nose which is either Roman nor Greek; more resembling a chunk of putty extends from two thick dark eyebrows to a scrubby, scrawny black mustache. The whole face is one which at first sight would be mistaken for that of a low-class immigrant—the kind of face you see bending over the coats and trousers in the sweatshop rooms and later see directing these same sweatshops with unfeeling, hawk-eyed gaze—the kind of face which seems to sleep, yet watches everything. Sweatshop director—that is Johann Hoch at first sight and fits him to a doff.[23]

Chapter Four

Brynhild Poulsdatter Størset was born November 11, 1859, in Selbu, Sør-Trøndelag County, northern Norway, among the fjords and the tallest, sheerest cliffs of the far north, not far from the border of Sweden. Established on January 1, 1838, Selbu borders nine municipalities—the largest is Trondheim—famous later for being peacefully taken over and occupied by 500 soldiers of the German Wehrmacht without a shot being fired as the town slept at the crack of dawn on April 9, 1940.

Selbu, its name derived from the ancient Norse *Selabú*, which is drawn from nearby Lake Selbusjøen, and *bú*, meaning district, is not so much a district as it is a rural hamlet. Even today, its population barely numbers 4,000 inhabitants—mostly engaged in the agricultural and forest management professions, although snow-packed Selbu enjoys a worldwide reputation for the quality of its finely crafted, knitted mittens and clothing items as well as the development of a special knitting technique perfected by local woman Marit Emstad (nee Marit Olsdatter, 1841–1929). At the age of sixteen, Emstad knitted the first pair of "two-thread mittens" using two different colored threads instead of one, adding a complete rose pattern to adorn the whole of the mitten, giving rise to a cottage industry that was barely in its infancy when Brynhild Størset, the youngest of eight children, was born into abject poverty to Paul Pedersen Størsetgjerde (1808–1890) (descendants use a shortened form of the last name, Størset) and Beret Olsdatter Langli (1817–1885), who maintained a farm in Selbu.[1]

Mittens, murder, and the mystery of Belle Gunness shrouds much of the history of Selbu and Belle's enduring legacy in these parts. According to the first published accounts of the Gunness tragedy, which appeared in 1908, Belle's parents were circus people living a nomadic, hand-to-mouth existence dependent on carnival hucksterism and the small change they received in order to survive. This unverifiable, sensationalized version of Belle's early family life was accepted as fact for many years, but it seems to have had more to do with local Indiana gossip and Indiana folktales than with the true facts surrounding her origins. A colorful bit of fiction has it that Paul was a "gypsy sword swallower" and his wife was a tightrope walker, although LaPorte historians Otto Salzer and Gretchen Tyler's research dismisses the notion as absurd.

Salzer and Tyler assert that the father was a husmann (a term for a peasant farmer, also called a cotter or crotter), which seems to be the actual case based on later, more conclusive research conducted by Torger Størseth of Selbu, who completed an extensive study of property records and uncovered the site, on a sloping hill located outside of the town, of the Størsethgjerdet farm at Innbygda, Selbu, as belonging to his distant relatives.[2] At this site Paul leased a small farm and grew barley, oats, potatoes, and a few sheep. During the unrelenting winter months, he supplemented the family's meager income by working as a stonemason. Suffering and deprivation characterized Brynhild's early life as she was sent to work as a dairy maid and cattle girl, someone hired to shepherd the livestock to the mountain pastures to feed.[3] The money she earned was turned over to her father.

Not much is known about the day-to-day travails of this peasant family, their way of life, or the ambitions of Brynhild Størset to sample the fruits of prosperity as she progressed into young womanhood. Brynhild's circumstances and her early years in Norway were anonymous until her crimes became a national story in 1908.

Up to that time, most people in the U.S. and around the world had never heard of Selbu or this remote corner of Norway. With its connection to the infamous Belle Gunness firmly planted in the public mind by the worldwide press, the awful shame of her deeds jarred the privacy and customary quiet reserve of the people living within the Scandinavian union. Author and researcher Janet Langlois uncovered a strongly worded editorial in the local newspaper, the *Selbyggen,* condemning Størset as a pox on the local community: "Here in Selbu she is remembered by many, and mostly they tell that she was a very bad human being, capricious and extremely malicious. She had un-pretty habits, always in the mood for dirty tricks, talked little and was a liar already as a child. People mocked her and called her '*Snurkvistpåla*' (meaning spruce twigs and Paul's daughter—the girl collected kindling from the spruce trees for the family fire)."[4] The demeaning, humiliating task and the cruel nickname subjected the girl to mockery and public ridicule.

Brynhild occupied the lowest rung of a sharply defined economic caste system. Small resentments multiplied within the troubled girl until a defining tragedy in her early life fueled powerful anger and a recurring pattern of violent retribution toward men.

In 1877, at age seventeen, a traumatic and life-altering tragedy befell the shy young woman and forever clouded her disposition and attitudes toward men and child rearing. Brynhild, who had been confirmed in the Evangelical Lutheran Church, discovered that she was pregnant, scandalizing the family—and bringing shame and scorn down upon herself. Following this scandalizing news, she attended a country dance one night and was physically accosted by the scion of an old and well-to-do local family—a man far above Brynhild's lowly station in life.

It is likely that she fought hard to resist the young man's sexual advances. Rebuffed and filled with anger, the young knave brutally kicked her in the abdomen. Brynhild miscarried, but officials in Selbu did not prosecute the offender. Then the attacker suffered a malady of the stomach and died mysteriously. In light of her crimes in LaPorte, there was some speculation that Brynhild poisoned the offender in what amounted to a revenge slaying—thus claiming her first victim.

Was murder a biological part of the genetic makeup of Brynhild Størset, or did this jarring event from her early adulthood permanently alter her moral precepts and sense of right and wrong? Women make up only 10 percent of all murderers. Psychologists agree that the difference between the sexes is linked to differences in biology. Women are "pro-social"—that is, chemically predisposed to be the so-called "gentler sex," preferring appeasement through nonviolent means rather than physical confrontation. Women tend to perpetrate less violent types of crimes such as fraud and embezzlement. But when murder is the outcome, the female killer usually preys on those with whom she has close personal involvement—husbands, lovers, and family. Criminologists Robert Holmes and James Deburger, authors of the 1988 volume *Serial Murder: Studies in Crime, Law & Criminal Justice*, cite three factors applicable to the female serial killer: (1) "almost always a sociopathic personality pattern; (2) an intrinsic locus of motives that makes sense to the murderer but may not be apparent to others; and, significantly, (3) rewards and gains which reinforce the killer's behavior are almost always psychological."[5]

In his seminal 1943 paper "A Theory of Human Motivation," Dr. Abraham Maslow posited a "hierarchy of five basic human needs": physiological needs; safety needs; needs of love, affection, and belongingness; needs for esteem; and needs for self-actualization. Maslow notes:

While *behavior* is almost always motivated, it is also almost always bio-logically, culturally and situationally determined as well. In our society the thwarting of these *needs* is the most commonly found core in cases of maladjustment and more severe psychopathology. Love and affection, as well as their possible expression in sexuality, are generally looked upon with ambivalence and are customarily hedged about with many restrictions and inhibitions. . . . Practically all theorists of psychopathology have stressed thwarting of the love *needs* as basic in the picture of maladjustment. Many clinical studies have therefore been made of this *need* and we *know* more about it perhaps than any of the other *needs* except the physiological ones."[6]

Forensic psychologist and criminal profiler Dr. Micki Pistorius of the South African Police Service builds upon Maslow's theory of security deprivation, noting: "Although wealth may seem to be an external gratification to others, female serial killers kill for money to gratify their deep, deprived psychological need for security."[7] The deprivation of this sense of security at a young age may be the key to understanding the psychological motivations of the serial killer Belle Gunness in later life. Although nothing could be proven to link the young woman to the death of her assailant in Norway, her personality markedly changed over time. She became increasingly morose and resentful; illusions of romance and settling down with a caring, tender man vanished. "Money," as her sister Nellie Larsen insisted, "was her God." Like her contemporary Johann Hoch, she seemed bent on escaping the rural provinces in order to make her way to America, where popular myth held that even a person of the most humble origins could make their fortune. She was hard and bitter and lacked empathy but clung to the illusion that America promised her a chance at a comfortable existence.

Over the next three years, she saved her money with one objective uppermost in her mind: escaping the humiliation and the drudgery of her peasant toils in Norway for fresh opportunity abroad. She labored in the slop of the pigpens, milked the cows at the crack of dawn, and tended the horses until her older sister, whose name, curiously, was also Brynhild, agreed to help her pay for passage to New York.[8] The older sister had left for America in 1874 and married a Chicago man named John Larsen. By the time the younger Brynhild arrived, the Larsens were content and well established on Chicago's Northwest Side.

Turning her back on the scruffy little town that had caused so much personal sorrow, Brynhild Petersen, as she identified herself to the immigration authorities, boarded the steamship *Tasso* of the Wilson

Line and made the Atlantic crossing via Trondheim, Norway, and Hull, England, on September 8, 1881—four years before her mother died.[9] Leaving behind her other siblings in Norway, she made her way to Chicago, where Norwegians were counted among the city's largest ethnic settlements. In 1893, the same year Magnus Andersen captained a replica Viking ship across the Atlantic on a voyage to promote the theory that Leif Erickson had discovered America (and which he exhibited later that same year at the World's Columbian Exposition in Jackson Park, Chicago), the Norwegian population in the Windy City ranked second in the world only to Oslo, the capital of Norway.

Life with the Larsens offered security but proved to be an unfulfilling arrangement. The young woman worked hard to support herself as a domestic. Her duties likely involved cooking for well-to-do families and caring for their young. She may even have supplemented her modest income as an unlicensed midwife.[10] By now Brynhild had Americanized her first name to the familiar Belle or Bella in the custom of her sister who had scrapped her name for Nellie—popular American names for women of the era—but relations between the two women were often strained. Nellie and John were thankful when Bella met and married the department store watchman Mads Sorensen, a man of warm and pleasant wit, in 1884. They exchanged vows at the Norwegian Bethania Lutheran Church at Peoria and Grand Avenue (now Indiana Avenue) in front of the Reverend Mr. John Z. Torgerson and settled in to a quiet, rather ordinary life at 58 Marian Court.[11] It was a plain existence without incident or fanfare and one that offered up few clues pointing to the murderous path Belle was destined to follow.[12]

Their life together revolved around Norwegian fraternal societies, the Lutheran church, and daily routines—although in a revealing moment she confessed to her sister a lack of affection for the husband she had settled in with. "I would never remain with this man if it wasn't for the nice home he has," she confided. Nellie Larsen remembered Mr. Sorensen as kind and decent and ". . . [he] was one of the nicest men I ever knew and was a good husband to her but she never appeared to care for him."[13]

A physically strong and imposing woman in her own right, Belle cooked and cleaned and worked outside the home in the shop of a meat butcher for a time. The skill and ability she developed slicing up animal carcasses proved useful in LaPorte, when she wielded her hatchet on the remains of a dozen murdered suitors. It was during her Chicago years when Peter Gunness boarded with Mads Sorensen and Belle in their building with the Sorensens' two little girls, Myrtle and

Lucy—who likely were not Belle's own. Mrs. Sorensen had a mania for children—taking in the boys and girls no one else seemed to want or whose parents could not afford to clothe and feed them. That Belle was incapable of giving birth to a child of her own following the vicious assault she had suffered as a young woman in Norway seems to have fed her desire to adopt children off the streets. Among the Austin residents, rumors swirled that the grocery store was a blind. Her real business, some would say, was running a "baby farm"—the buying and selling of infants.

R.C. Ganiere, a professional portrait photographer at 299 Grand Avenue, counted Mrs. Sorensen as one of his most loyal and devoted customers. He, too, noted her obsession with children. Belle made frequent visits to his studio to be photographed with the children that she attired in their finest Sunday clothes. "Although neighbors regarded Mrs. Gunness in the nature of a hermit, she appeared jovial whenever she came to my place," he said. "She dressed stylishly and was rather handsome. What troubles existed between herself and her husband I did not know, but there was much ill feeling, and the man, a midget in comparison with his wife, seemed to fear her."[14]

Nellie Larsen was very aware of Belle's fixation with children after Nellie's daughter Olga went to live with her aunt for six weeks. When it came time for Olga to return home to her parents, Belle offered to adopt the little girl, but Nellie refused, and angry words were exchanged. Nellie and her sister broke off communication for many years after the falling out.

In February 1894, Belle and Mads bought the grocery store business on Grand Avenue and paid Charles Christiansen $12 a month to rent the living quarters.[15] To economize, the family slept in small apartments at the rear of the store. Their otherwise drab existence was punctuated by angry quarreling over money issues. Belle was disappointed with the store's income and warned Mads that they would be compelled to give up the business if matters did not improve. Then she suggested to her husband that he should increase his life insurance coverage as a hedge against insolvency.

Mrs. Sorensen berated her husband for problems that were largely of her own making. She was sullen and often rude to the customers, said little to them, and made as few acquaintances as possible. "Mrs. Gunness was a powerful woman at that time," said Catherine Burke, who purchased her groceries from the store. "Many times as I went into the store to make purchases, I noticed her muscular appearance. She seldom spoke, even when addressed, and her husband it appeared, would almost crouch at her approach. He appeared to be in fear of her. The two beautiful daughters she claimed as daughters were dressed in the finest clothes and people often wondered where the owners of the small grocery store secured the profits to dress the girls in style. During the time Mrs. Gunness and her husband conducted the store, they never had any visitors that I can recall."[16]

But were the little girls really *her* daughters? The sudden appearance of baby Axel in the Sorensen home in Austin raised eyebrows. Belle passed the infant off as her own, but Dr. J.B. Miller, a North Avenue physician, who rented space in the Sorensen home, related a rather curious tale. "A few days before the appearance of little Axel I was asked by Mrs. Sorensen to hold myself in readiness to attend her for a confinement case [a term for birth and the recovery period that follows]. To me as a physician this announcement came as a surprise. I had seen Mrs. Sorensen often, having rented up a few days previously two rooms in her house at 620 Alma Street for my office," Miller related. "When Mrs. Sorensen came to me with this statement I concealed my surprise and of course replied I would be ready to take the case."

A few days later someone shoved a note under Miller's door advising him that he was "wanted" immediately and to proceed at once to Belle's bedchamber. "This looked peculiar to me as I had passed the evening in my office and had slept in an adjoining room but had heard no one. I hurried right over to Mrs. Sorensen's room and there found her in bed with an infant. 'Why doctor,' she exclaimed: 'Where in the world were you? I aroused the whole town trying to find you and had to get somebody else.' There was nothing I could do but say I had been at home. I never learned with any degree of satisfaction what doctor attended the woman."[17]

Belle claimed that she gave birth to four children, but it struck the neighbors as exceptionally odd that the woman had no children of her own in the first eleven years of her marriage but had allegedly delivered four within the span of the next three years. "I went to her house one day and found an infant lying on a couch. It was crying hard," stated Mrs. William Diesling. "'Why don't you feed the baby?' I asked. 'Oh I haven't got time to take care of it,' she answered. I asked her whose baby it was and she said a relative had just sent it to her to take care of. The next day that baby had vanished and Mrs. Gunness told different stories about where it had gone. It was about this same time that a man drove to her house. He disappeared the following day but the bay mare and his carriage remained and were used by the widow. They are both in her barn today."[18]

According to the burial records, Assistant Police Chief Herman Schuettler discovered that Caroline Sorensen, a three-month-old girl, died on August 24, 1896, and an infant boy named Axel passed away in April 1898. Both children exhibited symptoms of acute colitis—inflammation of the large intestine—and both were buried in Forest Home Cemetery. Colitis was likely superinduced by the consumption of poison. In each instance Belle collected significant insurance claims.

Though he was unsure that the Sorensen home in Austin could be described as an actual "baby farm" as some suggested, neighbor Andrew Olson also found her actions peculiar and disturbing. "It is a fact that Mrs. Sorensen never nursed any of her children," he said.[19]

Studio wedding portrait taken in the middle 1880s of Johann Hoch and an unknown victim taken in Chicago. It was customary for Hoch to marry in a church and have the wedding portrait taken before he swindled the money and abandoned or killed a victim. Photo obtained by the *Chicago Daily News,* courtesy of the Chicago History Museum, DN-0001079.

Two murdered wives of Johann Hoch: Mary Schultz of St. Louis *(left)* and Justina Loeffler of Indiana. Ms. Loeffler's relatives made a futile effort to determine if the missing woman might have been slain by Belle Gunness three years after Hoch's death.

Left to right: Three of Johann Hoch's jilted wives—Emma Rankan, Anna Hendrickson, and Amelia Fischer— wait to testify in court in February 1905. Amelia Fischer married her sister's murderer, reported him to the police, then had a change of heart and fought to save Hoch's life. Photo by the *Chicago Daily News,* courtesy of the Chicago History Museum, DN-0003589.

Criminal defense attorney Isadore Plotke *(center)*, pictured here in 1906, fought hard to save the life of Johann Hoch but was fired by his client. Photo by the *Chicago Daily News*, courtesy of the Chicago History Museum, DN-0002601.

Judge George Kersten, who presided over Hoch's trial, photographed outside of the Cook County Criminal Courts Building in 1910. Photo by the *Chicago Daily News*, courtesy of the Chicago History Museum, DN-0008533.

Chief of Police George M. Shippy, photographed here in 1907, led the Johann Hoch investigation and later survived an assassin's murder attempt in 1912. Photo by the *Chicago Daily News,* courtesy of the Chicago History Museum, DN-0006073.

Cool and defiant, Johann Hoch *(seated, left)* is surrounded by his jailers at the Cook County lockup in February 1905 following his extradition from New York. Photo courtesy of the Chicago History Museum, DN-0003590.

HOW JOHANN HOCH MARCHED TO THE GALLOWS

Remarkable Picture of the Actual Procession to the Gallows by American's Photographers and Art Staff.

Johann Hoch's long walk to the gallows at the Cook County Jail after a last-ditch appeal for a stay failed. *Chicago American*, February 23, 1906.

Johann Hoch serenaded his female victims with a zither, a German stringed instrument, then allegedly hypnotized them with his arresting gaze. At his trial, the spectators' gallery was filled with women. *Chicago American*, January 31, 1905.

Artist's sketch of *Chicago American* reporter Evelyn Campbell interviewing Johann Hoch inside his New York City jail cell in February 1905. The drawing appeared in the paper on February 6, 1905, and wildly exaggerated Campbell's role in the arrest of the bigamist.

The *Chicago American* pushed hard on the theory that Johann Hoch had been employed by H.H. Holmes, the serial killer featured in Erik Larson's recent best-selling book *The Devil in the White City*. A *Chicago American* newspaper sketch artist of the day drew him with demonic features and published this image on February 9, 1905.

POLICE NOW SAY HOCK WAS A PUPIL OF BLUEBEARD HOLMES

Believe That Fugitive Was Guilty of Many of the Crimes Laid to the Englewood Man Ten Years Ago

HOCK WAS AN ACCOMPLICE OF HOLMES, SAYS WOMAN

Evelyn Campbell Finds Witness Who Knows His History.

BY EVELYN CAMPBELL.

A TREMBLING woman, frightened by the weight of a secret which she has kept for thirteen years, has given to me most startling evidence concerning the career of Johann Hoch, or Jacob Schmitt, the bigamist just captured in New York.

The unreliable opinion expressed by Chicago Police Lieutenant James O'Donnell Storen in the *American*—that Johann Hoch was an accomplice of H.H. Holmes—was accepted by the newspaper and played up as fact by Evelyn Campbell.

Chapter Five

Shortly after midnight on the evening of August 19, 1895, three terrifying explosions shook the South Side Englewood neighborhood—and within minutes the most sinister building in Chicago was consumed in pillars of flame. The explosions and the clanging of the gongs of the hook and ladder wagons roused the Englewood neighbors living on 63rd Street from their night's rest as the fire threatened to consume the wood-frame apartments nearby. Flagman George Meyer of the Western Indiana rail crossing had turned in the fire alarm, but by the time firefighters arrived, clouds of smoke were rising above the roofline, and bright flames burst into the sky.

Disoriented, the local people spilled into the streets to see what all the commotion was about. By now the roof of the four-story "Holmes Castle" had fallen in. "It is the hand of providence!" cried out one resident while others urged the firemen to turn off their hoses and just let it burn down.[1] Through the open upper windows of the structure, the spectators glimpsed asbestos material falling from between the walls as the fire devoured the building. Later, questioned by police in the light of day, persons living in the neighborhood said they remembered seeing a strange man lurking near the rear entrance. He had seemed nervous and uneasy.

At the time of the destructive blaze, the castle's former owner-occupant, Herman Webster Mudgett, answering to the pseudonym H.H. Holmes, was incarcerated in Philadelphia's Moyamensing Prison awaiting trial for a string of homicides committed over a 17-year period. Holmes has long been regarded as America's first true serial killer for the atrocities he committed in Chicago. Here was a diminutive, nimble-minded practitioner of torture-murder and gruesome alchemy who did his killing from inside this sinister dwelling he called his "castle." Today, following the publication of a recent best-selling work of literary nonfiction by Erik Larson, H.H. Holmes has been resurrected as the "Devil in the White City," a terrible figure carved from the late Gilded Age.

Chicago, with the excitement and majesty of the 1893 World's Co-lumbian Exposition, replete with gala pageantry and bursting fireworks in nearby Jackson Park, provided the backdrop for Holmes's unspeak-able deeds. "[B]esides being a sort of human shambles, [the castle] had been the scene of disgraceful orgies," the *Tribune* reminded its readers the morning after the mysterious fire [2] "Holmes managed to draw nearly all persons with whom he had dealings into some transaction which closed their mouths by other methods. It is evidently the opin-ion of the police that some of these 'interested' people . . . set fire to the old trap, which no doubt silently holds secrets dangerous to some of those associated with Holmes." [3] One such figure believed to have been associated with Holmes who might have had some dangerous secrets of his own was Johann Hoch.

Reporters familiar with the odd configuration of the building's in-terior recalled that the staircases did not end anywhere in particular. The twisting passages brought the visitor back to where he had started from, disoriented and bewildered. The mysterious second floor was a maze of 35 rooms, secret chambers and vaults with 51 doors, many of which led nowhere. Standing three stories tall and measuring 162 feet long by 50 feet wide, the most puzzling aspect of the building was the steel-jacketed vault on the third floor next to Holmes's office and study. Only Holmes could open this door to the vault. And only Holmes and a mysterious accomplice named Jake Hatch manipulated the gas pipe that was fed into the vault and used to asphyxiate victims.

The real horror was in the castle cellar, where Holmes had added an elaborate furnace that he used as a personal crematory. There was also a tank containing a noxious mix of oils that was strong enough to kill a person in less than a minute. Another tank, this one 14 by 16 feet long, made of sheet iron, and closed with a door, contained quicklime. It was in that tank that the police unearthed bone fragments of the murder victims lured to their deaths by the diabolical Holmes. The human remains, it was determined, were mostly women.

The interior of the Holmes castle was gutted. A ghoulish scheme to remodel the building and open it to the public as a dime museum stocked with "relics" that once had belonged to the killer was thwarted —and the Englewood neighbors gave thanks. The killer languished in a Pennsylvania prison awaiting a final rendezvous with the rope, but questions were asked about the fate of an accomplice of Holmes: a shadowy, elusive figure known around Englewood as Jake Hatch had slipped away and was nowhere to be found. Who was Hatch, and what peculiar knowledge did he possess of these grisly murders?[4]

Herman Webster Mudgett was a scapegrace as a boy—an incorrigible young rascal who caused his father, Levi Mudgett, and his wife, Theodate, both devout Methodists, torment and many sleepless nights in the little town of Gilmanton, New Hampshire, where he was born on May 16, 1860, in an 1825 white clapboard colonial home located on the corner of Province Road and Cat Alley, directly across the street from the town hall. Levi was the local postmaster. He also owned a small farm where his son Herman toiled in the fields and attended school only in the winter—or whenever it was convenient for the father to spare the boy from his chores. Resentful of the shackles of honest labor, Holmes relied on his cunning nature and his ability to absorb information at a rapid rate. He was a fast learner who devoured the novels of Jules Verne and Edgar Allan Poe, and in time he also mastered the fundamentals of science.

Considered "bookish" and somewhat effeminate by nineteenth-century standards of manhood, Mudgett was pale complected with deep-set blue eyes and a low, soft voice that women found enchanting. From late adolescence onward he was a lady's man and was betrothed at age twenty to Clara Lovering, the 18-year-old daughter of a well-to-do farmer in Loudon, New Hampshire. The young couple ran off to be married on the Fourth of July, 1878, in the town of Alton by Squire John W. Currier.

Mudgett had accumulated some money, and his passion for medicine was encouraged by his young bride, who worked as a dressmaker to help him meet his expenses during his freshman year of college at the University of Vermont in Burlington. Then he transferred to the University of Michigan at Ann Arbor to begin his studies on September 21, 1882, with the backing of one Nathan Wright and a widow who was pledged to marry Mudgett (who had abandoned Lovering) once he attained a medical degree. He was mentored by Edward Swift Dunster, a distinguished academician and professor of obstetrics and diseases of women and children.

Holmes was given every advantage and shown great consideration, but he soon exhausted his finances and turned to insurance fraud as a means of satisfying his tuition bills. With a hired accomplice, he commenced his criminal career by insuring a cadaver and filing a claim. In a moment of inspiration—Mudgett claimed he was dissecting a corpse in an anatomy class when the idea struck him—he inveigled his business partner to get his life insured for $12,500. A corpse was obtained. Then a bogus claim was filed, but the insurance company paid up promptly, and the money was divided evenly between Mudgett and his Canadian confederate.

With a theoretical knowledge of medicine but bored with the routines of university life, Mudgett jilted the widow and slipped out of Ann Arbor in the summer of 1884 to accept a teaching job in Mooers Fork, at the northern tip of New York State in Clinton County. Impressed with his gentlemanly manner, the trustees of the school district appointed him principal. He practiced medicine on the side. Mudgett represented himself as a single man and boarded with one W.H. Vaugh while playing the gallant to the prettiest girls in the village. Eyebrows were raised when Clara and her child turned up unexpectedly at the train depot, forcing Mudgett to spin a yarn to the young woman to whom he proposed marriage about his pending divorce action with Clara. Clara and her infant son had been living with her parents in Loudon, patiently waiting for her husband's return. In desperation she traveled to the tiny upstate New York hamlet of Mooers Fork to urge him to come home and be a father to the child, but her husband would have nothing to do with her or the boy.

He lingered in Mooers Fork another year, but the strange death of a local man named Clark whose daughter was romantically linked to Mudgett aroused suspicions. He ran up an unpaid bill at a lodging house with his new landlord, D.S. Hays, who cornered Mudgett in his office one morning just as he was finished packing up his belongings and loading them onto a lumber wagon in preparation for a fast exit out of town. Hays blocked his path, but Mudgett drew a revolver, whipped up his horse, and sped northward to the Canadian border, leaving behind a jilted fiancée and more than one angry creditor. By now Mudgett was concealing his true identity through a series of aliases—he preferred H.H. Holmes or Henry Howard—and was off and running on a kaleidoscopic crime career.

In the winter of 1885–1886, Holmes turned up in St. Paul, Minnesota, to cultivate business, establish trust, and mulct the unsuspecting. He was appointed receiver for a local restaurant, stocked the place with goods on credit, sold off everything in a whirlwind 48-hour spree, then walked off, leaving the bondsman, the provider of cash bonds for criminal suspects indicted or under arraignment, holding the forfeit. Next, Holmes absconded to the well-to-do Chicago suburb of Wilmette to commit his first bigamous act: a marriage to Myrtle Z. Belknap, daughter of Jonathan Belknap, a local merchant whose sizeable estate he aimed to steal through a forged deed. But that was a long-range plan that had to wait while he invested in an Englewood drugstore owned by one Mrs. E.S. Holden on the ground floor of the building that was to become his murder castle. Mrs. Holden conveniently disappeared in 1887. "Gone to California!" exhorted Holmes to the inquiring neighbors, as he installed a new manager and assumed ownership of the business.

Marriage vows were exchanged between Myrtle and Holmes on January 28, 1887. Their daughter, Lucy, was born not long after, but she was cared for in her maternal grandfather's home after Holmes removed himself from the Chicago area, leaving his Englewood drugstore and Myrtle behind. He established his next temporary base of operations in Terre Haute, Indiana, with a new sidekick in larceny, one Benjamin F. Pitzel, a water-eyed sot with a wife named Carrie and six hungry children. Pitzel was a desperate man who was always short of cash. H.H. Holmes specialized in committing insurance fraud, and Pitzel, sensing a rich harvest, was a party to the schemes. But he was promptly arrested by Indiana authorities on a charge of forgery. Holmes provided straw bail—a worthless bail put up by a front man or third party "strawman" with no legal credentials—for his partner, and the two were soon on their way.

Not long after making the acquaintance of the Pitzels, Holmes was back in Chicago in 1891 promoting a new venture, the Warner Glass Bending Company, which purported to be a well-financed corporation scheduled to deliver decorative glassworks for the home and office to the residents of Englewood. From his office in the Chemical Bank Building, Holmes applied for a patent in the name of Warner, the presumed inventor of the process. Machinery was purchased on credit from the Perkins Wind Mill and Axle Company of Mishawaka, Indiana, with a note of credit in the amount of $15,000 guaranteed in the name of little Lucy Belknap, now four years old. Lawyers retained by the firm spent the next ten years in a futile attempt to recover the monies due them from the Belknaps, the estate lawyers, and Holmes's criminal defense attorney—but to no avail. What happened to the equipment? Holmes had disposed of it wholesale, of course.

Eager to cash in on the opportunities awaiting men of enterprise and daring who were looking to get rich at the World's Columbian Exposition and through the influx of thousands of visitors from across the nation and around the globe descending on the city, Holmes acquired his 63rd Street hotel in 1892 and employed carpenter and a jack-of-all-trades Patrick Quinlan, a taciturn man who had lost his entire family in a fire, to oversee construction and Joseph Owens, a cleanup man and janitor. As the renovation work went on and the monstrosity took shape, the name on the title kept changing. First Holmes transferred the ownership deed to his mother-in-law, Mrs. Belknap, then Hiram S. Campbell, and then A.S. Yates, a name linked to the Campbell-Yates Company, a shell corporation with no assets or even a principal business, which was to become the vehicle for defrauding Chicago area retailers. Holmes ordered expensive furniture from the Tobey Company on Wabash Avenue to fill every room, crockery from the French, Potter & Company, mattresses and bedsprings from the Schultz & Hirsch Company on Des Plaines Street, and gas fixtures from the Schroeder & Williamson Company. As a commercial hotel fitted up to receive World's Fair guests, the venture was a costly failure, and Holmes soon fell into debt. When he failed to pay his bills, creditors grew suspicious and, over the course of the next twelve months, deputy sheriffs were dispatched to the castle armed with writs and warrants.

There they found Quinlan, who knew considerably more than what he was at first willing to reveal. Old Pat was a man of many secrets, but he seemed to be the one who was in charge. His signature, "P.B. Quinlan," was affixed to nearly every department store invoice and delivery slip. Clearly he had an important role to play in the operation.

Quinlan led the police from room to mysterious room—but all were empty. The furniture and the fixtures had seemingly vanished. The investigators were dumbfounded. Where was Holmes? Had he sold all of his ill-gotten loot and gone on the lam? "Surely[,] man[,] you must know where all of the merchandise has gone! Speak up!" the officer said. Quinlan smiled uneasily and suggested that $50 would help loosen his tongue. After receiving the money, the carpenter-janitor approached a blank wall and tore away the decorative paper to reveal a hidden door that led to an anteroom where Holmes had stashed a large portion of the Tobey furniture items. Additional chairs and tables and the French Potter crockery were removed from the crawl space between the top floor and the roof. It was soon apparent that the entire building was honeycombed with secret rooms, trapdoors, and mysterious hidden places—all constructed by various contractors and work crews hired and fired by Holmes on a whim. In that way only the master of the castle—and perhaps Quinlan and one or two others—understood the curious layout of the place.

On November 22, 1893, a meeting of 25 creditors seeking redress from Holmes was called in Chicago. H.H. Holmes nervily presented himself to the gathering to say that he could not possibly pay the $25,000–$30,000 demanded of him, claiming that his revenue projections for the hotel venture had fallen well short of his most reasonable expectations.

The next day, as arrest papers were drawn up, Holmes skipped town, leaving behind a mountain of debt, strange secrets, and a collection of grotesqueries yet to be discovered. In the coming months, the remains of possibly 27 people who had been gassed, cut up, and buried in the basement were uncovered. "He skipped out," explained an attorney for the creditors, "and went straight to Philadelphia. He branched out and did a $20,000 job on a Fort Worth, Texas[,] bank, one in St. Louis and another in Indianapolis. He is one of the slickest all around swindlers I ever saw."[5]

In the general excitement of the Chicago World's Fair, little attention was paid by law enforcement to the outrageous swindles and costly hoaxes Holmes perpetrated against the unsuspecting. His most daring and memorable ruse was convincing city inspectors that he had invented a method of converting Lake Michigan water into natural gas, which, he explained, the city could manufacture for a quarter of a cent per million cubic feet. Holmes, claiming to hold a patent for the enormous basement generator that resembled a washer-boiler mounted on stilts, had an emissary of the gas company carefully inspect the device and observe a stream of water running in at one end of the machine but not coming out at the other end. A smell of gas hung in the air, which made the contraption seem all the more convincing.

Holmes was asked to light every gas jet in the house, raising the meter to 3,000 cubic feet. For ten straight hours the inspector remained in the basement with the peculiar machine, and for ten hours it performed as capably as Holmes promised. An offer of $25,000 was made, but in the following week when workers returned to cart the generator off to the city power plant where it would be run through its paces, the fraud was easily revealed. Holmes had managed to bore into the gas company's main. Embarrassed, the gas company deigned not to prosecute, hoping that the humiliation would escape the eyes and ears of Englewood and quickly be forgotten. But Holmes had another mischievous trick to pull on his Englewood neighbors. Not long after the natural gas hoax, he announced that the enormous hole in the basement floor where the gas generator once rested had opened up an artesian well of purifying mineral water.

Holmes ran a pipe up from the basement and connected it to the soda fountain in the first floor drugstore he had acquired from Mrs. Holden, who had by that time vanished and was presumably dead. It was said that all of Englewood crowded around for a taste of the five-cent elixir that Holmes, in the company of a paid ringer posing as a learned chemist, vowed to be the most healthful and natural essence in all of the land—guaranteed to forestall old age and cure impotency! So marvelous was it that future plagues of cholera and diphtheria might even be permanently eradicated, so Holmes said. For the neighborhood alcoholics looking to end their drinking habit, Holmes bottled the water, sold it at a discount, and enrolled the inebriates in his "Silver Ash Institute," a fraudulent forerunner of Alcoholics Anonymous that he originally chartered in Kalamazoo, Michigan, in 1891. The excitement ground to a halt when a real chemist said that the potion everyone was so excited about was nothing more than common lake water. The neighborhood wiseacres glanced at one another knowingly. There was mirth and amusing stories to tell, leaving the people of Englewood shaking their heads, but still no arrest.

When he wasn't swindling retail emporiums and insurance companies, or patenting useless contraptions to peddle to the greedy and the gullible, this charming and otherwise entertaining little humbug with a pleasant, disarming manner gained the trust of his victims before killing them. His "castle" was built on the installment plan—loans secured in the name of a man answering to the name of Gott, a restaurant owner who accepted Holmes's checks for the lodging of the construction workers putting up the crooked and misshapen castle interior. The checks bounced, and Gott could not collect a cent from Holmes.

Inside the castle with its maze of trapdoors, hidden gas jets, and the stolen furniture, visitors to the fair who were seeking accommodations rented rooms by the week. Many were never heard from again. Estimates vary from 10 to 30, although Holmes's gallows confession pegged the actual number at 27. The fiend was particularly interested in luring young, pretty women inexperienced in the ways of life but in possession of useful office skills acquired in business colleges.

He was a womanizer and a compulsive seducer. He hired young girls for meaningless jobs as stenographers and typists. They were tempted with the offer of the flattering title of notary public (considered a highly coveted attainment for a working woman in those days) and were often promoted to "company directors" of his various incorporations as a means of drawing them close. Pretty 17-year-old Emily Van Tassel worked in a candy store in which Holmes had a financial interest. The mother of the girl encouraged her daughter's interest in this successful businessman—a "model of virtuous manhood"—who took Emily out for carriage rides in the city. Later he murdered her in the store and cut up the body into small pieces.

On the third floor of the castle Holmes constructed a murder vault—a tiny chamber large enough for one person to stand in. Holmes would place a bowl of noxious benzene and fuel oil in a bowl. When the doors were closed, the oxygen was absorbed by the acid, and the victim died a horrifying death. Afterward, the remains would be stripped of the flesh, the bones bleached, and the skeleton re-articulated by a specialist named M.G. Chappell who made a living this way. Chappell would then mount the skeletons on brass fittings and sell them to medical colleges. Between 1865 and 1890, the number of medical colleges in the U.S. more than doubled, fueling a black market for fresh cadavers and human skeletons delivered by graveyard profiteers conveying them directly to the classroom from the backs of their wagons, no questions asked.[6] Holmes as a serial killer emulating the crimes of William Burke and William Hare, the notorious Scottish graverobbers who murdered 17 victims in 1827–1828 and delivered the cadavers to the Edinburgh Medical College, went about his gruesome tasks with the profit motive uppermost in his mind.

Such was the unhappy fate of Julia Connor, wife of Davenport, Iowa, jeweler Icilius "Ned" Connor and the mother of a 12-year-old girl named Pearl. Ned Connor came looking for a job as a watchmaker in September 1889 after hearing that Holmes was advertising for a tinkerer and repairman. Holmes offered him a salary of $12 a week, but it was the comely Julia who really caught his attention and sealed the bargain. So he agreed to take Julia on as cashier, taught her basic bookkeeping, and set them both up in a flat he owned at 7403 Honore Street. Soon Ned Connor became suspicious of the arrangement and threatened his wife with violence after noticing how friendly she had become with his employer.

Holmes launched the jewelry business on August 15, 1890, and made Julia a company director. This was his usual ploy with his intended female victims: give each of them important responsibilities, a title of perceived importance, and a false sense of security before springing the trap. Not long after these developments, Ned Connor separated from his wife—presumably after confirming the details of her affair with his employer. Charging her with desertion, Connor filed for divorce but held out hope that the woman would come to her senses and reconcile. But Julia was deeply enamored with Holmes and refused to bend to her estranged husband's incessant demand that she leave Holmes's employ; however, she could not possibly know that he was still married to Myrtle Belknap and Clara Lovering.

Julia happily accepted an offer to have the title of the drugstore transferred into her name—along with an insurance policy taken out on her daughter, Pearl, another warning to Ned that Holmes was up to no good. Then the mother and daughter suddenly disappeared. Holmes offered the feeble explanation to Ned that she had moved to St. Louis—but the address he supplied turned out to be a cheap boardinghouse for male transients. When pressed further, Holmes said they had all gone "off to Lacota, Michigan," with the daughter of Pat Quinlan. Connor demanded to know for what purpose. "Vacation," Holmes replied. "Mrs. Quinlan has relatives in that part of the state and likes to spend the summer up there." Later, when the basement of the charnel house yielded up its secrets, Connor identified an oil-stained garment hanging from a hook as belonging to his wife. In his written confession, Holmes stated that he poisoned the little girl, Pearl, after bungling an abortion on the mother—who was allegedly pregnant with his child at the time.

Julia Connor had been done away with after another new woman came into Holmes's life—the refined and educated Minnie Williams, a graceful Southern belle and graduate of the Conservatory of Elocution in Boston, who accepted a position as Holmes's stenographer and principal secretary of the ABC Copier Company. Hearing that Minnie and her sister, Anna (called Nannie), a schoolteacher at the Midlothian Academy in Texas, were in line to inherit some valuable real estate in Fort Worth, Texas, Holmes invited the sister up to Chicago after Minnie and Nannie's father had been killed in a train accident. Full of hope and eager to visit the World's Fair, Nannie came north from Midlothian, Texas, to live with her sister and Holmes on July 7, 1893, prior to their wedding and two months after the Fort Worth property at Rusk and Second Street was deeded over to one Benton T. Lyman, an alias of Holmes's drunken sidekick Benjamin Pitzel. The Texas property was intended for the construction of a second "castle" using the same blueprints drawn up for 63rd Street. The Texas castle was to be built under Quinlan's guiding hand, but Holmes cashed out and sold the pile of boards, tar paper, and lathes after vociferous objections were raised by Fort Worth real estate owners. The $80,000 the sale netted was then used to further his swindling schemes.

Holmes provided living accommodations for the Williams sisters at 1220 Wrightwood Avenue on the North Side of the city. But over the coming weeks he moved the sisters and the reprobate Pitzel around the city into various lodging houses and hideaways, including the elegant Plaza Hotel overlooking Lincoln Park, as he plotted new and outlandish insurance frauds, thus making his little circle of followers complicitous in a scheme to torch the castle and collect a cash settlement. The hotel desk clerk at the Plaza Hotel remembered that Minnie Williams, a woman of medium height, large brown eyes, and a well-developed figure, had identified Pitzel as her brother. It all seemed curious to the clerk.

Early in November 1893, the castle erupted in flames. Although the building was saved, Holmes claimed $80,000 worth of property damage from the Fidelity Insurance Company. The "proof of loss" was signed and attested to by Campbell and Yates, names linked to Holmes's shell corporation via which he defrauded Chicago area retailers, but Fidelity Insurance requested an investigation. Insurance inspector F.G. Cowie was put on the case by company officials who were eager to get the goods on Holmes. Upon examination of the insurance documents, it was soon discovered that the signature of Campbell suspiciously resembled that of Ben Pitzel. Neither Campbell nor Yates could be tracked down, of course—the men were an invention—as Cowie drew ever closer to learning the truth about Holmes's swindling activities. The insurance man said: "I was continually running across evidence that Holmes was leading a double life—in fact that at times, it might be said he was leading a *quadruple* life. He had a wife and three children at Wilmette, and I learned he had built a fine house there. Investigations showed that not a stick of this house had ever been paid for and it was deeded to a relative of his wife."[7]

Cowie confronted Holmes in the office of the insurance company, and while he was detained, Minnie Williams was tracked down in the Plaza Hotel and compelled to admit the fraudulent character of the fire and her role in the swindle. "When this was done my work was at an end," Cowie explained. "I had no further interest in the case and do not know what became of the outfit after I was through with it."[8]

Amazingly, the police took no further role in the matter after Cowie turned over his findings for follow-up. For the time being, the insurance fraud investigation fizzled, but Cowie's relentless pursuit succeeded in driving Holmes out of Chicago. The swindler slipped out of the city with his traveling party intact, in order to pursue a new woman and a fresh bigamy scheme. Minnie Williams—always the willing accomplice but never the bride—accompanied Holmes to witness his marriage to yet another smitten young damsel he had seduced and coaxed into matrimony. Miss Georgianna Yoke was a tall, willowy blonde from Franklin, Indiana, who, like many restless young girls from the hinterland, had a yearning to come to Chicago to experience the thrills of the World's Fair, secure a position, and quite possibly find a dashing suitor to pass the time of day with. In time she found work as a clerk in the Siegel & Cooper department store on State Street—a drab counter job that got her by until Holmes engaged her as a secretary for one of his many side businesses. The hapless but devoted Minnie allowed herself to be introduced to Miss Yoke as Holmes's "cousin."

Holmes passed himself off as the nephew of Henry Mansfield Howard, a prosperous Denver man, all the while coveting the $3,000 belonging to Georgianna's grandfather's estate, which she was scheduled to inherit. Holmes deposited a portion of the money received from his most recent insurance settlement into the Merchant's National Bank of Franklin as a good-faith gesture to demonstrate his commitment to providing for the girl's future.

Miss Yoke, the daughter of an Indianapolis school principal and herself an estimable young woman well liked by her Franklin neighbors, went through with the ceremony in a Methodist church on January 17, 1894, and became Holmes's last wife—but her honeymoon was spent alone inside a Denver hotel. For mysterious reasons, Holmes said he "could not be seen there" during the daytime hours. The union, like all others, was short-lived. He abandoned her a few months later after being informed by her family's attorneys that the grandfather's estate would not be settled for many months, thus tying up the $3,000 inheritance. Humiliated and jilted by her husband's betrayal and rumors assailing her character, Georgianna Yoke fled to Montreal, Canada, to escape the verbal sting of the town gossips. She is counted among the fortunate few who escaped from Holmes's web.

After December 15, 1893, the Williams sisters were never seen alive in Englewood again. According to Holmes's death house statements to Detective Franklin Geyer, the Philadelphia gumshoe obsessed with unraveling the mysteries of this enigmatic killer, Anna/Nannie was "attacked by acute insanity" in the spring of 1893. Possessed of a wild, jealous streak, and thinking that Holmes would marry her after she confessed her undying love and eliminated her sister, Anna murdered her sister, Minnie, with a hard blow to the head from a small wooden stool. Holmes said he was an innocent spectator to the fury of the sister and claimed to have placed the body in a large trunk, loaded it in his carriage, and dumped Minnie's remains into Lake Michigan.

To allay suspicions about the Williams sisters, he had each of them dispatch letters to their aunt Lucy Marshall in Terry, Mississippi, assuring the woman of their benefactor's generosity and his sincerest intentions for both of them—and his promise to send the girls on an extended European tour to Germany, London, and Paris. The tactic of forcing the victim to write a letter to loved ones to allay suspicions leading up to their murder is common among many modern serial killers.

After Minnie's murder, Anna ran off to Europe, forcing Holmes to hire a temporary replacement, Emeline C. Cigrand, who had previously worked at the Keeley Institute, a sanitarium in Dwight, Illinois. While employed as a stenographer and record keeper for the sanitarium, she met up with Patrick Quinlan, who was sent there to dry out following his latest alcoholic binge. After taking "the cure"—a concoction of gold powders and seltzer water—Quinlan referred Miss Cigrand to Holmes for a position with the Campbell-Yates Company that would pay her $18 a week, more than she was being paid by Dr. Keeley. Emeline was a woman of delicate features—tall, fetching, with beautiful flaxen hair, and possessing a great intellect. She was motivated, ambitious, and engaged to be married to one Robert E. Phelps from her hometown of Lafayette, Indiana. Although Phelps was a wealthy man, he too was looking for a job that Holmes was more than willing to provide. Emeline, who lived in an Englewood boardinghouse from May through October 1893, confided to a neighbor that she was afraid of her employer, had second thoughts after observing his callous behavior toward other employees, and desired to return to her previous position in Dwight, 100 miles west of Chicago. Her statements were at odds with the sworn testimony of music teacher J.B. Corbett, who said he was hired by Holmes to teach Emeline to play the guitar so that she could accompany Holmes, who had taken up the violin, in duets. "She is my cousin," Holmes told Corbett and others, but that struck a number of people oddly because Holmes seemed a little "too friendly" with the girl.

At the end of each workday, Emeline and Holmes had become accustomed to riding bicycles together in Englewood. On other occasions they attended theater together. Then, just before Emeline could complete her music lessons, she simply vanished. "I have said a hundred times that there was something wrong about the departure of Miss Cigrand," said Mrs. Maurice Lawrence, who, with her husband, rented a room in the castle. "It would seem impossible and wholly unlike the girl, knowing me as well as she did, not to say anything about going away or getting married as Holmes claimed she had done."[9]

In December 1893, Dr. Peter Cigrand cabled Holmes with an inquiry about his missing daughter and the whereabouts of her fiancé. In a typewritten letter to the father, Holmes said that Emeline and Phelps had traveled to Michigan, where they were married, and then sailed to England, where Phelps allegedly pursued a promising new business opportunity with his father. After two years passed with no word from Emeline to her family, Dr. Cigrand and his wife, desperate to find out if their daughter was alive or dead, hired a well-known

Indiana spiritualist in a misguided attempt to communicate with the afterworld in a séance. After they had sat in a dark room for nearly two hours, the distant voice of a young woman supposedly transmitted from beyond the grave whispered in otherworldly tones, saying, "This is Emma. I went into the spirit land two years ago and was far from home. Oh, it was terrible!"[10]

It is unclear if her parents believed this kind of hoodoo or not, but mysticism and séances—often merely organized crime rackets—were common in Victorian America, and the medium at this séance wasn't so far from the truth. Holmes had in fact murdered both Emeline and Phelps after they had pressed him one too many times for payment of their wages. The family of the missing girl believed that Holmes had run out of funds and stopped paying their salaries.

In October 1893, two months before the disappearance of the Williams sisters, Pitzel was arrested in Terre Haute, Indiana, for passing forged checks to local merchants. Holmes came down from Chicago and secured his release on bail, anxious to explain to his witless sidekick that he had figured out a surefire way to scam $10,000 from the insurance company. The swindle perpetrated against the Fidelity Mutual Life Association of Philadelphia was worked through Jeptha D. Howe, the brother of the city's public defender and an affable but indiscreet St. Louis attorney who consorted with and represented shady characters.[11] Holmes, continuing to use the name H.M. Howard, which he had recorded on his most recent marriage certificate, had already taken out a $10,000 life insurance policy on Pitzel, who naively assumed that it was to be a simple matter of locating a cadaver, burning it beyond recognition, and then convincing the authorities that the deceased was indeed Ben Pitzel. But this time Holmes dispensed with the body-double plot and murdered his faithful accomplice. Pitzel, masquerading as B.F. Perry, was a victim of chloroform poisoning inside a dank Philadelphia row house at 1316 Callowhill Street, where Holmes had opened a patent agency. A sudden explosion inside the building September 4, 1894, charred the corpse, making Pitzel's identification difficult but not quite impossible. A broken bottle of benzene and a pipe—the kind of smoking implement Pitzel carried with him at all times—were found next to the body and identified.

The burned remains of the deceased were buried in a potter's field, and an insurance claim was promptly filed. Jeptha Howe, representing the grieving widow, Carrie A. Pitzel, claimed the money, just as Holmes had directed. Previous to this, the Pitzels' young son, eight-year-old Howard Pitzel, had been murdered and stuffed inside a chimney in an Irvington, Indiana, residence that Holmes had rented in October

1894—although this fiendish crime had not yet been detected, and Carrie was deceived into believing that her son was traveling with Holmes and unhurt.

The mother of Howard was sent by Holmes from town to town to carry out one foolish errand after another, while she was caring for her sickly one-year-old infant and her 16-year-old daughter Meda. As she did this, her two other daughters, Alice and Nellie Pitzel, were removed from the Albion Hotel in Toronto, done away with, and buried at 16 St. Vincent Street in the cellar of a residence belonging to Frank Nudel, chief clerk of the Toronto Department of Education. Holmes rented the man's house in October 1894 and asphyxiated the children inside a locked trunk. Detective Geyer, aided by the Toronto police, unearthed the remains and confirmed their identities.

Although wanted by Chicago detectives for his earlier insurance frauds, Holmes might have gotten away with his latest caper and retreated back into the shadows for the time being if not for the confession of Marion Hedgepeth (1856–1910), a revengeful St. Louis con man and convicted train robber who was serving a 25-year stretch for looting $75,000 from a Missouri-Pacific train. Hedgepeth was well acquainted with H.H. Holmes because they had briefly shared space in the lockup after Holmes was incarcerated for an earlier fraud he had perpetrated against the Merrill Drug Company.[12] Hedgepeth, the leader of a gang of cutthroats known as the Hedgepeth Four, had provided Holmes with a referral to Attorney Jeptha Howe and believed he was entitled to a promised $500 finder's fee, which of course Holmes had no intention of paying. Weeks later, after Holmes had secured his release on bail—courtesy of the obliging Mr. Howe—Hedgepeth wrote a letter to Major Lawrence Harrigan of the St. Louis Police Department telling what he knew of the Philadelphia insurance swindle in return for the promise of a reduced sentence.

Chief Harrigan immediately notified the Philadelphia insurance company, and the local authorities in the City of Brotherly Love commenced a manhunt. Philadelphia Coroner Ashbridge next issued a warrant for arrest after Pitzel's identity was established by his widow, who identified a bruised thumbnail and an unmistakable wart on the back of the victim's neck that was instantly recognizable, even though the face was blackened and blistered from the burns. Two dollars were pulled from the decedent's pocket, and after an autopsy was conducted, the remains were conveyed to a potter's field.

The arrest warrant made its way to Massachusetts, where the district attorney in Boston tracked down Holmes and dragged him into custody on November 17, 1894. The long string of insurance scams, including the murders of 27 people—quite possibly more—was finally over. "Pitzel's alive and well in San Salvador," Holmes declared. He said that the body found on Callowhill Street was a cadaver that he had imported from New York, but at that point, his statements were impossible to believe. As the complex threads of this story slowly unraveled, the nation was shocked by the savagery of the crimes. In a chivalrous age such as the late Victorian Era, the murder of women and innocents was all the more appalling to public sensibility and was considered a crime against nature. They called Holmes a "Modern Bluebeard"—and much worse. "The idea of Holmes escaping the death penalty is too painful to be entertained," opined the *Chicago Tribune* on July 17, 1895. "Such escape would be a libel on justice and an everlasting disgrace to anyone who could stoop to defend him."

Inside his Philadelphia jail cell, Holmes talked casually and freely of his life, reveling in the press attention and unafraid of the trial ahead of him—although he expressed grave concerns that the state of Texas might insist upon his extradition. In 1894 it was common practice to hang horse thieves in the Lone Star State—and among Holmes's many deceptive practices was a gigantic horse swindle carried out in Fort Worth while posing as O.C. Pratt as he gained control of Minnie Williams's inheritance.

What would they do with the likes of this Yankee swindler? Holmes wondered as he called the murder charge "foolish." He declared that he would defend himself in open court, saying: "After all, the worst they can get me for in Philadelphia is an insurance fraud."[13] Nevertheless, J. Carroll McCaffrey, Samuel P. Rotan, and William A. Shoemaker were retained as co-counsel when the trial commenced in the Philadelphia courtroom of Judge Michael Arnold on October 28, 1895. Proceedings lasted four days, and despite the tawdry twists and turns of the defendant's life, the trial would have been unremarkable if not for Holmes's decision to dismiss his lawyers and undertake his own defense. The proceedings of the court and the intricacies of the law of the Pennsylvania Commonwealth eventually overwhelmed Holmes after he bungled his cross-examination of witnesses. At that point the defense team was engaged once more.

The bitter denunciation of Georgiana Yoke, summoned to the stand as a prosecution witness, provided moments of high drama and revealed the first crack in Holmes's placid demeanor. Only then did he appear to lose his nerve and display sorrowful emotion. It was quite apparent that he was taken aback by her testimony, in which she attacked him as the devil incarnate, a monster who had shamed and humiliated her and attempted to make her a party to his awful deeds. Carrie A. Pitzel followed her to the witness stand and essentially made the same pronouncements. Holmes did not testify, and his legal team waived their closing arguments. There was consensus among the members of the press that the prosecution had not proven their case beyond a shadow of a doubt. In fact, many superstitious observers believed Holmes was likely to beat the rap because he had the devil in him, and Satan was certain to fix the outcome. Inside his jail cell the archfiend made unsettling pronouncements that Satan had taken possession of his soul. The proof he offered was in his rapidly changing appearance. "I am convinced that since my imprisonment I have changed woefully and gruesomely from what I was formerly in feature and in figure. I mean in fact that my features are assuming nothing more than a pronounced satanical aspect. From what I can see I believe fully that I am growing to resemble the devil; that the osseous part of my head and my face are gradually assuming the elongated shape so pronounced in what is called the degenerate head, and that the similitude is almost completed. I am convinced I no longer have anything human in me."[14]

The jury retired on November 2, 1895, and came back with a resounding verdict of guilty. "In the name of almighty God I state that I have not taken human life!" Holmes solemnly declared. But in the weeks and months leading up to his scheduled appointment on the gallows, Chicago police were kept busy digging in the basement of the castle. And only then, as piles of human bones were extracted from underneath the flooring, was the full magnitude of Holmes's crimes revealed to the world. Chicago police were desirous of extraditing him back to Chicago to answer for the murders of Julia and Pearl Connor, but the date of execution had already been set for May 6, 1896, in Philadelphia. There was no going back.

The condemned man spent five sleepless nights reading his Bible before being led to the gibbet by Sheriff Samuel M. Clement and Assistant Superintendent Alexander Richardson of Moyamensing Prison, who were tasked with affixing the black head covering and fitting the noose securely around Holmes's neck. "Don't be in a hurry[,] Aleck!" Holmes cautioned because there was a dying declaration he wished to make. "Gentlemen, I have very few words to say. I would make no remarks at this time but for my feeling that in not speaking I would appear to acquiesce in my execution," Holmes began. "I wish to say only that the extent of my wrong-doing in taking human life is the killing of two women—they having died by my hand as the result of criminal operations." Holmes here claimed to have performed illegal abortions on both Emeline Cigrand and Julia Connor, sending them to their deaths unintentionally. He continued, "I wish also to state here, so that there can be no chance of misunderstanding hereafter, that I am not guilty of taking the lives of any of the Pitzel family, the three children, or the father[,] Benjamin Pitzel[,] of whose death I was convicted, and for which I am to hang today. That is all I have to say."[15]

"Are you ready?" Sheriff Clement asked as 60 spectators inched forward in their seats for a closer look.

"Yes, don't bungle! Goodbye!"

The freshly made rope tightened, and the drop fell at 10:12 a.m. in the prison corridor. "My client died like a man," observed Attorney Rotan. "He was collected perfectly and was cool up to the moment the trap fell and apparently he was less affected than anyone in the corridor."[16] Showing no sympathy, Detective Geyer called Holmes "an expert liar" and expressed satisfaction with the outcome. He traveled to Chicago not long after to observe the ongoing excavation of the castle basement and to gather fresh material for a forthcoming book he planned to write claiming personal credit for solving the H.H. Holmes mysteries through relentless methods of police detection. Although Holmes was deceased and his remains would molder in an unmarked grave encased in 10 feet of concrete in Holy Cross Cemetery, Delaware County, Pennsylvania, neither the vainglorious Geyer nor a host of latter-day armchair detectives and historians could truthfully claim that this case had been entirely resolved or that there ever was an "official ending" to the story.

Like Banquo's ghost, the specter of H.H. Holmes lurked in the shadows of Englewood, and the tales of his crimes never escaped the public memory even as a stranger legacy began to unfold: tragedy befell many who were involved in the prosecution and defense of Holmes, suggesting a demonic, beyond-the-grave curse—if one placed credence in such superstitious beliefs. J. Carroll McCaffrey, a man in good health and one of the defense attorneys, died suddenly on September 11, 1896. The foreman of the jury, Linford Biles, was accidentally electrocuted by a live wire on the roof of his home. Attorney William Shoemaker was disbarred from practicing law after attempting to foist upon the court a bogus affidavit. George S. Graham of the prosecution team was defeated in his efforts to be made a director of the prestigious Union League of Philadelphia. Judge Michael Arnold took sick and nearly died days after the trial concluded, and William K. Mattern, the coroner's physician who had conducted the autopsy of Pitzel's body and testified against Holmes, died of blood poisoning. The deaths of these men occurred within a year of the execution.

Patrick Quinlan, whose stock and trade was carpentry but whose lips remained sealed right up until the end, brought a $40,000 civil lawsuit against the Chicago Police Department in September 1895, charging the detective bureau with defamation of character by branding him a murder accomplice, subjecting both him and his wife, Ella, to the third degree "sweat," and detaining him for three weeks with violent criminals and assorted ne'er-do-wells within the dank armory lockup on Harrison Street, Chicago's equivalent of the infamous Tombs Prison in New York City. In the ghoulish courtroom display that followed, city attorneys exhibited skulls and skeletal fragments believed to be Julia Connor and Emeline Cigrand in order to demonstrate that at the very least Quinlan was guilty of trafficking human remains with local medical schools. The civil suit was called frivolous and dismissed. Unable to clear their names or restore their reputations, Quinlan and his wife, Ella, left Chicago. The former keeper of the castle committed suicide at his farm in Portland, Michigan, on March 6, 1914, saying he could no longer sleep through the night. Before drawing his final breath, Quinlan told the attending physician that he had ingested strychnine in order to escape his earthly torment.

Troubling reminders of Holmes's misdeeds and a trail of human bones kept surfacing in odd places long after he was gone. On September 18, 1896, a bank bookkeeper found a crudely dug grave in the dense woods between the adjoining Chicago suburbs of Evanston and Wilmette. A curious mound of dirt devoid of underbrush convinced A.H. Parker and his wife that something unnatural rested just below the surface. Workers were summoned to the site, and, using shovels and a pickax, they dug down—unearthing rib bones and a woman's skull, but no items of clothing or personal artifacts to suggest the identity of the victim. It appeared that the remains were actually two people, but, lacking modern forensic techniques, identification was impossible. Pointing in the direction of the former Holmes residence in Wilmette, which stood less than 1,000 feet away, it was deduced that these remains must have been deposited by none other than the 63rd Street monster while he was still in residence on the North Shore with Myrtle Belknap. But that opinion was by no means conclusive.

More skeletons—presumably from Holmes's castle—were unearthed on September 11, 1914, on the site of the Van Kirk farm in Momence, Illinois, 40 miles due south of Chicago. A plowman breaking an old field that had lain fallow for many a year turned up the scattered bones of a woman. Two other skeletons were dug up nearby, reminding Kankakee County residents that teams of investigators swarming through the area in 1895 had previously dug this field but turned up nothing. Those investigators of 1895 had acted on a tip that the bodies of the missing Williams sisters might be buried there; however, time had long since destroyed whatever clues could be gleaned from an examination of the old bones in 1914.

Remarkably, the Holmes murder castle withstood two fires set by arsonists, and condemnation proceedings assured that the structure remained a curious Englewood landmark for another 43 years before the wrecking company finally reduced it to a pile of rubble in January 1938. The U.S. Government paid $61,000 to 88-year-old Emma Anderson, a resident of the Sovereign Hotel and the recorded owner of the castle, for the title to the premises. Before demolition, Anderson leased the ground floor retail space in the creaking old castle to a used magazine and book dealer and a commercial sign manufacturing business. After she had sold her interests, the castle was torn down so that construction could begin on the Englewood branch of the U.S. Post Office. The old W.P.A. post office still stands today in a squalid, gang-infested slum that suffers the highest murder rate per capita of any neighborhood in Chicago. It might be argued that the modern-day horrors of everyday living in Englewood are in some ways representative of the grim legacy that Holmes left behind on this distressed corner of the city.

The final and most compelling mystery associated with Holmes and his murder castle is the true identity of the elusive and mysterious Holmes accomplice Jake Hatch, aka Dernberg and many other aliases. In July 1895, a man identifying himself as a machinist and claiming to possess intimate knowledge of Holmes's operations paid a call on the desk sergeant at the Cottage Grove Avenue police station. He said he had worked for Holmes several years earlier and though he said he was not a party to the murders or any of Holmes's con games, the man had something very interesting to show police in a deserted house out on the West Side near the Cook County Hospital.

The police peppered Mr. Dernberg with questions, but he played his cards close to the vest until entering the West Side address. Then Dernberg lifted the lid of an old-fashioned Saratoga trunk, revealing the half-articulated skeleton of a woman and a set of medical books, treatises on the art and science of articulation, a three-cent piece with a hole bored through the edge of the coin and likely worn as a jewelry charm, and a tintype photo of an unknown woman. The tintype was thought to be a relative of the victim. Chicago Police Inspector John

E. Fitzpatrick, who led the local portion of the nationwide investigation, drew an audible gasp and ordered the trunk taken by wagon to his private office downtown. It was ascertained from Dernberg that the old and battered trunk had been carted away from the castle at Holmes's insistence in June or July of 1893. At the time of delivery to the West Side, the trunk had contained the body of a nude woman. The date, June or July of 1893, coincided with the disappearance of Julia Connor and Emeline Cigrand, but there was no way for Dernberg to positively confirm that the body was either of these women. Holmes gave specific instructions to have the body taken to M.G. Chappell, the bone articulator, where Chappell was to remove the tissue and skin and mount the skeleton. Dernberg said he knew this to be standard procedure because he had been to the castle many times before and pointed out locations in the basement where he had observed other bodies awaiting dissection.[17]

The man was taken to the interrogation room downtown where he was subjected to the notorious third-degree sweat—the barbaric art and technique of grilling witnesses and criminal suspects perfected in Chicago in the 1890s by police inspectors Herman Schuettler and John Fitzpatrick and copied by police departments across the country. The sweatbox at Central Station was a plain, neatly furnished room with a rolltop desk and three chairs—nothing more. A prisoner might be confined to the room for one day or four weeks—it did not matter to detectives because it was the admission of guilt that counted, not a respect for civil liberties. This was certainly true in the brutal and violent world of Chicago policing in the 1890s. In time the extortion of confessions from detainees became a contentious issue that wound its way through the higher courts of Illinois prior to codes being enacted to check the impulses of violent police interrogators. Dernberg, if that was in fact his real name, acquitted himself well under such intense scrutiny and convinced police that he was just an innocent middleman from the West Side earning a tough living locating and dropping off cadavers to the Cook County Hospital medical school. He said his motive in leading police to this charnel house and the discovery of the grisly remains in the trunk arose from a sense of civic duty, adding that he had "suspicions" about Holmes. Dernberg said he was anxious to assist the investigation any way he could, but why he had waited so long was puzzling.

The trunk containing the books and the bones was locked away in a dingy, windowless evidence room in back of the main elevators in City Hall. The room and the adjoining vaults were maintained by Custodian of Property John D. Hall. There the remains of Julia Connor or Emeline Cigrand languished until the storage area was cleaned out and a caretaker with a conscience would see that the bones were taken to the coroner for proper interment.

The comings and goings of the persuasive Mr. Dernberg, aka Jake Hatch, were of passing interest to police investigators after he was permitted to leave the sweatbox and was released from custody. Hatch, who had alternately worked as a carpenter, janitor, and machinist, was alleged to be a party to the Fort Worth swindle. According to Holmes's statements to the press from his cell in Moyamensing, he had placed Howard Pitzel in the custody of his sidekick Hatch until October 11, 1893, when he was to pick up the boy at the Detroit train station. "The boy was not with him," Holmes maintained. "Hatch told me he left Howard with Minnie Williams. I thought the child was safe. But I hardly think Hatch is in prison. If he was I would have known it. He was engaged with me in several of my business enterprises. It is for the police investigators to find him . . . if they can." As he said this, there was a smirk on Holmes's face, and the tone of his voice was riddled with sarcasm. "I am confident they will not find him in prison. I think he is in the West between Chicago and San Francisco. I have not heard from him."[18]

Was it Hatch who escorted the boy to Irvington, Indiana, to chloroform and murder the lad in the rented house, or was this Hatch a contrived figure—an alter ego—sprung from the psychotic brain of the delusional psychopath H.H. Holmes as some have theorized? Another possibility was that Jake Hatch was Dernberg the bone-man or an Arkansas horse thief named J.C. Allen (who also answered to the aliases Caldwell and Mascot) who inspired subliminal fears in the edgy and nervous caretaker Patrick Quinlan. Quinlan told police that Allen was a real person, and as janitor he was subordinated to the whims of this man in the pecking order established by Holmes inside the castle. "He engineered all of the big deals for him [Holmes]," Quinlan testified. "I was not good enough for the *fine* work."[19]

Allen corroborated Quinlan's statement to the extent that he was the "confidential man" for Holmes and had received the deed to the Fort Worth property from Minnie Williams but denied that he had anything to do with her murder. In an attempt to reduce his fifteen-year sentence for horse thieving, Allen revealed to the warden of the Arkansas State Penitentiary in Little Rock that Quinlan—not he—was "in on" the murders of the two sisters all along. He said that he had overheard Holmes and Quinlan whispering plans for Minnie's removal from the premises. Until this confession was made public in the newspapers, many considered Hatch and J.C. Allen one and the same.

Jake Hatch, real or imagined, was never found. He vanished and was forgotten by time, meriting little interest to the police once Holmes was hung. His name did not become a matter of public record again until 1905, when Evelyn Campbell, the ambitious Hearst reporter for the *Chicago American,* played a hunch and began poking around the old Englewood haunts of H.H. Holmes and his former henchmen. Campbell sought out neighbors and acquaintances with long memories of the Englewood nightmare in the hope of establishing the startling evidence to prove that Jake Hatch was none of the original suspects—but in fact was the murdering German bigamist and mixer of poisons, Johann Hoch.

Chapter Six

"Strong and self-determined" was about the kindest description the townsfolk of LaPorte were willing to grant Belle Gunness. Deliverymen, farmers, neighbors, and shopkeepers told stories of her amazing physical strength, calling her a female Paul Bunyan. As her infamy spread, stories began to circulate that she wasn't a woman at all but a man in drag always seen dashing about town in a man's fur coat and a sealskin cap during the cold winter months.

"Mrs. Gunness was a woman of unusual appearance," Dr. Harry H. Long, coroner of LaPorte County, conceded. "She was large, bony, powerful looking, with square jaws and black eyes. She was a woman who would attract attention anywhere from her lack of womanly characteristics. Her long strides, together with her remarkable countenance and her generally vicious appearance gave her an aspect that was almost terrifying."[1] People remembered her "large, grotesque" hands, ideally suited to slicing up pig carcasses and cooking up ham, bacon, and pork shoulders. On butchering days the men from the adjoining farms would shoot the animal, bleed it, and gut it—leaving the women to take care of the rest. Belle, however, performed these messy tasks herself. Mrs. C.C. "Frances" Lapham, a LaPorte neighbor for nearly nine years, provided vivid descriptions of a wide leather belt containing pouches and variously sized knife sheaths that Belle wore underneath her loose-fitting housedresses. This hand-tooled holster belt held various carving and paring knives ideal for cutting up farm animals, a side of ham—or a human being.

"She was a strong enough woman to be able to kill a man of size if she took him unaware," opined Cook County Coroner Peter Hoffman. "As to her ability to cut them up afterwards she needed no practice as a skillful surgeon to accomplish that. The woman was simply a good carver."[2]

The question of Belle's true gender was raised many years later by author Lillian de la Torre in her 1955 potboiler *The Truth about Belle Gunness*. The issue was probed in greater depth in Janet Langlois's 1985 volume focusing on the folkloric and feminist dimensions of the case. Langlois asked: "Was Belle Gunness a typical farm woman or was she not? A series of questions—Was her strength magnified by tellers whose rules for gender were formed under more urbanized conditions? Was she a disguised man using the stereotype of the peasant woman once again to gain his own ends?"[3] Attaching greater sociological significance to Belle Gunness than she probably deserved or is entitled to, Langlois wrote: "In fusing men and women's spheres in the agricultural domain, the Belle Gunness figure actually duplicated the transitional roles of women in the American work force under the urban influence at the turn of the century."[4] With this statement, Langlois seems to suggest that increasing industrialization in the U.S. at this time was creating new opportunities for women in the workplace as they stepped outside the home to accept jobs in factories, department stores, and offices.

Gunness used and manipulated her gender to suit her purposes and achieve her aims, just as Johann Hoch was doing concurrently in Chicago and across the U.S. By no stretch of the imagination, however, could Belle Gunness be compared to the "Gibson Girl," artist Charles Dana Gibson's idealized, iconic image of fashionable American femininity at the turn of the last century.[5] But neither was she a cross-dressing lesbian, a man in drag, or even a mythic figure carved from local Indiana storytelling and legend. All she amounted to was a physically strong, willful criminal sociopath and clever manipulator who used her gender to the greatest advantage. While many considered her mannish and physically unappealing for the eye to behold, others, such as the Chicago photographer R.C. Ganiere and her church minister in LaPorte, noted her stylish appearance and commented favorably on her maternal skills.

Questions about Belle's sexual identity were first asked by her La-Porte neighbors in the spring of 1903, following the arrival of baby Phillip Gunness. Mrs. William Nicholson found the doors to the Gunness manse bolted shut when, in neighborly fashion, she volunteered to assist Belle in the delivery of the baby; however, under no circumstances would Belle permit anyone to witness the birth. Dora Diesslin Rosenow related how odd it seemed to her that Mrs. Gunness was out in the yard chasing after her pigs and washing the baby blankets in the cistern just two days after birthing a son. "Ah, in the old country they never go to bed after they got a baby!" Belle said and laughed.[6]

If Gunness had indeed managed to give birth to Phillip, she would have been a 44-year-old mother—not a physical impossibility, but nevertheless it seems rather unlikely. Midwife Mary Swenson told investigators that she remembered being called to Brookside Farm but arrived too late to assist the mother. When she set eyes on little Phillip for the first time, she was astonished to find the child washed and clothed and looking much too old to be a newborn.

The rural LaPorte women echoed the same dark suspicions as Belle's Chicago neighbors in Austin had—that Belle Gunness was faking pregnancies and claiming other people's children as her own. No birth certificate for Phillip was ever tracked down, and rumors circulated that the child was "dropped off" at the Gunness farm in the dead of night. Frances Lapham spoke up for the rest of the gossipy neighbors and boldly stated that Belle had murdered another woman and took the victim's baby. "Belle was as big as a man," she said. "Maybe she *was* a man."[7] After interviewing a score of LaPorte people, a *Chicago Journal* reporter concluded that Mrs. Gunness was a "female Hercules."

With the strength of Hercules, Belle smashed the skull of her second husband, Peter Gunness, on December 16, 1902—nine months after their church wedding. At the inquest, Belle described the circumstances of her beloved Peter's death as a terrible, terrible accident—not an act of willful murder. On the night of December 16, he was sitting next to the kitchen stove, and while reaching over to pick up his shoe, his body weight jarred the shelf above, dislodging a sausage grinder and a stone jar containing hot water. Both items crashed down on his head, resulting in a deep cut to the scalp. Belle attended his injury and applied Vaseline to ease the pain. Peter did not lose consciousness but lay down on the couch to rest. Then he fell asleep. At three o'clock the following morning, Belle was awakened from her slumber by the sound of her husband groaning. She went to his side but before a physician could arrive, Peter Gunness was already dead.

Dr. B.O. Bowell, who worked as a physician for Coroner Long, determined that death was caused by skull fracture. He measured the distance of the fall, weighed the machine, and concluded that no foul play was involved. But wasn't it rather puzzling that Mr. Gunness did not lose consciousness immediately after sustaining the fatal wound?

Gust Gunness, the dead man's skeptical brother who never countenanced Peter's marriage to this woman in the first place, was summoned from Minneapolis to come down to LaPorte. "I stayed there several days," he said. "Mrs. Gunness begged me continuously to stay with her and manage the farm. 'We can get along nicely together,' she said, 'and we will make good money here for I know you are a good farmer.' I didn't like her eyes and I didn't like the place so I refused. I didn't think we could get along. I had no money to speak of. I tell you—I'm glad I didn't take up that offer."[8]

The following spring, Gust returned to LaPorte to remove his niece, Swanhilda, from Belle's care. The girl was lonely and desperately wanted to live among her blood relatives, but Belle refused to let her go. "She will be well cared for here," Gust Gunness was assured. Failing in his attempt to hire a local attorney to sue Belle for a division of his brother's $3,500 life insurance policy intended to benefit the orphaned girl, Gust and his brother Carl contrived to remove Swanhilda by stealth methods. Under the cover of night, the brothers spirited her away from LaPorte to Edgerton, Minnesota, a small rural town located in the southwest corner of the state. "When my papa married that woman," Swanhilda stated in a later interview, "he took us down there to live with her on a farm. She treated me all right when papa was around but all of us were afraid of her, even Myrtle and Lucy, and Jennie Olsen was too. After papa died she treated us worse than ever. Pretty soon after papa died that woman began having men to see her. I stayed there almost a year when Uncle Gust came and got me and I came away to where my grandma lived."[9] The uncles were convinced that their decisive action spared the life of their brother's daughter, and it probably did.[10]

The surviving "daughters"—Jennie Olsen, Myrtle, and Lucy—drew away from Belle and rejected her terms of endearment, but they knew better than to defy her authority and were considered by all to be sweet and well-behaved children. Each week they rode to the Methodist Sunday School in a cart drawn by a little pony. "Mother loves you more than all of the world," Belle would entreat them, "and will make rich women of you some day." Instead of embracing her with loving affection, the girls would often recoil and cast a wary glance in her direction as they ran through the yard with Belle's collie dog, Prince, and played their childish games on the property.

The girls' recollections contradicted Nellie Larsen's memories of Belle and her supposed "fondness" for children. "When she came to Chicago she would attend the children's picnics at Humboldt Park and would get up on the platform and offer to take care of the children," Larsen said. "I have heard her get up and say, 'Are there any children in the audience who want to go home with me? Are there no young ones who need a home and will come with me to my farm? I will care for them.'"[11]

Following the death of Peter Gunness, a succession of male visitors turned up at Brookside Farm. Most were unattached men of Nordic descent hailing from small towns in the Upper Midwest and Great Plains who had answered her lonely hearts placements in the matrimonial notices of the *Skandinaven*. Emil Greening, a 17-year-old carpenter who had worked with his brother Fred performing handyman chores at the Gunness farm, admitted to a romantic infatuation with the pretty, blonde-haired, blue-eyed Jennie Olsen. He remembered the peculiar circumstances surrounding the arrival and disappearance of so many middle-aged men from the farm. "Mrs. Gunness received men visitors all the time," Greening said. "A different man came nearly every week to stay at the house. She introduced them as 'cousins' from Kansas, South Dakota, Wisconsin and from Chicago. Most of the men that came brought trunks with them but they rarely took the trunks away. Mrs. Gunness kept the 'cousins' with her all the time in the parlors and her bedroom. She was always careful to make the children stay away from her 'cousins' who rarely tried to show them any affection. I believe that many murders were done right under my nose."[12]

Day laborers hired by Gunness for seasonal work disappeared just as quickly as her out-of-town suitors. Olaf Lindboe was a 35-year-old Wisconsin man who moved from a dairy farm in Rockefeller, Illinois, to accept Belle's offer of employment. He labored on the Gunness farm from March to July 1905 and then vanished. Chris Christofferson, who lived at 702 D Street in LaPorte, met Olaf Lindboe, a lighthearted and easygoing man, three or four times by his recollections until one day at the height of the plowing season—when Lindboe was most needed—he was suddenly gone. "Probably it was the last day of May or the first part of June 1905, that I went to Mrs. Gunness and found her plowing corn on a riding plow," he stated. "I expressed surprise at finding her at this enterprise. She explained that she had to herself plow as Lindboe had left her. I expressed surprise that he had left her in the midst of plowing. She said that he had gotten a letter from a land grant and that he could get [a] free ride to the St. Louis—that he had gone to St. Louis to the fair and that he was going to buy some land. I said it was funny that he did not come around and bid goodbye to me. She said no—he had gotten in a hurry to leave."[13] Belle changed the story and told her inquisitive neighbors that Lindboe had "gone back to Norway" to witness the coronation of King Haakon VII following passage of the resolution by the Norwegian *Storting* to dissolve the historic union with Sweden.

Henry Gurholt, another migrant Wisconsin man, succeeded Lindboe but lasted less than five months. Christofferson remembered the day that Gurholt arrived at the farm to begin work. "I helped him carry his trunk upstairs into the room over the sitting room in the brick part of the house," he said. "I remember his saying to Mrs. Gunness when he had come down from carrying the trunk up, that she had given him a nice room. She said, 'Oh yes! I always like to have it neat and nice for a person who works for me,' or something like that. Along in August 1905, Mrs. Gunness had Gurholt cut some oats for her. Then she came down and got me to stack the oats. She said Gurholt had, after cutting the oats, said he was sick and could not stack the oats, but that he had left her."[14]

Throughout his travels, Gurholt had kept in close touch with his family in Scandinavia, Wisconsin, but the last letter home was dated July 4, 1905, to his brother Martin who supplied Coroner's Clerk Charles Mack with a verbal summary of the original document on May 25, 1908. "In the letter dated April 20th, 1905, he is in good health and that he likes the farm where he is—that on the farm are apple trees, pear trees, and peach trees and that they are starting to blossom; that it is one of the nicest places in the neighborhood. He goes on to say that the house is of brick with thirteen rooms—that there is a grove of nice green trees planted around the house and that he is being treated almost the same as one of the family—that LaPorte is an awful nice village. In the letter dated May 16, 1905 he says there are practically no Norwegians about LaPorte but there are a few Swedes."[15] Following his disappearance, Belle explained to his family that Henry had left her place in August in order to go to Chicago to work as a horse trader in the Union Stock Yards. He had abandoned his trunk and fur overcoat, and both became Belle's property. She was seen wearing the coat all over town during the January chill.

George Berry of Tuscola, Illinois, came to LaPorte that same month with $1,500, the intention of working on her farm, and eventually marrying Mrs. Gunness—but that was the last anyone saw of him. An unidentified, 50-year-old Ohio man replaced Gurholt, but he disappeared at oat-cutting time. He left behind a horse and buggy that Belle put to good use. Gurholt had a black mustache, and Lindboe's was reddish—descriptions that matched two corpses later unearthed at the Gunness murder farm.

In June 1907, Gunness hired Ray Lamphere, a curly-haired, 37-year-old Indiana man, for carpentry work and assorted odd jobs. Lamphere was a jack-of-all-trades who was talented with a hammer and nail but otherwise dull-witted, plodding, and unimaginative. He claimed to have worked as a builder for twenty years and said that he carried a membership card in the Carpenter's Union in Chicago Heights. From a fellow carpenter, Lamphere received a job referral concerning work that needed to be done out at the Gunness place, and soon he met up with Belle at a pre-arranged time on the street in LaPorte. He was hired immediately.

As their relationship unfolded, it seemed that there was nothing Lamphere wouldn't do to please the "Mistress of McClung Road." By his own admission the two became sexually intimate despite a 12-year age difference between the older woman and the younger man in her employ. Gunness was 48 in 1907; Lamphere was 36. He said that as the relationship evolved, Mrs. Gunness had proposed marriage to him on several occasions and encouraged him to take out a life insurance policy naming her as the sole benefactor. She said she would promise to pay the premiums providing that he would agree to marry her. His refusal to agree to these terms led to a bitter and acrimonious falling out, but during the time he remained in her good graces, Lamphere kept her secrets and respected her wishes to the point of aiding and abetting murder. As a hired hand, Lamphere knew better than to attempt to break into Belle's "secret room" on the second floor of the farm house—the "Bluebeard death chamber"—where presumably all of the gruesome work of cutting up the bodies was carried out, although the basement cellar was another area of the house where the grisly "leather apron" tasks were believed to have been carried out. Belle held in her possession the only key to the second-floor room.

Ray Lamphere was a watery-eyed sot, the ne'er-do-well son of William Lamphere, an elderly produce farmer who had once been a justice of the peace and one of LaPorte's most prominent and respected politicians until hard times set in and reduced his circumstances. The elder Lamphere always said that his son "was a good boy," but the only thing against him was his love of drink.

On any given night Ray could be found imbibing alone or in the company of one or two confidantes in the dimly lit barrooms of LaPorte, and always in the far corner, away from the door and the prying eyes of the other patrons. When he was drunk—which, according to the testimony of locals, was nearly all the time—he was gloomy and bitter as he contemplated his sorry predicament as the keeper of Belle's secrets. While in his cups one night at "Dockie" Shoemaker's place on McClung Road, he boasted to Bessie Wallace—one of his saloon mates—about his alleged "control" over Mrs. Gunness. "I got the old she-devil where I want her! I know enough to make her get down to her knees to me. I could send her to the gallows for what I know about her! See these clothes? They cost $40. She paid for them. But that isn't enough. I need money bad and I am going to get it from her."[16] In his more sober moments, this mask of self-bravado evaporated because Lamphere knew and understood that Belle was aware of a few of his own painful and incriminating secrets—that he was a bigamist and a scoundrel with several wives scattered across the country. Those wives included a jilted and abandoned woman in Allegheny, Pennsylvania, who had hired a private detective named George Roman to track him down.[17]

The tortured relationship between Gunness and Lamphere was peculiar but was clearly one of parasitical codependency. Belle obsessed over what he might say and what he would choose to keep to himself. So she watched him closely, causing Lamphere to shudder nervously each time he passed by the Gunness graveyard, knowing that if he wasn't careful he just might end up in the same shallow plot of ground as his predecessors.

Chapter Seven

In 1892, Johann Hoch fled from New York State and a trail of broken-hearted spinsters and widows who knew him for a time under a dozen different aliases to which he answered. Chicago, the World's Fair City and a vista of opportunity for persuasive con men, now beckoned.

His background, his personal interests in medicine and anatomy, and indeed his circuitous path along the Eastern seaboard, mirrored that of H.H. Holmes. Identical in age and temperament and possessed by a predatory, yet disarming gentility, Holmes and Hoch were flip sides of the same coin: both men were driven by an insatiable greed, lack of conscience, and narcissistic personalities. Neither held women in high regard, and they viewed their victims with withering contempt.

Hoch was sarcastic, glib, and quick with a joke—masking his true feelings toward his female victims with candy, flowers, and gifts. Just as Belle Gunness engendered warm, nostalgic memories of "home and hearth" in her seductive letters to prospective bachelors, Johann Hoch also knew how to exploit his victims' inherent fears of loneliness, separation from kinfolk in the old country, and isolation in a new land. He spiced his lies and half-truths to the authorities with personal asides and boasted about the art and technique of maneuvering credulous females into his web.

Gunness was never as vain as Hoch—although she was the more deliberate and calculating of the two, effectively plotting her strategy like a skilled chess master anticipating an opponent's next move before the opponent had even thought of it. While Gunness "nested," Johann Hoch lived in the moment; Hoch was a treacherous phantom scurrying from place to place, rapidly adapting to new people, places, and situations—making up the rules of the game as he moved along. "If you want to kill your wife and get the money and at the same time avoid suspicion, be a devout husband," Hoch advised in a rare moment of self-reflection.[1] His was an indiscriminate, frenzied existence.

Settling in Chicago with murder in mind, Hoch rented a flat at 2951 Keeley Street, which was in the German North Side 9th Ward neighborhood. The location was fifteen miles due north of the Holmes Castle in Englewood but was easily accessible via the Metropolitan elevated line linking up the South and North sides of the city. The vast network of public transit lines inaugurated into service in Chicago during the early 1890s made it possible to traverse once distant and remote areas of the city in relatively short periods of time—and criminals were no longer confined to one neighborhood or precinct.

Hoch had deep connections in South Side communities. He had, on several occasions, solicited employment in the town of Pullman, south of Englewood, and worked in the machinery shops for a time. He was no stranger to the side of town where Holmes carried out his abysmal deeds during the years 1888–1893. Later he established a permanent residence on South Union Avenue, a block south of 63rd and Wallace. The trail of evidence and the suspicion that Hoch was the alter ego of Jake Hatch, the elusive Holmes henchman, is at best circumstantial—but neither can it be easily discounted. The swindling techniques employed by both archfiends were remarkably similar in their planning and execution.

Hoch engaged Fred Magerstadt & Company at 901 Milwaukee Avenue in the Polish quarter on the Northwest Side to provide the furnishings for his living quarters. Hoch said he would pay on the installment plan, and no questions were asked of him. The scheme was to demonstrate to his intended victim that he was a sincere man of some importance with a finely appointed "bachelor's den" to show off, thus necessitating his frequent dealings with furniture retailers. He had no intention of satisfying his debt with this firm. At approximately the same time and employing the same modus operandi, Holmes was bilking the Tobey Company. Hoch's bill was $47.80.

Three weeks after he rented his flat on Keeley Street under the pseudonym C.A. Mayer, Hoch's first Chicago wife passed away under mysterious circumstances. Her name had disappeared to history by the time Hoch was questioned in his jail cell in 1905 about this crime. He couldn't remember it and said there was no point in even asking.

Posing as H. Irick, the little fat man with the red, round face and oily manner married his second Chicago wife scarcely one month later in June 1892, moving her into comfortable surroundings at 481 Franklin Street, with additional items of furniture purchased for $115 from Magerstadt. "I asked him why he changed his name every time he got married and he said he had been so unfortunate with his wives that other women might object to marrying him," the furniture dealer reported.[2] The explanation seemed entirely reasonable at the time—this was, after all, a superstitious age. It was a widely accepted belief that a percentage of men by their very nature were unlucky in love or jinxed by repeated misfortunes.

Two months is the longest period of time that Hoch was known to have lived with one wife. He took his pick of the German widows and made them happy for all of a day or two—on average. If he discovered that a dowry was less than $300, he quickly dispatched that wife to an early grave forthwith. The ink was barely dry on the marriage certificate when some unknown "illness" would strike a wife down. He had no time for a poor woman deceiving him by masquerading as someone of financial means.

His second Chicago wife—her name also vanished from the record—expired just thirty days after the ceremony. "What happened to Mrs. Irick?" Hoch was asked later. "How should I know?" he snapped. "Mebbe' she ain't dead. Mebbe there ain't no woman by that name! Besides that's so long ago I have forgotten!"[3]

Hoch laid low in his marital pursuits through much of 1893—which is coincidentally when Holmes, Pitzel, and the mysterious Hatch were active in Chicago, Fort Worth, Denver, and Indianapolis. In the early winter months of 1894, not long before Holmes was seized and incarcerated in Philadelphia, Hoch resurfaced on Chicago's Northwest Side, where he opened a neighborhood tavern at Milwaukee and Western Avenues; he had acquired the tavern from one Louis Witte through matrimonial swindling. By the time of the tavern purchase, he was wooing and marrying his next victim, Mrs. Jacob Schmidt. During the courtship and engagement of Mrs. Schmidt, he reverted back to his German birth name.

Hoch sold the unpaid furniture from his marital adventures to third parties, and with the cash proceeds, he had enough money in hand to fool Magerstadt into believing that his business dealings were aboveboard, and therefore Magerstadt need not fear extending the credit line to him for a *third* purchase. When Hoch approached Magerstadt for more new furniture for the third time, once again the Milwaukee Avenue dealer happily obliged. The merchandise was delivered to 1008 N. Western Avenue, but soon Hoch sadly announced to Magerstadt that his new wife had run off. "This must have been one of those ladies who wandered off and their folks couldn't find them no more," Hoch declared.[4]

Hoch passed a busy year in 1894. In June he was married to the widow Julia Steinbrecher of 333 W. Belmont by Justice Moritz Kaufmann in the home of his best man, Benno Lechner, a saloon keeper at 394 Larrabee Street who first drew Hoch's attention to the lonely German woman living across the street from Lechner during her period of bereavement. "Two weeks afterward Hoch came to me—he was calling himself 'Heh' at that time—and told me that his wife was very sick and that he wanted $10 to buy medicine. I let him have it and went over to see Mrs. Heh," Lechner related. "She was very sick and said: 'That man is poisoning me.' I was just going to taste some of the medicine on the table when Heh came into the room and saw me," Lechner reported. 'Stop that!' he yelled. 'That is for the woman!' The next thing I heard was that Mrs. Heh was dead and that her husband had sold her property for nearly $4,000."[5]

The death scene was witnessed by the victim's grown foster son, William, who said he had stood by and observed Hoch as he administered a white powder to Julia on several occasions. "Hoch always sat beside her bed all the while. He would allow no one else to give her medicine," William recalled. "He constantly gave her a liquid in which he had mixed a white powder. I tasted this once when he was no[t] looking. It tasted like citrate of magnesia or sweetened lemon. Always after drinking it my mother had cramps in her stomach for half an hour. She called me to her bed one day and said: 'This man is not what he pretends to be. He wants to get my money! He is slowly poisoning me.'"[6] However, the son did not believe the accusation because her words were uttered while in a state of delirium. The victim's daughter-in-law reported Mrs. Steinbrecher to be in perfect health two months before her untimely death, a death attributed to nephritis, a painful disease of the kidneys for which there was no known cure. Strangely, both the son and the daughter-in-law waited *ten years* to report this information to the Chicago Police Department.

Mrs. Steinbrecher died at six o'clock in the evening. Hoch stripped her of her rings and earrings, and when the undertaker came to lay her out, Hoch kept saying: "*Mach geschwindt!*" [Hurry! Hurry!] Julia was interred at nine o'clock the next morning. Hoch did not intend for the neighbors to participate, but a large throng of well-wishers turned out to pay their respects anyway. While en route to Graceland Cemetery for the interment, the Steinbrecher funeral hearse and mourner's carriages were abruptly halted by a deputy from the Cook County coroner's office who demanded to see some papers. "I have been informed that this woman said on her death bed that her husband poisoned her!" the official declared.

A faint murmur was heard from the funeral procession as the deputy conferred with Hoch. "There is something wrong here," opined John Latheron, a family acquaintance. "A coroner's inquest *ought* to be held on this woman!"[7] It was a cold day, but Hoch perspired nervously. Hoch's attitude with this man was indignant, and he scolded the deputy for his impertinence. The horse-drawn carriages were allowed to proceed only after Hoch nervously produced a burial certificate signed by a physician appropriately named Dr. Grimme.

Hoch's abbreviated period of mourning ended one week later when he moved out of the Steinbrecher home, leaving behind the grieving young children and the maid, Annie Ebert, to whom he had proposed marriage in the kitchen following the funeral. Miss Ebert threatened to sue him for breach of promise after Hoch jilted her, but just a week after jilting the maid, Hoch zeroed in on his next intended victim, Mrs. Emma Rankan, a portly, middle-aged widow living at 375 Ward Street in Chicago—Hoch's temporary residence until the Steinbrecher children and the maid vacated his property. Emma Rankan, however, was nobody's fool: she was on guard and would not be swindled or murdered by a cad out to steal her money—and she was just as adept at playing the marriage game as Hoch. Mrs. Rankan, alias Warneke, alias Dumke, had been married a number of times and had collected sizeable sums of money from a score of ex-husbands *she* had swindled. Mrs. Rankan was wanted on a charge of bigamy and larceny in Jefferson Park, a neighborhood northwest of downtown Chicago. She responded—with the same motive in mind as Hoch—to Hoch's personal ad that appeared in the *Abendpost* a day after Julia's funeral. Emma Rankan's favorable reply to Hoch read:

> Honored Sir: Have read your advertisement in the *Abendpost* that you are looking for a housekeeper and that you are a widower, which causes me to write to you since I myself am a widow and am all alone. I have property and am living in a beautiful part of Chicago. Should you desire to make my acquaintance, kindly call and we can talk the matter over verbally. I think everything will be agreeable, but before you call please write a few lines. Address: Mrs. Emma Rankan, 375 Wells Street.[8]

Hours after nuptials were exchanged, Hoch escorted his bride to the former Steinbrecher home, unconcerned about the morbid impression that his actions must have made on Rankan. "I have a $1,400 mortgage on this place, and I need your money to pay the debt," he demanded. Rankan had hidden $3,000 in her residence—a tidy sum of money in those days—but refused to part with her life savings to help Hoch satisfy the obligation of her deceased predecessor. She found the tone of his voice threatening and noted with alarm that he owned a handgun. One day she emptied the cartridges from Hoch's revolver after observing him tucking the weapon into his desk drawer. She was certain at that point that he was going to kill her and had taken precautionary measures to ensure her safety.

The couple lived together in a South Side flat for all of three days, until Hoch grew impatient, pushed the weapon into her breast, and forcefully demanded the $3,000 after his more restrained and polite requests for her to part with the money fell on deaf ears. "I told him I would have to go to the safety deposit vault in the bank to get it, but first I had to go to my sister's house to get the key. Then I ran out the back door. I heard him snapping the revolver at me. I never saw him afterward," Rankan eventually revealed to police—but her own shifty background as a bigamist coupled with apprehensions about answering to criminal charges sealed her lips until the police turned up on her doorstep ten years later.[9]

Martha Herefeldt, wife number 7, exchanged vows with Hoch (who had adopted the alias Adolph Hoh) in the residence of Rev. Rudolph John, pastor of St. Paul's German Lutheran Church. She was another in a lengthening list of Hoch's victims who chose silence over prosecution. Hoch had located the woman through a shady matrimonial and employment agency at 2208 S. Wabash Avenue run by Gustav Strelow, a confederate who had been a party to several of Hoch's earlier schemes. As part of his duties, Strelow published a portrait of Hoch in his newspaper and circulated it among a bevy of housekeepers looking for work; these housekeepers were the widows and spinsters who registered at his office. He made it his personal business to know the financial circumstances of his female clients through background checks, the conducting of surveillance of likely targets as they transacted their business at the teller windows of banks, and discreet inquiries made with cooperative bank officials.

After his introduction to the companionable Martha Herefeldt, Hoch made his proposal in a calm, businesslike manner that appealed to Martha's practical side. Hoch soon gained possession of her entire estate, valued at $1,800. The couple moved into a building belonging to the woman's sister, Mrs. Mary Burmeister, at 198 Ontario Street on the North Side of the city. But after two months, Hoch announced that he was going back to Germany to claim a large fortune left to him by his late mother. At that point he deserted Martha. After waiting three months for a letter or postcard from her dear husband, Johann, Herefeldt concluded that she had been swindled and betrayed. Left nearly destitute, she fled from her sister's home to resettle in Pasadena, California.

The women Hoch abandoned (but left physically unharmed) preferred to hide behind a curtain of silence and anonymity rather than draw in the authorities and endure the unwanted attention and pain of a police investigation in which their names would show up in the newspapers. In the case of Martha Herefeldt, she lacked the funds to bring a civil lawsuit against Hoch or Strelow for recovery of her savings, but her unwillingness to file a criminal complaint made it possible for Johann Hoch to continue his lonely hearts manipulations that culminated in death for at least a dozen more women in Chicago and across state lines for the better part of the next decade.

It had been a busy and financially prosperous year for Hoch in Chicago. Up until 1898, the police had not made contact with him nor had they made any indirect inquiries that he was aware of. He reasoned that the police were either oblivious to the intrigues, too busy, or simply unconcerned. Lonely hearts fraud was an annoyance but not a pressing matter in police circles. In 1894, the city was in the throes of an economic depression and was suffering high unemployment following the close of the World's Fair. Hard times had set in across the land. Homeless men and an army of beggars roamed the downtown streets. Of even greater concern was a labor dispute in the town of Pullman that pitted the American Railway Union (ARU) against intractable officials of the Pullman Palace Car Company, where Hoch had been employed at various times; the dispute had erupted into violence and bloodshed, forcing the President of the United States to send in federal troops to quell the disturbance. In the wake of these large-scale problems, the bitter betrayal of a handful of elderly women by a fortune hunter received scant attention and was deemed a minor offense not worthy of a "copper's" time—even after a victim stepped forward to register a complaint. The encounter with the coroner's deputy gave Hoch a moment of nervous pause, and he knew that there was only so long before Magerstadt pressed his claim for the unpaid bill, but otherwise Hoch felt secure in the belief that he was smarter than the police; he was also aware that he was being protected by the embarrassed silence of the spinsters.

With his accumulated wealth acquired through deceit and murder, Hoch set out in February 1895 from Chicago for Wheeling, West Virginia. Posing as a wealthy Chicago man and going by the new alias

Jacob Huff, the squat little bigamist opened a saloon and *brauhaus* at 4728 Jacobs Street in Wheeling's German 8th Ward. The saloon was remembered as an agreeable public place appealing to the immigrant German population, where good lager flowed freely and Hoch serenaded patrons while accompanying himself on the zither, a stringed instrument he often used to impress ladies during courtship rituals. As was the case in Chicago, Hoch's involvement in the saloon trade made it possible for him to meet up with the right sort of people.

A nineteenth-century saloon of the type Hoch operated was more than a place of escape for hard-drinking men to drown their sorrows. It was also a focal point of community life where people socialized, exchanged useful information about job opportunities, voted in elections, and gained a rightful sense of belonging—all of which were especially important to newly arrived German immigrants who were accustomed to their nostalgic longing for the "continental Sundays" in the beer gardens of the old country.

Without Strelow's Chicago matrimonial bureau to provide fresh leads, Hoch joined the Wheeling "Mozart Singing Society" to meet some "quality, cultured women." Then for good measure, he struck up a friendship with a trusting local parson, the Reverend Herman C.A. Haas, to supply the necessary introductions to German-speaking widows in his congregation. Haas had noted with alarm Huff's harried, almost incessant pursuit of a score of eligible women but dismissed his feelings of unease toward Hoch (aka Jacob Huff), hoping he would settle down with one woman. The minister introduced him to Caroline Miller Hoch (he took this woman's married name as his own, and it became the most common alias he employed through his future pursuits), a widow with a house, $8,000 in the bank, and a $2,500 insurance policy. Reverend Haas married them at St. Matthew's Church on April 18, 1895, and the groom took up residence in Caroline's abode that same day.

Less than two months later, on June 14th, the good reverend was summoned to Caroline's bedside. She had lost considerable weight, and her complexion was pallid. Jacob Huff had been observed administering a white powder to his sickly wife, who protested at having to ingest this bitter-tasting medicine, raising Haas's suspicions. Not wanting to falsely accuse a man of trying to poison his wife without firm proof, the reverend hesitated in mentioning this to the authorities. When Caroline's condition did not improve, the reverend consulted Dr. Gregory Ackerman, a famed local surgeon and expert on diseases of the stomach, for an opinion.[10] Caroline's hands were swollen, she vomited continuously, and her stomach was distended by the ordeal. The following morning, the woman passed away from what Jacob Huff's attending physician, Dr. Ford, described as acute peritonitis.

Medical ethics were such that Dr. Ackerman dared not challenge a colleague's diagnosis, but when Reverend Haas went to the woman's home, he found the place empty and the body unattended. Jacob Huff was at the barbershop having his thinning hair and mustache trimmed when the reverend walked in and demanded an explanation. Huff broke into tears and buried his head in his hands as the barber stood back. "What is the meaning of this?" Haas demanded. He expected that the widower would be at home, in quiet mourning—not trading jokes with the town barber. "Have you no respect for the dead?"[11] Huff's spontaneous show of sudden grief seconds after he had laughed at his barber's joke convinced the reverend that this man was not only ice-cold but had blood on his hands.

That afternoon, Haas made the rounds of the local drugstores to see if anyone matching Huff's description had recently purchased a white, powdered medicine for relief of stomach troubles but was told that nothing had been dispensed by any of the druggists he visited. Next, an inquiry at the local real estate office revealed that Huff's saloon was being closed down. The proprietor had not paid his bills to the Belmont Brewing Company as well as a score of creditors, including Dr. Ford.

Caroline was buried the following day at the Red Men's Cemetery, a private burial ground for the members and family members of a local fraternal lodge in Wheeling. Adolph Hoch, Caroline's first husband and a steelworker from Ritchietown (South Wheeling) until his death at age 31, on July 7, 1892, was interred in the same plot.[12]

Meanwhile, Haas conducted a thorough search of the woman's sickroom but could not locate any mysterious bottles of medicine left behind. By now Huff/Hoch deduced that the reverend was on to his game and moved quickly to close out his business in Wheeling but not before paying a final "visit" to the home of Reverend Haas.

On the second Sunday following Caroline's death, Haas was alarmed by the sound of an intruder in the second floor of his residence. Rushing up the stairs to investigate, he was stunned to discover Hoch/Huff snooping around his bedroom. "What in God's name are you doing here[,] Huff? How did you get in?" he demanded. Looking flustered and perspiring, Hoch replied that he only wanted a private word with Haas, but given the late hour, it could easily wait. "I did not see you in the parlor, so I came upstairs thinking you might be here. I am so sorry," he replied unconvincingly. Hoch turned and bolted down the stairs and ran out of the house through the front door. Shaken, the reverend immediately emptied the contents of his personal medicine bottles into the toilet, fearing that Hoch might have dispensed his deadly poison into the medical nostrums on his dresser. Had he not panicked at that moment and considered the matter further, Haas might have had the good sense to turn the bottles over to the police for chemical analysis.

After the jolt of panic wore off, Reverend Haas reported his suspicions to the police, who then went in search of the widower Huff. But no trace of him could be found anywhere in the town—until the following morning when his coat, hat, vest, shirt, trousers, shoes, a silver pocket watch, and a copy of the will of Caroline Huff were retrieved in a grove of willows lining the shore of the Ohio River near the government dam. Hoch had been last seen the day before while buying a train ticket to Chicago; he had been nattily attired in a new suit of blue clothes, russet shoes, and a straw hat. He had drained Caroline's savings from the German Bank and settled a few minor debts before checking out.

Was he dead, or had he flown the coop? The police wondered.

The police force dragged the waterway but could not find a body. After a full day, the search was abandoned, and Huff/Hoch was declared legally dead. It was supposed that a grieving husband had killed himself in a fit of depression as his footprints were found leading into the water. The police believed there was nothing more to it—despite eyewitness accounts of Hoch's purchase of the train ticket and the banker's statements about his cash withdrawal.

Haas would have none of it, and several days later he demanded action from the police. "This man is alive I tell you! He was seen just the other day on the streets of Zanesville [located 73 miles west of Wheeling in East-Central Ohio] by Conrad Fitschle from Bellaire [Ohio] with a new woman!"[13] One hundred photographs of Hoch/Huff were immediately circulated, but it was too late to track him down. At the same time a gruesome discovery was made: it was noted that Caroline's grave appeared to have been tampered with the night before Hoch's alleged suicide. Someone had turned a shovel in the dirt, suggesting that a grave robber was lurking about. The significance of the grave's disturbance was not readily apparent to these country gendarmes, and no investigation was ordered. Torn by guilt, and believing he was responsible for the tragedy, Reverend Haas was determined to pressure the courts and the police to take action.

Hoch had long since vanished—gone west into Ohio like a thief in the night with $2,500 of the victim's money in hand. But he had not counted on the angry determination of the Wheeling pastor, who, for the next five years, meticulously scanned the matrimonial notices and obituaries of the German newspapers in his search for clues to the whereabouts of Caroline's killer. Although Haas eventually left his Wheeling congregation and transferred to Utica, New York, he clipped every possible lead involving the sudden deaths of middle-aged women from across the country and the descriptions of the men they had associated with at the time of their passing—and he personally contacted a prosecuting attorney in Mainz, Germany. In 1898 Haas's sleuthing paid off when he learned that Hoch's real name was Jacob Schmidt, and he was wanted on a charge of fraudulent bankruptcy and deserting a wife and children in Germany. It was only a matter of time, Haas reasoned, before this catalog of information would prove useful to the police in some distant city.

Chapter Eight

The question of accomplices and their level of complicity haunt the Gunness murder farm investigation. Did an actual ring of co-conspirators exist who provided her with referrals to potential victims that she intended to lure to their deaths, or did the black widow carry out her butchery alone?

Early clues pointing to an accomplice assisting Belle in her murderous schemes first surfaced when one Julius G. Truelson, Jr., the son of an upstate New York piano manufacturer, told Ralph N. Smith, LaPorte prosecuting attorney from the 2nd Judicial District, that he had arranged for Belle to kill his new bride in the summer of 1907. Truelson was a 22-year-old wastrel who had once attempted to pass himself off as Jonathan Thaw, a cousin of Pittsburgh millionaire Harry K. Thaw, who committed the sensational 1906 murder of his wife's lover, the architect Stanford White, in Manhattan. "She was Mae O'Reilly of Rochester, New York," Truelson said of his wife, the presumed victim. "There were reasons why I was anxious to rid myself of the woman and I wrote to Mrs. Gunness telling her that I wanted to bring Mae there. We killed Mae one night and buried her by the side of the Pere Marquette tracks that run along behind the Gunness farm."[1]

Truelson, utterly unreliable and a first-rate fraud, was locked up in a Vernon, Texas, jail for writing bad checks when he made his startling confession to Smith, but Truelson quickly retracted the story when authorities told him that he would be extradited to Indiana to face a likely murder indictment and criminal trial. Smith believed the boy's yarn was absolutely true, given the vivid descriptions and salient details that Truelson supplied. But then John Peel, an uncle of Miss O'Reilly, reported that his niece was alive and well and living at 11½ Fifty-Sixth

Street, in New York City. Truelson said that he had fabricated the story in a poorly thought-out attempt to escape the charges against him in Texas, but LaPorte County Sheriff Albert Smutzer found it impossible to believe that Truelson had fabricated the entire story. "The crime he described dovetail[ed] with known facts we have, and, in addition, he gives us details which have been known to us alone and could not have reached him through a newspaper."[2] Even so, Truelson was eventually ruled out as a suspect.

Later, a Cleveland man named Fred Halle notified LaPorte authorities of a peculiar encounter with a Chicago man who had intimate knowledge of the Gunness farm. His letter, written in 1961, to La-Porte authorities was accompanied by a small photographic image bearing some resemblance to a younger, trimmer Belle Gunness. The Cleveland man wrote:

> Dear Sir: Last August while waiting for a streetcar in our Public Square, I was approached by a man who began a conversation with me. He stated he was in Cleveland on a speculation and that cattle was his line. After some time he endeavored to find out regarding my family and asked me if I was married. In a spirit of fun I said no and he immediately began to tell me about a rich widow who resided in LaPorte, Indiana[,] who was looking for a man. He claimed she was the owner of a large ranch stocked with cattle and that she was looking for a man. He also gave me a picture of the woman who was supposed to be looking for a husband which I enclose herewith and I do this merely thinking that I might be of assistance in the matter of Mrs. Gunness. This man claimed that Chicago was his home. He had a reddish complexion, smooth face, dark hair and wore a black soft hat, blue suit, and had the general appearance of a man pretty well to do.[3]

Strong circumstantial evidence pointing to the existence of a Chicago connection puzzled investigators in Illinois and Indiana. An expressman's record of five large trunks consigned to Belle and sent from the Windy City to the sprawling 48-acre Gunness farm in LaPorte over a six month period led to the theory that she was operating a "clearinghouse" of murder, and wealthy men were being waylaid and killed in Chicago, packed inside their portmanteaus, and shipped down to Indiana for burial; however, a drayman reported that two of these trunks had never left Chicago. An exhaustive search commenced, but the mystery trunks were never found—at least not in the usual room where Belle stored the personal effects of her other "gentlemen callers." In Chicago, Assistant Chief Schuettler discredited the body-in-the-trunk theory. "I do not find the trunks," he said. "I think it extremely unlikely that any person would ever try shipping bodies around the country in the manner suggested. Detection would be, you might say, inevitable."[4] If the trunks did not contain the bodies of victims murdered in Chicago by third parties, they held the worldly possessions of a succession of lonely men who naively believed they were going to settle contentedly into LaPorte for the remainder of their days with a woman who would love them, feed them, and bed down with them for many a night. Belle Gunness and Johann Hoch counted on the trusting faith of these lonely, desperate people.

Liverymen John Welker and Clyde Sturgis of the Foster & Degarrno Express Company remembered delivering eight trunks to the farm—two of them labeled "Potatoes" and "Wall Paper." Sturgis remembered that the trunks were old, very heavy, and corded. Leo Wade, an assistant to Welker, said the experience was most unpleasant. "She wouldn't let Welker and me into the house with some of the trunks. We put some on the front porch." Like Dante and Virgil descending into the infernal fires of hell in the *Divine Comedy*, the expressmen vividly recalled the uneasy feelings of dread that overtook them. "Another trunk, at her orders, we carried to the house after dark. There was no light in the house and she did not strike one when we entered with the trunk. She led us through two dark rooms into a third and opened the door. But I told Welker I had enough and we dropped the trunk in the third room and left." Sturgis related another delivery he made that gave him pause. "Mrs. Gunness told me to carry them into the cellar way [sic] of the house. I started to un-cord them for her, but she told me to leave them alone and they weren't my business so I got out," he said.[5] Did the trunks contain the dismembered corpses and personal belongings of dozens of victims sent down by business agents of marriage brokers?

Suspicions pointing to an agent in a Chicago matrimonial bureau acting on Belle's behalf seemed to be the only logical explanation for the disappearance and presumed murder of Herman Konitzer, the 48-year-old scion of a wealthy family in Posen, Germany, who disappeared from the boardinghouse of Olive Johnston at 701 N. Halsted Street in Chicago in October 1905. Konitzer had been educated in a Berlin university and was a recent émigré to the U.S. He had managed the estate of a countess before making the Atlantic crossing and was in possession of a sizeable bankroll. He had rented rooms in the Bismarck Hotel and was getting situated in his surroundings when he spotted

Johnston's advertisement for lodgers in a German-language newspaper. He transferred his belongings to the Halsted Street address and was accompanied by a traveling companion, a Catholic priest. Several weeks later, Konitzer left Chicago bound for LaPorte with a small grip in his hand. He told the landlady that he would soon return to retrieve his wardrobe, which was valued at several hundred dollars—but she never heard from him after that.

Mrs. Johnston believed that Konitzer was carrying $5,000–$10,000 cash with him at the time of his disappearance. He had sold all of his possessions in Germany in order to finance his new life in America. The landlady was also positive that a female letter writer from Indiana who had sent a dispatch to Konitzer at the Halsted Street address was Belle Gunness. Konitzer had previously confided to Mrs. Johnston his ambition to marry and settle down on a farm.

If this communiqué was sent by the mistress of McClung Road, how did Belle succeed in making contact with an immigrant German when her matrimonial notices only appeared in the Scandinavian press? The letter supposedly written by Belle was in German, strengthening the belief that Gunness, like Johann Hoch, who was actively engaged in Northwest Indiana at the same time as Belle, operated through the contrivance of a confederate in Chicago who made it his business to inquire as to the wealth, status, and history of unmarried, unattached people of means.

Men of good will and trusting nature answered Belle's clarion call for companionship through the lonely hearts ads in the ethnic press. One example of her lonely hearts notices read: "PERSONAL—Comely widow who owns a large farm in one of the finest districts in LaPorte County, Indiana[,] desires to make the acquaintance of gentlemen unusually well-provided with views of joining fortunes. No replies by letter considered unless sender is willing to follow answer with personal visit."

John O. Moe of Elbow Lake, a small agricultural town in Grant County, West-Central Minnesota, subscribed to the *Skandinaven*. After an exchange of letters beckoning him to come to Indiana to sample her wonderful cooking, share her bed, and run the farm, he hurried down. Moe was last seen in Elbow Lake on December 20, 1906. He said he was going east of Chicago—but provided no further details. Two days later Moe presented to Alfred Peglow, Assistant Cashier at the First National Bank in LaPorte, two drafts for $1,100 drawn on the National Park Bank of New York. "Mr. Moe wished to use the money in LaPorte to pay off a mortgage but that he had no one in LaPorte to identify him and that they would deem it a favor if we aid him in the matter. He seemed very anxious to have the cash but we finally took the drafts for collection, sending them to our New York correspondent and asking them to wire us when these drafts were paid," the cashier remembered.[6]

"Moe was with Mrs. Gunness almost constantly," the carpenter Emil Greening told investigators. "When he left, his trunk stayed behind and no one saw him go. It was several days before Mrs. Gunness announced that he was gone. Moe's trunk was in the Gunness home on July 11, 1906 when I left the place. His was not the only one. There were about fifteen other trunks, and one room was packed full of all kinds of men's clothing which Mrs. Gunness said her 'cousins' had left and she was not certain if they would be back for them."[7]

Widower Ole Budsberg lived on his own farm in Iola, Wisconsin, with his three grown sons, Mat, Oscar, and Lewis, when he left home on April 5, 1907, bound for LaPorte to "run the farm" for Mrs. Gunness. Ole was barely conversant in the English language, but he received his news from the *Skandinaven,* which was published out of Chicago, and the *Decorah Posten,* another prominent Norwegian news journal with national circulation. From one of these two papers, presumably the *Skandinaven,* he made his first contact with Belle and was encouraged to travel to LaPorte with $800 in his valise and a draft for $1,000 in exchange for the promise of marriage. On April 6th, he appeared at the LaPorte Savings Bank with Belle and asked Assistant Cashier James Cartwright Buck to send a $1,000 mortgage note to the Farmer's State Bank in Iola, Wisconsin, for collection. The cash was counted out, and that was the last Mr. Buck thought of the matter until October when the Iola bank sent a note of inquiry asking about Ole's whereabouts. The sons had not heard anything from their father in months and expressed the normal concerns. "Shortly after the receipt of this letter, I, at the request of the cashier of our bank went out to Mrs. Gunness' and inquired if Mr. Budsberg was there," Buck related. "She said he wasn't. I asked her when she saw him last. She said she didn't know—that she didn't keep any track of dates—that the last she saw of him he left her house to catch the two o'clock train, and that he was going to Oregon to see about buying some land, or something like that."

To allay the suspicions of the family, Gunness wrote a letter to Mat Budsberg, contriving a story to put him at ease and throw off suspicion. "In it, she said she wanted to send him some letters and papers that had come for him after he left her house, so she wanted to know whether he was at his home [back in Iola] to receive them if she sent them over," Matt Budsberg testified. "She said too, she hoped he was not offended by her not marrying him. She said she hoped if he was going out west, he would find some land as a homestead, but if she were in his place, she would go to the old country and visit. The letter was written in the Norwegian language."[8]

The remains of Budsberg were unearthed from the Gunness graveyard in May 1908. There was enough of the contour of his face left to make it possible for Oscar and Mat to make a positive identification. In a quiet whisper, one of the sons told LaPorte authorities that he was surprised by Ole's decision to leave Iola. "My mother had been dead only four years and all of us children never thought of his getting married again."[9]

Belle was an expert poisoner who administered strychnine in the food she served Ole and the other men she welcomed to her kitchen table.[10] Strychnine, an alkaloid extract obtained from the dried ripe seeds of *Strychnos nux-vomica*, a small tree of the East Indies, stops the inhibitory reflex in the victim within twenty minutes of ingestion. Strychnine is a common component of industrial rat poison, and it induces a particularly horrifying death. The victim immediately experiences muscle spasms that escalate into painful and agonizing convulsions in the central nervous system—convulsions that lead to lactic acidosis (too much acid in the body), hyperthermia (abnormally high body temperature), and rhabdomyolysis (the rapid breakdown of skeletal muscle). Death results from asphyxiation caused by the paralysis of the neural pathways that control breathing.

Standing over her victims in the throes of their violent death struggles, a depraved look of smug satisfaction crossed Belle's face as she experienced a sense of exhilaration while watching their lives ebb away within minutes. This was more than simply the "business of murder for profit" carried out with the detached indifference of Johann Hoch, who, unlike Belle, paid the cost of the funeral and burial for his known victims. Belle disposed of the remains the same way a sane person would haul the household trash out to the garbage can. This was serial murder on a more personal level: these were acts of pure hatred, born out of years of a bitter memory of the brutal assault she had endured as a young woman in Selbu.

At the point of death, or after her victims had died, Belle dragged them from the kitchen floor down into the cellar of the main house for butchering, where she dismembered the bodies by the light of a lantern or single candle. Inside this medieval chamber of horrors Belle had installed a wooden table next to a vat filled with chloride of lime solution. Using cutlery drawn from her leather holster—the same knives that she used to slice up pork bellies—she severed the limbs of the men she had lured into her deadly trap. The room was kept strictly off-limits to Ray Lamphere, the neighbors, and especially the children.

Miss Jennie Garwood, a teacher at the Quaker school that the Gunness children attended, noted with alarm one morning the unhappy appearance and tears of the little ones. Garwood asked Myrtle what the trouble was, and the girl said that they had been beaten and whipped by their mother. "Why is that?" the teacher demanded to know. "Mama told us to keep out of the basement but while we were playing we went downstairs. She caught us and before we got to the bottom of the steps she brought us back. She always kept the cellar door locked and got awful mad when anybody started near it. She told us that she would punish us worse if we ever tried to get downstairs again. Then she whipped us."[11] Garwood said it was the first time she had seen the children behaving so, and she was very surprised.

Little Myrtle had also confided a deadly secret to one of her playmates, a story that was later disclosed to LaPorte Police Chief Clinton Cochrane. "If you never tell anyone, I will tell you something," the girl whispered. "Well, if you promise never to tell, my mama killed my papa. She hit him on the head with a meat cleaver but don't you tell!"[12] Hearing all of this later, Mayor Lemuel Darrow of LaPorte was convinced that Belle had stored a cadaver in this temporary morgue and was afraid that the girls would discover it. Darrow had his eye on Belle for several years. At the time of Peter Gunness's death, he insisted that the circumstances were suspicious, but a serious investigation was never launched. Poor police investigative policies and procedures greatly aided both Gunness and Hoch through the years.

Body parts were wrapped in gunnysacks and buried in holes in the Gunness private graveyard—a plot of land measuring 75 by 125 feet and circled by a double fence of large and small wire mesh standing 8 feet high. To the south, the ground sloped downward into a marsh that was once a part of Clear Lake. Belle would pour quicklime to speed decomposition. Then, for good measure, she'd pile on cane and bricks to accelerate the action of the lime. Greening remembered that during his time working at the farm, Mrs. Gunness had asked him and several other men to dig up large tree stumps on the property and refill the holes with soft dirt. Human body parts that she did not toss into the pig trough for consumption by the swine were dropped into soft, shallow depressions in the ground.

Fred Richman, one of Belle's many itinerant farmhands hired for seasonal work, was asked to dig a five-and-a-half-foot-deep hole and mark it with a stake. He was handed two silver dollars for his work and invited in for a glass of wine with Belle and two men who had driven up in a green automobile. The wine, he said, contained a drug. Richman managed to make it home, collapsed into bed, and awakened hours later. Not long after, Gunness had a shed erected over the site of the mysterious hole.

A nearby pond was another likely location to dispose of human remains that were impossible to identify once they were unearthed. John Zach, a house-mover employed by Gunness from time to time, said that on three separate occasions he was engaged to move the pigpen to different locations on the property. "I wondered why she was so particular but it never entered my head that bodies might be buried in the place where she wished it. Now I am convinced something was wrong."[13]

Few were safe from Belle's scheming, and only one of her invited guests was known to have escaped with his life. That was George Anderson, a 39-year-old Swede from Tarkio, Missouri, who was told that he needed to come up with more money than he had brought with him in order for him to stay on and allow Gunness to "pay off her mortgage" before she could marry him. Anderson owned a 32-acre farm that Belle asked him to sell. The man wired his bank in Tarkio asking for the necessary fund transfer and then bedded down in the guest room for the next two nights. On the third evening he awoke from a restless twilight sleep to find Belle leaning over the bed, peering down at him in a menacing way. He mumbled a few words, and Belle left the room without replying. Frightened for his safety, he lied awake the rest of the night and bolted out of the bed at the crack of dawn. He hurriedly dressed, then raced out the front door without looking back.

Belle Gunness was a master criminal to the core and a living blueprint of the vicious sociopath whose repertoire encompassed the crimes of arson, fraud, and murder. And no one understood the mind of this female Borgia better than her Austin physician, Dr. Charles E. Jones, who provided the best contemporary analysis and insight into Belle's motivations for becoming a murderess in midlife. "I can explain psychologically to my own satisfaction the causes that started her on her terrible work," he said. "I remember her well as a religious fanatic type. The sudden wealth, comparatively speaking, that came to her at her husband's death I believe may have had for her an irresistible suggestion of the ease with which money might be obtained. In the incident of her [first] husband's death her temptation to commit the alleged atrocities may have had its birth."[14]

What really motivated Belle Gunnesss? Was it a personality disorder? Mental illness, perhaps? The horrifying abuse and ridicule she had endured in Norway as a young girl? Or, more likely, a case of simple greed? Greed is a monster that feeds on itself, and the ease with which Belle dispatched her first two husbands without the Chicago police, the insurance company investigators, and the coroner's office taking immediate action fueled the lust for riches and emboldened her to become arguably the worst female serial killer in U.S. history.

Chapter Nine

Johann Hoch covered his slippery trail of bigamy and murder with the greatest care and skill. He played upon his victim's sympathies by acting out the part of a brokenhearted widower left to face the relentless cruelties of a hostile world all alone. Cunning and unpredictable, he avoided the usual traps likely to get him into trouble with police and private detectives. He learned from Holmes's poor example that insurance fraud, in the main, was a bad idea, as it left behind an incriminating paper trail that led even the cleverest insurance swindler straight into a death sentence if murder could also be proven. Hoch wisely limited himself to plundering his wives' bank accounts and acquiring their physical property—assets much easier to dispose of in the long run. That was his modus operandi, and it served him well in Chicago and as he traversed the country after his brush with the law in Wheeling, West Virginia, and the meddling, bumpkin minister, Herman C.A. Haas.

From Zanesville, Hoch changed trains in Chicago and continued west to the Cripple Creek gold strike in the Colorado Rockies, where he invested in a worthless mine that was salted with just enough gold nuggets to convince him that he was about to strike it rich. Hoch claimed that he sunk $45,000 into the venture, but once he realized that he had been swindled by a crooked mining agent, he took matters into his own hands. "I was out of my element and they robbed me with my eyes open," he related. "Still the men who sold it to me didn't have much to crow about. I melted up some of the nuggets he fooled me with and cast them into my .44. They tell me he is carrying one of them around now in his hip joint."[1]

In desperate need of funds, Hoch next turned up in San Francisco, establishing his base of operations in a rented room at 30 Turk Street. The notice he had placed in the San Francisco newspaper drew a favorable response from the widow Barbara Brossert, said to be in possession of $1,465.[2] Hoch lingered in the Bay Area long enough to romance and marry Mrs. Brossert on September 22, 1896, before heading back east to Cincinnati and new conquests. Mrs. Brossert, deserted and penniless at 108 Langton Street, had few options and reportedly worried herself into an early grave.

Hoch charmed two new, willing victims in Cincinnati, "The Queen City," and married them both within the shortest span of time possible in 1896–1897. Weeks after fleeing San Francisco, he stood at the altar with Clara Bartels, the recent widow of Henry Bartels, who had passed just four weeks earlier. They were joined in matrimony as Mr. and Mrs. Schmidt as Hoch chose to revert back to his birth name. Clara joined her first husband in eternity less than two months after her nuptials to Hoch. The official cause of death in that primitive age of patent medicines and rampant quackery was, not surprisingly, reported as gastritis.

Following the funeral, Hoch lived in the Bartels residence for two months before trading vows with Julia Doess, a widow from Hamilton, Ohio, whose late husband had kept a saloon at Mohawk Place, Cincinnati. Hoch deserted her after stealing $600 and her entire wardrobe, though it's unclear why he took the latter. He abandoned Julia with the explanation that he was leaving for Germany immediately because word had reached him that his poor old father had suddenly taken sick and was teetering between life and death. Fortunately for Mrs. Doess and her future prospects for happiness, she recovered from her despair and humiliation and married a man named Fetzer and reportedly lived quietly thereafter.

The entire Cincinnati adventure required less than five months of his time to wrap up before moving on. Considering the furious pace of seduction and marriage proposals he made after winding up his affairs in West Virginia, California, and Ohio during the early winter months of 1897, reconstructing Hoch's travels is tricky business. In an age of tremendous social mobility, when economic chaos and the turmoil of war, famine, revolution, and continuous upheaval drove millions of people to U.S. shores, Johann Hoch was shielded by his anonymity throughout his travels. He simply never slowed down, paused to reflect, or lived contentedly off his illicit gain. He did not dawdle for a moment, and his many falsifications covered his trail. With a manic energy and compulsion born out of a monstrous, narcissistic ego that undoubtedly masked a sense of inadequacy, he preyed upon society's most vulnerable victims—lonely, insecure widows and spinsters.

He made few friends and traveled alone but always carted about a large valise containing a magician's costume of sorts, with an assortment of wigs and hairpieces, and two other important possessions—a top hat and a long black coat to impress upon his next bride that he was a wealthy society man of considerable means. Among his personal belongings was a diploma issued by Professor L.A. Harridan's Correspondence School in Jackson, Michigan, certifying Hoch as a "master hypnotist." Victims of his confidence game attested to his ability to put them in a hypnotic trance as he strummed soft melodies of love on his zither.

Those who knew him contrasted his ordinary, unassuming appearance with his superficial charms. "He could pass anywhere as a typical German-American of the lower middle class with a fair education," recalled Dr. Francis W. McNamara, former Chief Physician of the Cook County Jail. "He had an oily tongue, an ingratiating manner and a mild blue eye. His big round head suggested intellectual capacity; his soft voice and amiable behavior would have suited a kindly *paterfamilias*. Nothing about him suggested the horror of deed, the depravity of souls with which his story deals. Beneath his plausible exterior Johann Hoch was a character out of nightmares, but he never revealed his essential malignity."[3] Indeed, Hoch was no Don Juan, but he always believed he was too smart, too cunning, and so great of an expert in the foibles of human nature that the authorities could never hope to catch him. Of course, the limitations of local law enforcement in Victorian America greatly benefited his caliber of crime.

The exchange of useful information and levels of cooperation between big city police departments conducting criminal investigations was poor. Interstate criminals moving from one city to the next had more to fear from the Pinkerton National Detective Agency and other private detection agencies than the bungling metropolitan police departments, burdened as they were by the drag of political interference, big city vice rings, and violent street crime in tough inner-city neighborhoods. Despite the formation of national police associations during this time and a growing sense of professionalism, there was no nationwide method of cataloging criminal offenders. Job techniques were learned on the street by rookie recruits walking the beat with older, experienced veterans. Fingerprinting as a method of modern law enforcement did not become a standard of detection until 1904 when it was successfully introduced at the St. Louis World's Fair.

The Bertillon system of body measurements and profile photography used to catalog offenders in the rogues gallery common in all detective bureaus and precinct stations was inefficient, cumbersome, and poorly managed. Records were often lost, destroyed, or transferred to a distant warehouse and forgotten due to their sheer volume. It would be nearly impossible today for a modern Bluebeard to replicate the marriage swindles of Johann Hoch on so massive a scale and for such a length of time. There were many bigamists running loose in America in the 1890s, but none were quite as prolific or elusive as Hoch.

This man of many aliases slipped quietly back into Chicago after his San Francisco foray ended, with the intention of remaining in his home city for the near term. He chose as his new residence a rooming house directly across the street from a restaurant at 2210 S. Wabash that was owned by the American-born Janet Spencer, a fetching widow of forty who was raising a young son.

In 1898 when Hoch settled into this South Side neighborhood, it was inauspicious and run-down. The area was gradually being given over to vice mongers, pimps, dope fiends, and prostitutes migrating southward from the old Custom House District, formerly located at the southern edge of downtown Chicago. Spencer struggled to hold on to her restaurant and boardinghouse and keep the building respectable, but all around the neighborhood "concert saloons," gambling dens, bordellos, opium joints, and disreputable dives displaced legitimate businesses under the watchful "protection" of the two pernicious bosses of this new and vicious "Levee," a segregated vice district on Chicago's South Side—Alderman "Bathhouse" John Coughlin and his henchman Michael "Hinky Dink" Kenna. Together they made this Chicago's 24-hour "tenderloin," a Mecca of sin and vice.

Spencer, beautiful but desperate and unhappy, was vulnerable to the attentions of Hoch, who introduced himself as N.H. Chalfont, Superintendent of the Hote National Advertising Agency on River Street, near the open-air produce markets lining South Water Street. After a gala, whirlwind romance, with nights of champagne toasts and floral bouquets in the dining rooms of Chicago's splendid downtown hotels—among them the Great Northern, the Congress, the Richelieu, the Sherman, and the Palmer House—Hoch suggested marriage, and Janet Spencer counted her newly found blessings. She looked forward to carefree days, relief from financial worries, and a new daddy to love and care for her 10-year-old son, Boyd.

Janet wanted to be married in Chicago—but Hoch (aka Chalfont) thought it might be much more romantic to tie the knot in the Bluegrass State of Kentucky. So, at his suggestion, she sold her business holdings and realized $2,000. She provided Chalfont with money to buy a suit of wedding clothes and defray the costs of the wedding tour.

After the ceremony was performed, they proceeded to Muncie, Indiana, and then to Gaston, a tiny hamlet in Delaware County where it was suggested to the new bride that she consider buying a farm near Elwood, Indiana; however, the deal was never closed, and Mr. and Mrs. Chalfont returned to Chicago on April 15, 1898. They secured comfortable apartments at 49 and 51 Rush Street, north of the river.

Janet still had $1,700 left to her name—but she entrusted the entire sum to her new husband, who said that he had a pressing business engagement at the Palmer House, and he wished her to accompany him to the luxurious State Street hostelry while he attended to the matter. Chalfont/Hoch left his wife and the little boy in the waiting room for the next two hours. When he did not return, she summoned a carriage and was returned to the Rush Street rooms only to discover the sad truth: her gallant new husband had packed up all of his clothes and personal effects into two valises and fled, ruining her life and leaving Janet and her son stranded and broke. The police were notified, and two plainclothes detectives were sent out to find Hoch, but their search was futile.

Within a year, the cozy little restaurant that Mrs. Spencer had worked so hard to maintain at 2210 S. Wabash became Gilbert's Saloon, a licentious, all-night dive operated by one F.D. Stephens, who permitted gamblers and Levee prostitutes to congregate inside the establishment into the wee hours of the morning. Afterward the drunken revelers and their consorts repaired to Janet Spencer's former hotel across the street, which was now an assignation house.

Not long after stranding Janet Spencer, Hoch fell into the hands of the Chicago Police Department after a complaint was filed by the Simon Strauss Furniture & Carpeting Company at Blue Island Avenue & West Harrison Street for the same old swindles perpetrated against the Magerstadt Company earlier—selling unpaid, mortgaged furniture to third parties. Arrested on March 28, 1898, Hoch landed in the Cook County Jail on Hubbard Street for retail fraud. He was sentenced to one year of confinement by Judge Frank Baker of the Criminal Court, Branch 6.

The Chicago detectives who called on Hoch did not know what to make of the man in their custody or the full measure of his transcontinental crime spree. Hoch said his name was Martin Dotz, and he listed his place of residence as 1266 W. Fifteenth Street on the West Side—another successful dodge for the wily little con artist because the police were still oblivious to the recent and sudden disappearance of the woman who had lived at that address. Strauss, the furniture supplier, just wanted the return of his money. He related the details of the merchandise scam but could provide no useful information as to the nature of the scheme

Hoch (aka Martin Dotz) had hatched or details of any alleged murders of German widows. Nor did he much care to find out.

One afternoon, as Hoch wiled away the hours in the bridewell—smoking cigars, telling jokes, and otherwise ingratiating himself to the inmates and guards—he was suddenly confronted by an unexpected and most unwelcome visitor: Mrs. Mary Burmeister, sister of the jilted Martha Herefeldt. Burmeister had come to see him about the money he had stolen from them several years prior. In reduced circumstances, Mary still could not afford to prosecute the case on behalf of her sister. Gazing at the woman through the bars of his cell, Hoch feigned insanity. Waving his arms and gesticulating wildly while making weird, guttural sounds, he played the role of a madman to perfection, and Mrs. Burmeister was led away shaking her head and sobbing.

Hoch served his time without incident and was scheduled to be released on July 31, 1899. Before the cell doors swung fully open, however, he was questioned at length by Chief of Detectives Captain Luke Colleran, who had been castigated by the Chicago Civil Service Commission in a blistering internal report as an example of the kind of officer "more devoted to politics than to the apprehension of criminals. Captain Colleran is a man who spends more of his time in caring for Mayor [Carter] Harrison's favorites than he does in anything else. . . . [T]he Chief's record will be looked up. The Police force of Chicago is thoroughly rotten."[4] Already under fire for gross negligence in his mishandling of the Detective Bureau, Colleran was in possession of the incriminating letter written by Pastor Haas of Wheeling, West Virginia, a letter laying bare the evidence before him of Hoch's flight from German justice on a charge of fraudulent bankruptcy and for deserting his wife and children in Horrweiler. In the letter, Haas related his suspicions about the death of Caroline Miller Hoch in Wheeling, but none of these facts struck a responsive chord with the captain, who conducted an obligatory interview with the inmate.

Colleran was inclined to dismiss the preacher as the kind of annoying, second-guessing crank who was the bane of every big city police department detective, but later Colleran decided to elicit more information from Haas. He wrote to Haas:

November 1, 1898.

In reply to your letter relative to Jacob Adolph Hoch, serving a year's sentence here for bigamy under the name of Dotz or Doesing [sic] I desire to inform you that I sent an officer with the photo you sent me to the Bridewell, and Hoch or Doesing acknowledged at once it was his but denied knowing any person in Wheeling. Now we learn from a cousin of his deceased wife that he kept a saloon at No. 4728 Jacobs Street, your city where he married his wife. Friends here are positive he poisoned his wife to get her money. He is said to have married several women to get their money. Lay the whole matter before your Chief of Police and have him hunt all criminal evidence in the matter. Obtain indictment if possible, for murder. Forward papers to us and we will turn him over to our chief.—L.P. Colleran, Chief of Detectives

The Bureau was already aware of Hoch's many aliases and his subterfuge in coaxing different women into marriage, but in their view it did not add up to very much.

As Colleran awaited a reply, Reverend Haas proceeded immediately to Wheeling State's Attorney William C. Meyer's office with a request to exhume the grave of Caroline Hoch. The order was issued on November 14, 1898, and the coffin was pried open, and only then, after three years had passed since the interment, was the grisly evidence of Hoch's handiwork revealed. Inside the pine box was what seemed to the trained observer to be horrifying evidence of a crime but for very odd, and unexplained, reasons, it did not register with the police. Caroline's midsection had been cut open and the vital organs had all been removed in order to eliminate any trace of poison from the digestive system. Given public sensitivities, newspaper reports of this gruesome discovery were sanitized and censored. Dispatches from Wheeling simply stated that no traces of poison could be found in her system upon exhumation, "owing to the effects of the embalming fluid."[5] There would be no charges of homicide directed against Hoch. Superintendent Clemens of the Wheeling Police sent his reply, reporting that "Johann Hoch is not wanted for any crime."[6]

Just as Hoch was waving good-bye to his fellow inmates in the county jail, Fred Magerstadt, the Milwaukee Avenue furniture dealer, came with his lawyer in tow and presented his bill of particulars for the earlier thefts by deception. There was the matter of Hoch's unpaid $150 bill of March 1898. Again Hoch was indicted, and once more he was convicted and sentenced to another year in the Cook County Jail. He accepted the verdict of the court with good cheer, did his time, and walked away in October 1900. Having outwitted the police twice, he was freed to kill again.

Greatly amused by the cupidity of Colleran and the Chicago Police Department gumshoes, Hoch embarked on another marital safari across the hinterland. The unrelenting grind of it all, the long and tiring hours of rail travel—none of it seemed to matter to him. He was a middle-aged man of inexhaustible energy driven by the excitement of the game and eager for the next chance to test the gullibility of the victim and the fallibility of the police. The game was always afoot.

Only Johann Hoch could provide an accurate, detailed record of the many cities and towns he went 'a courting' in between 1900 and 1905. His later statements to police and prosecutors were confusing, self-contradictory, and full of embellishments. It seems remarkable in hindsight that he could have been in so many places in so brief a period of time.

Scores of middle-aged women from all over the country, many claiming to be former wives of Hoch, eventually came forward—often with conflicting stories to tell. Mary Murtha of St. Louis, friend and companion to Mary Becker-Schultz (who had perished from what was later determined to be arsenic poisoning in 1901) remembered Johann Hoch aka Jacob Schultz as kind and generous. "Hoch was a model husband," she said. "He was kind, considerate and thoughtful of the welfare of his wife. He did everything in his power to comfort her in her dying hours. He spent nights at her bedside comforting her and nursing her." The physician who signed the death warrant said his suspicions about the manner of death were allayed because Hoch and Becker-Schultz "were such a devoted couple," and Hoch was such a "model husband."[7]

With the passage of time, many of these women were undoubtedly mistaken in their initial identification of Hoch and might have confused him with some other roué with striking similarities to Hoch who had absconded with their savings. The bigamy racket was big business, and Johann Hoch was not alone in his pursuit of riches.

The shopkeepers, boardinghouse matrons, and German widows who succumbed to his ruse and survived to regret their trusting faith relied upon fading memories, or they simply connected the published accounts of Hoch's crimes in their hometown newspapers to personal misfortunes whether there was any validity or not. Their eagerness to extract a measure of revenge against the scoundrels who ruined their lives and reputations was understandable, and consequently an impossible number of women from all over the country contacted the police with that thought uppermost in their minds. But as it turned out, often they were mistaken. Following Hoch's movements and placing him in one locale long enough to commit the crime was another daunting task. He moved quickly and left few clues behind to trace his whereabouts.

Love letters written by Hoch to Johanna Reichel in Chicago in February 1904 reveal that he traveled 2,000 miles from St. Louis to a rooming house at 1104 Clay Street, San Francisco. Hoch kept room and board just long enough to entice two new victims, a "Miss. Loughran" and one Susan Maynard, the latter of whom was much younger than his other victims. Maynard was only twenty-seven. Hoch claimed that Maynard's death was not his doing. "We were married six weeks . . . and enjoyed one week of married happiness, when some enemy of mine poisoned her in a mysterious way and she died suddenly one night at my side in a theater. Understanding my previous painful experience with the ignorant American police I withdrew her money from the bank and left town. Many and many times I have wondered whether it was a jealous wife or a jealous rival who caused her death. I am afraid these mysterious things in my life will end in my undoing."[8]

Meanwhile, in one of his letters to Mrs. Reichel in Chicago, Hoch explained that his fictitious employer had "transferred" him from St. Louis to the Bay Area, where he spent much of his free time enjoying the temperate winter climate in the San Francisco public parks. "I am from 7:00 a.m. until 5:30 p.m., in the business and the rest of the time in the park. Every evening there is music in the park. And I am there every day. I cannot say enough of the nice things of nature. The flowers I sent you I picked with my own hands and I like it very well here. I took this position for three months only that means until May 1. In case I do not like it I always have the right to become a detective in Pullman." Then he wrote ominously: "Now I would not say anything of what I intend to do. I am pretty tired of life. I would like to have my own business again. In time I think you can give me advice, Mrs. Reichel."[9]

The man of many names with an irresistible fondness for separating widows from their money returned from the West Coast—with a "stopover" in Wisconsin to brutally victimize and kill two more women—before continuing east to Baltimore and then New York, where he set sail for a short European sabbatical before his courtship with the two sisters on Chicago's North Side. After returning from Europe, where he enjoyed a brief reunion with his legitimate wife and the children he had abandoned in Horrweiler years earlier, there were to be no more days of sunlight and serenity. The many threads tying together his tragically fated victims with this peculiar little man unraveled inside the rented five-room flat at 6430 S. Union Avenue after Hoch returned from Europe to steal the affection and the money of Marie Shippnick Walcker and her estranged sister Amelia Fischer. Amelia was worth $750 if Hoch could figure out a way to do in Marie and seduce Amelia.

Hoch suggested reconciliation between the sisters as a way to get in Amelia's good graces. After much coaxing, Marie agreed to a meeting at the home of Anna Held at 241 Vine Street. There Hoch was presented to Amelia as her new brother-in-law. Up to that moment Amelia had not known that Marie was married to this man and showed bewilderment. She was cordial to Hoch but was frosty to her sister. "Would you like to shake hands and end this nasty business?" Hoch suggested. "I want no misunderstandings in the family. There is no reason not to get along." After much coaxing and persuasion, a truce was effected.[10] But Hoch began paying more than the customary or proper attention to Amelia. In unguarded moments he whispered words of endearment and confessed to Amelia—a rather dour looking, frumpy matron of no special physical appeal—that he often pressed her photo to his heart and that if he had met her first she, not Marie, would have become his wife.

Hoch encouraged Amelia to come by and visit their happy little home on Union Avenue, and over the next few weeks she was a frequent caller. While Marie cooked and cleaned, Amelia and Hoch conducted little tête-à-têtes in the parlor, whispering and giggling like smitten schoolchildren; therefore, it was not so surprising that on December 20, 1904, Marie took sick. The other sister, Bertha Sohn, who, unlike Amelia, was on excellent terms with Marie, was informed by Hoch that his wife had caught a cold, but Bertha noticed eruptions on Marie Walcker's mouth. She also noted that Marie's complexion had turned a deadly shade of yellow. "Oh Lord how badly you look!" exclaimed Bertha. Whereupon Hoch shrugged his shoulders and said, "Well, that will be better again after a short time."[11] Mrs. Sohn cheerfully suggested that if she were up to it, Marie ought to come over for Christmas dinner and enjoy the holiday merriment. A turkey feast would restore her color. Hoch interjected: "A great many things may happen and you know that cannot be done because I will not leave her alone over night."[12] Hoch suggested in the strongest terms that Amelia spend the holiday with Mrs. Sohn at the Union Avenue address, because he "had a great deal of work to do."

On December 21, word reached Bertha Sohn that Marie had taken a dramatic turn for the worse. Dr. Joseph Reese, who maintained an office above William Schleizer's Englewood Pharmacy at 63rd and Halsted, where Hoch had purchased a rubber syringe and sheeting for the "care" of his wife, had been summoned to Union Avenue. Hoch informed Bertha that he had been ordered to administer enemas to the stricken woman. Dr. Reese later denied giving such a directive—nor was he aware of Hoch administering any medicinal potions other than a prescription of powdered opium and gum camphor that he had prescribed to relieve her discomfort. Reese also prescribed pepsin to be taken after dinner, carbolic acid, and subnitrate of Mallinckrodt's bismuth, and three-to-four-quart hot douches for Hoch to administer every day. "I thought that I had a healthy wife as I had much misfortune in my life in that line," wrote Hoch in a dispatch to Mrs. Sohn. "But now it so happened in the same way again. I had hoped I would not have to accompany my wife to the grave and look down into her grave, but I hoped my wife would close my eyes and not I hers."[13] Bertha was skeptical of the whole thing. She believed her sister was suffering from blood poisoning.

On January 4, as Marie's condition worsened, Dr. Reese assigned a nurse to attend to her needs, but Hoch insisted that he didn't want or need the assistance of an outsider. For the six days that Nurse Gussie Hotzapel attended the sickroom before she was sent away, Hoch had no opportunity to mix the arsenic into the food or medicine prescribed by Dr. Reese. As she expelled the arsenic in her system, a gradual improvement was noted in the patient's condition. After the nurse departed on January 10, Hoch once again began administering the deadly white powders from a small tin box secured from the Englewood drugstore. The poison was mixed in with the rectal enema and administered. Marie drifted in and out of consciousness and complained of burning in her throat and stomach. The next evening, January 11, in her weakened state, Marie quarreled with Hoch as Amelia prepared supper in the downstairs kitchen. Amelia overheard her sister cry out: "Why go on and marry her! Go on and marry her after I am dead!"[14] By now Marie had deduced that her sister had shown some reciprocal interest in Hoch, and in her final agony, Marie was tormented by jealousy, bitterness, and the certain knowledge Amelia was a husband stealer. Amelia raced up the stairs to intervene. "Is that the thanks I receive for what I do?"[15] Amelia fired back. "If it was not for your illness I would answer you entirely different!" "You are a human sow!" Marie gasped. Her pain and discomfort was made worse by her jealous anger. Her condition was unendurable. In tears Amelia said she wanted to leave the house, but given the lateness of the hour, she accepted Hoch's invitation to sleep downstairs in the parlor rather than return to the North Side. The last words of Marie Walcker were words spoken in anger and remorse to Hoch at 3 o'clock the following morning: "Go and take her, you can marry her if you want to! Go and take her!"

With the first rays of light peaking through the curtains, Doctor Reese returned to 6430 S. Union Avenue to pronounce the patient dead. After conferring privately with the doctor, Hoch informed Amelia that the cause of death was kidney and bladder disease—a diagnosis Amelia at first seemed willing to accept. Amelia gave the sickroom bedding a good washing and airing out. She washed and dressed the body of her sister and hung the bedroom linen on the clothesline while the much-relieved Hoch smashed bottles of Marie's medicine against the wall of the adjacent house. He showed little compassion or empathy for his late wife and her sufferings as the tinkling of shattering glass bottles punctured the silence of the morning. "Well there goes a lot of money. There is a lot of money wasted. We will never use that medicine again!" he said.

After the household duties were attended to, Hoch pulled Amelia aside. "Now sister-in-law, you see again, I am a single man now and you will stick to me and I will be good luck for you and your children. My wife told me you were a very good business woman. I intended to make your sister happy but it seem it could not be so," he said in a serious, low tone of voice. "Therefore I want to keep luck in the family and I want to make you lucky and I want to make your children lucky and happy. . . . You have had bad luck for so many years you deserve some good fortune. Promise to stick with me," he said further. "I am a man worth thirty to forty thousand dollars. You and I will open a hotel and we will run it together; I intended to do that with my late wife, but fortune was against me." The undertaker removed the body from the house at 8 a.m. This discussion took place in the kitchen of the house, moments ahead of the arrival of the funeral wagon.[16]

Amelia was taken aback. "This is not the time to talk about a matter of that kind," she said. But Hoch was urgent in his plea: "That makes no difference. The dead belong to the dead and the living, belong to the living. I intended to wait through a time of mourning, but inasmuch as my wife has taken all the love out of my heart for her, there is no use to wait any longer. I hope we will be able to arrange everything within a week. I have done my duty to her as a husband. Nobody can reproach me that I have not done my duty as a husband just as well as you have done your duty as a sister. "

In the next few days, Hoch spent many quiet hours with Amelia, entertaining her with stories from the Bible, quoting scripture, and vowing to bring her brood of nine abandoned children to America and care for them as his own. Hoch said he would rent out his Englewood cottage until such time as the children she had left behind in Germany crossed the ocean to join Amelia and her 19-year-old daughter, Martha, in a pleasant, three-story brick cottage he promised to build on the corner lot with his accumulated fortune. He suggested that they "keep quiet" about the marriage details, but he said that he would sail to Germany forthwith to fetch the young ones. Hearing this generous offer and believing it to be made in good faith, Amelia softened her attitude and warmed to the idea of marrying the grieving Hoch.

Setting aside his grief, at least for the moment, Hoch discouraged Amelia's suggestion that they plan an elaborate religious funeral procession, claiming neither he nor Marie put much stock in the church or its doctrine—contradicting his many religious pretensions. He moved quickly and ordered just two carriages to convey the coffin and mourners to the nondenominational Oakwoods Cemetery on the South Side, because this was all he had set aside in his budget. It was a well established fact—and Hoch understood matters perfectly—that it was almost impossible to convict in an arsenic murder case if the body is not examined before embalming. But in his haste to dispose of the body, Hoch made a fatal miscalculation: he neglected to inquire of the embalmer, John Long, whether or not arsenic was present in the fluid that Long injected into the corpse prior to burial. There was no arsenic in this particular consignment of embalmer's fluid, as it turned out.

Hoch swore a vow to Bertha Sohn that he would never marry again, because he "was born to misfortune." But when Amelia confided his intention to wed in a civil ceremony to Bertha, the woman became convinced that he was a no-good fortune hunter and was responsible for her poor sister's death. Bertha took a streetcar to the East Chicago Avenue Police Station to swear out a warrant for Hoch's arrest, but the clerk would not issue one without evidence. A citizen's accusation was, after all, not a criminal indictment.

On the Monday following the sparsely attended funeral, Hoch reiterated to Amelia his plans to travel to Paris and continue on to Germany, saying that his 82-year-old father had made provisions for him to inherit a vast sum. But before the arrangements for the Atlantic crossing could be made, he had to first settle some personal affairs, including the sale of the lots adjacent to the cottage on Union Avenue that he claimed to own. Hoch also claimed to be in desperate need of some traveling money because his cash flow was poor at the moment, and there was still the matter of a $1,000 mortgage left to pay on the cottage. Amelia was understanding and offered to front him the $750. "Well, I promise by all that is holy that I will repay it to the cent as soon as I get my money for the vacant lots," Hoch said.

The following Tuesday, January 17, Hoch and Amelia took a train out to Joliet, where they were married in a simple courthouse ceremony. Afterward they consumed a large dinner, toasted their good fortune, and returned to Chicago. The next day, Amelia withdrew the $750 from her bank, surrendered her passbook to Hoch, and together they took a carriage back to her flat on Wells Street to plot their future course.

Up to that point, things were going splendidly for Hoch—until, to his utter shock and dismay, he found Bertha Sohn in the kitchen engaged in a serious discussion with Mrs. Amelia Sauerbruch (one of Amelia Hoch's sisters), who also was living in the neighborhood. The subject being discussed was Johann Hoch, swindler. Mrs. Sohn declared that she had learned quite a bit about Hoch over the past 24 hours—that he had murdered her sister and was a bigamist. Sauerbruch turned to her new brother-in-law, pointed, and said: "Johann Hoch, you are a swindler and a bad man!" Hearing the loud and bellicose accusation that he was a murderer and a thief, Hoch turned pale and collapsed into an easy chair in the parlor.

"How you look! You are changing color so much," his new wife interjected—her voice faltering. "If you are not conscious of having done any wrong, why don't you come inside [the kitchen to answer the charge]?"

"No! No! I'm too excited," he stammered. Rising from his chair, Hoch swayed back and forth, then paced the floor, his mind racing.[17] He had not thought this out carefully enough. All of his planning had gone awry, and now he had to think fast.

Not wanting to engage this man any further, Amelia Fischer disgustedly shook her head and stepped back into the kitchen. Two minutes later, the sisters returned to the parlor to discover that Johann Hoch had flown the coop. Bertha Sohn wrapped a comforting arm around Amelia. "I wanted my children so much," Amelia sobbed. "He said he had part of the money ready but was a little short. I am a poor woman and the money I gave him I had got scrubbing floors!"[18]

Bertha nodded silently to Mrs. Sauerbruch and told her, "Go call the police—now!"

Studio portrait of the young Belle Gunness likely taken in Norway. Photo courtesy of the LaPorte County Historical Society, Inc.

Front view of the Belle Gunness home at 620 Alma Street (now Latrobe) in the West Side Austin community of Chicago. Photo courtesy of the LaPorte County Historical Society, Inc.

The backyard of the Belle Gunness home at 620 Alma Street. Chicago police decided not to dig for human remains, satisfied that Belle did all her killing in LaPorte. Photo courtesy of the LaPorte County Historical Society, Inc.

Belle Gunness and her three young children, likely all adopted: baby Phillip, Myrtle, and Lucy. Studio photograph taken by R.C. Ganiere, courtesy of the LaPorte County Historical Society, Inc.

Jennie Olsen was murdered by her foster mother, Belle Gunness. Photo courtesy of the LaPorte County Historical Society, Inc.

Joe Maxson worked for Belle as a hired hand after she let Ray Lamphere go. Photo courtesy of the LaPorte County Historical Society, Inc.

The smoldering ruins of the Gunness residence at Brookside Farm, LaPorte, Indiana. Photo courtesy of the LaPorte County Historical Society, Inc.

Panoramic view of the Gunness farm. Photo courtesy of the LaPorte County Historical Society, Inc.

A large crowd formed to partake in the public auction of the Gunness property following the tragedy. Photo courtesy of the LaPorte County Historical Society, Inc.

As the grim task of unearthing human remains at the Gunness farm continued, throngs of spectators and the idly curious gathered on the grounds to socialize, gawk at the workers, and otherwise enjoy the unexpected "carnival-like" atmosphere. Note the presence of children and their expectation of going for a pony ride on the killing field. Photo courtesy of the LaPorte County Historical Society, Inc.

Alaskan gold miner and prospector Louis Schultz sluicing the Gunness graveyard in search of human remains. Photo courtesy of the LaPorte County Historical Society, Inc.

The grim task of digging in the "Gunness Graveyard." Photo courtesy of the LaPorte County Historical Society, Inc.

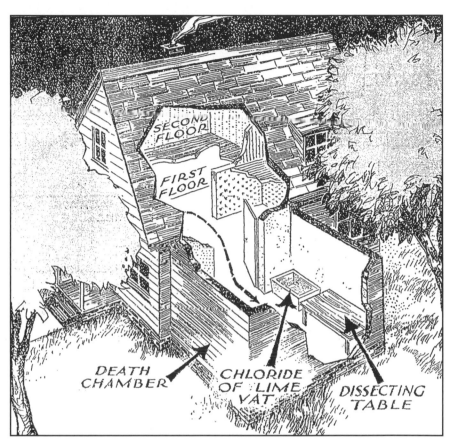

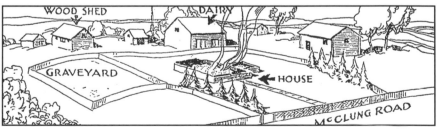

Schematic and layout of the Belle Gunness farmhouse and killing ground, LaPorte, Indiana. *Chicago Journal*, May 8, 1908.

Asle Helgelein, date unknown. Asle Helgelein traveled to the Gunness farm in LaPorte in search of his brother Andrew but found him buried in a shallow grave. Photo courtesy of the LaPorte County Historical Society, Inc.

Andrew Helgelein was Belle's last victim. Photo courtesy of the LaPorte County Historical Society, Inc.

The nearly intact remains of Andrew Helgelein unearthed. Photo courtesy of the LaPorte County Historical Society, Inc.

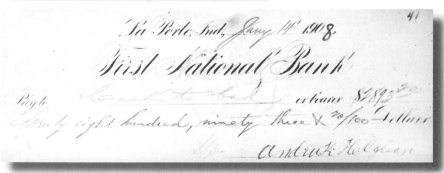

Bank draft from Andrew Helgelein written to "cash." The money—$2,893—was turned over to Belle Gunness. Photo courtesy of the LaPorte County Historical Society, Inc.

(right) Judge John C. Richter presided over the trial of Ray Lamphere. Photo courtesy of the LaPorte County Historical Society, Inc.

(below) Members of the LaPorte County jury who convicted Ray Lamphere of arson. Photo courtesy of the LaPorte County Historical Society, Inc.

Ray Lamphere's defense attorney, Herman Wirt Worden. Photo courtesy of the LaPorte County Historical Society, Inc.

LaPorte County Sheriff Albert Smutzer *(left)*, Coroner Charles Mack *(center)*, and unknown man. Photo courtesy of the LaPorte County Historical Society, Inc.

Esther Carlson may have been Belle Gunness. Photo from the *Chicago American*, February 12, 1961.

Chapter Ten

In the dark, whiskey-soaked recesses of his troubled mind, Ray Lamphere became convinced that Belle Gunness was plotting his death. The arrival of bachelor farmer and stockman Andrew K. Helgelein of Aberdeen, South Dakota, who came to town to win Belle's heart and "pay off the mortgage" on January 2, 1908, sparked a fit of irrational jealousy in Lamphere, who bored a hole in the floor of the sitting room in order to eavesdrop on the conversations of the two lovebirds from his position in the cellar. "I heard Mrs. Gunness plot with Helgelein to kill me," Lamphere revealed, although it seems farfetched to accept the handyman's yarn that the farmer from South Dakota was willing to aid and abet Belle in a murder plot. "She told him that she loved him and that they would have to get me out of the way. She was to give him the chloral and asked him how much it would take to kill a man. He advised her first to experiment on a dog. A dog I owned disappeared shortly after and I became watchful of their movements. I told a friend that in case of my death an autopsy should be held and informed him that Mrs. Gunness was a poisoner."[1] In the depths of his paranoia, Lamphere believed that Belle would attempt to commit him to an insane asylum because what he knew would send her to the gallows.[2]

Once "dear Andrew" arrived, Belle unceremoniously evicted Lamphere from her bed, fired him outright, then attempted to secure a peace bond—fearing that the enraged ex-farmhand might attempt to kill her or, worse, expose her to the community and law enforcement as a murderess. Oblivious to the intrigues afoot, Andrew Helgelein walked into the deadly trap. He was to become the last of the prospective husbands to fall victim to the fatal lure of Belle Gunness.

Historians and members of the greater LaPorte community who were close to the case and its chilling aftermath believe that Belle was responsible for up to 42 murders spanning the nearly eight years that she devoted to running the Indiana farm. It is impossible to verify with any degree of certainty that this figure of 42 individuals (the number that is most often cited) is accurate or not. Fourteen bodies were eventually unearthed from the Gunness graveyard, including the mostly intact corpse of Helgelein, who had been buried with obvious haste. As to the fate of the rest of the corpses, if the farm animals did not devour the small body parts directly, Belle buried the remains of her victims elsewhere on the property, or conceivably they were washed away in the nearby lake or hauled off with the rest of the trash. It was grimly noted that her chickens had grown extremely fat.

The story of the grisly and frightful series of events transpiring out on McClung Road and the discovery of the graveyard culminated with the unraveling of Helgelein's murder and the persistent efforts of the victim's brother Asle to strike at the truth. He refused to accept at face value the lies and distortions told by Belle in her seemingly friendly, homespun replies to his letters of inquiry concerning the whereabouts of the missing Andrew. Ironically, Belle and her jealous, sullen paramour Ray Lamphere ultimately were exposed from beyond the grave by Andrew Helgelein, the hesitant suitor from South Dakota that Mrs. Gunness had relentlessly pursued, nagged, and cajoled for a period of months. The evidence of Belle's plotting and conniving to secure this man's life savings pegged at $1,500 was revealed in a dozen personal letters chock-full of tender homilies, words of encouragement, loving affection, and motherly advice concerning the warm underclothes he would need to take with him on his long journey to Brookside Farm. The original Gunness letters to the Helgelein brothers are on file at the LaPorte County History Museum, and they paint a clear portrait of the woman the locals and the media dubbed the "ogress." One of her first letters to him read:

> August 30, 1906
>
> Dear Friend,
> Many thousand thanks for both of your letters and photograph. You impress me with being a good man with a strong and honest character. A real genuine Norwegian in every respect and it is difficult to find such a man and not every woman appreciates. There are plenty of those Americans or "doll men" [meaning gigolos] around here, but I would not even look at them, no matter how often they asked me. Take all of your money out of the bank as soon as possible as you do not know when you might lose them. Then get ready as soon as you can. You will have a much better chance to make use of your capital here, and you

can be sure that nothing will happen to them, but will probably make you independent for the rest of your life. If our closer acquaintance is such as I believe it will be, we can be the best of partners. My parents are both dead. I was the youngest child. I have a brother in Norway—a contractor or master builder in Trondheim and a sister there also. I also have a sister in Chicago.—Bella

When Andrew failed to show up in September, the tone of Belle's letters became more urgent and imploring. In October she wrote:

October 29, 1906
Dear Friend,
I received your letter Saturday evening, for which I thank you—my dear. I think it will be so cold for you up there all alone and only wish you were here where we do not have so much trouble. You must now hurry and come as soon as you can before the winter sets in. Clothe yourself well—on the way. Put on a heavy fur coat and good warm shoes and everything. You talk of leaving some of your money up there. This I would not do if I were you, especially when you are going so far away, rather, sell your things. If you read only just a little every day, you find the newspapers [are] full of bank robberies and bank failures; it is either one or the other. I am sure you will find just as good a place for them here as you will find up there. I will now tell you that I have a mortgage of $5,000 on a farm near LaPorte which is worth over $20,000. Another thing my dear is that you must be so very careful on the way, and keep your cash in a very, very safe place on yourself and sew them fast to your underclothes and do not say anything concerning it to anybody, not even to your nearest friend.—Bella

And still Andrew Helgelein hesitated. He did not make it down for Thanksgiving dinner as Belle had hoped he might, and after this her correspondence reflected a growing impatience. "She sent him pressed roses and wrote tearfully of the Norwegian Christmas," recalled attorney Herman Wirt Worden. "She drew pen portraits of herself and Andrew snugly ensconced by the big red, blazing stove in her back parlor next to the slaughter chamber where she cut up all her victims. The letters cover nearly two years. They run the gamut of emotion and veiled cupidity."[3]

Nearly eleven months more passed before Andrew could put his affairs in order and make up his mind to join up with Belle at her farm. In September, she expressed her delight that Helgelein "gave them [the Dakota people who objected to his excursion] the slip" in Aberdeen and was at last preparing to embark on a harrowing journey to find elusive, future happiness. With biting irony, she indicated how worried she was about the "thieves, robbers, and murderers" he might encounter along the trail that were out to do him harm.

LaPorte, Indiana
September 25, 1907

Mr. Andrew Helgelein,
My very best friend in the whole wide world:
I have received two letters from you for which I am so thankful. It makes me so glad and happy to think that you were so lucky to give them the slip in Aberdeen. I have always thought that was the case as nowadays there are so many thieves, robbers, and murderers. It is terrible to read about these things that happen in these times. Now dear friend, please be very careful [in] the little time you have left up there, if only you were here I would be so happy, but of course we find danger everywhere. This we both know but we must ask God to take care of us and he surely will do it, my dear friend. If you only know how I waited for you each day that passes. Now it is already the 25th of September and last year at this time I waited for you and you haven't come to me, but my dear friend I know you are a man I can trust and therefore I have waited so much longer and the fall is here again and I have the whole year managed the best I could without steady help because I have waited for you from one time to another as you have promised and promised and it seems as if you will never get your belongings in order up there. I would so much like to see and talk to you about one thing or the other and I should think you would feel the same way. It seems as if there is no end to your work up there. I have read in the newspapers that it has rained so much in your neighborhood that they had to stop threshing and I suppose you will have to wait long for them to begin again, to sell it where it is to someone or get some body to thresh it for you and come here. The weather is getting cold and it is getting so late my dear, the kindest man on earth. I think it would be best for you to take your creatures to Chicago and sell them there. At any rate you will get as much for them as at Sioux City and the small younger ones, if you do not think you get enough for them, you can take them over here and we will find room for them, my dear friend. Lately I have sold some of my cattle while the price was up because I thought you would bring some with you. Two young cows for butchering brought me $35 to $38 apiece. They were four years old but seemed to be poor milkers and several others according to their worth. As you, my dearest friend, asked me what I

thought best to sell, I think it would be best for you to take all you have to sell to Chicago, as you will come that way anyway and therefore it will save you from going some place else with them and save you from other danger and accidents. Now, dear friend, make up your mind as soon as possible as to what you really intend to do with everything. Forgive me for being so impatient, but I cannot help it, my dearest faithfullest [sic] and only friend in the whole world. In your next letter let me have the great happiness to hear that you are soon on your way here as then I will be the happiest and will know that I have found the best friend in the whole world. Now I must close for this time again, with best regards from your friend Bella Gunness.[4]

In a succession of letters to Helgelein spanning eighteen months, Belle promised that they would become so "cozy," and he would savor "some good homemade cake and some good coffee and cream pudding" and that they would "sit and talk and talk until we get so tired we cannot talk anymore." Belle painted an idyllic portrait of a fairy-tale Midwestern Christmas in the country with old-fashioned Norwegian home cooking spiced with tender descriptions of her perfect children and how much they loved playing with their "little Shetland pony."

With her comforting assurances, Belle finally succeeded in breaking down his resistance. Andrew at last agreed to come for a visit to preview a potential future home and then decide for himself one way or the other. He caught a train to Minneapolis and connected to Chicago. Before embarking on the journey, he told his brother that he would be back in about a week; however, nine days passed, and Asle heard nothing back. Alarmed, he contacted Minnie Cone, a mutual acquaintance of the brothers living in Minneapolis, who repeated what Andrew had told her earlier when he had stopped over in the Twin Cities—that he was going to look over the Gunness property with an eye on settling there permanently. Andrew had told Minnie Cone that he would be gone for only seven days. Asle then wrote to the postmaster of LaPorte inquiring about the farmer woman named Gunness, but there was no response. With mounting concern, he contacted the bank where Andrew had deposited his savings. In a letter dated April 10, 1908, Frank J. Pitner, cashier at the First National Bank, replied saying that he had conferred with Mrs. Gunness, who had told him that she would divulge all the information she had concerning Andrew.

Realizing her sudden vulnerability, and in a near-panic, Belle penned several unconvincing scenarios in a feeble attempt to allay suspicion and explain away Andrew's disappearance to his brother. On March 27, 1908, she informed Asle that "He wanted to take a trip to see if he could find your brother who had a gambling house in Aberdeen. He left Aberdeen the same day and he didn't find him in Minneapolis and he was going to make a thorough search for him in Chicago and New York. He always thought that he, the brother, went to Norway and he would go after him. I have waited every day to hear something of him."[5]

By then, Gunness had hired Joseph Maxson, another new man, to take over the chores of feeding the animals and managing the affairs of the farm after Ray Lamphere left her employ on February 8. Undeterred by threats of arrest and apparently unwilling to let go, Lamphere lurked in the shadows, keeping a reproachful eye on the widow and her every movement. The very sight of him made her squirm with nervous anxiety. Acting on Belle's complaint that Lamphere had repeatedly trespassed on her property and was cutting down the wire fence to spite her, the police arrested the spurned farmhand and jailed him on March 12 for committing an act of harassment. He was fined the paltry sum of $1, an amount allegedly advanced to him by Elizabeth Smith, an African-American woman whom the superstitious folk of LaPorte accused of engaging in voodoo and practicing the black arts. Using a crude racial epitaph, LaPortians ridiculed her as "Nigger Liz." She was central to the shocking chain of events that unfolded.

Belle filed a second complaint on March 28, and a $19.10 fine was assessed by Justice Robert C. Kincaid against Ray Lamphere by a Stillwell, Indiana, judge. Wirt Worden represented Lamphere in the proceeding and asked Belle a series of pointed questions about the suspicious deaths of her first two husbands, but a stream of objections were put forth by her lawyer and the questions were never answered. Justice Kincaid was later asked to describe Belle's demeanor during her testimony. "The woman, when the first questions were asked her, was composed," he said. "Then she trembled and was agitated as the questions became more numerous. The questions were leading and not relevant and at the time seemed somewhat insulting to the woman by intimating that she killed her two husbands for the insurance. She protested against the cross-examination and left the stand agitated which might of course be true of any decent woman resenting insinuation."[6] John Wheatbrook, who owned a farm in Springville, six miles north of LaPorte, obligingly paid the fine and put the shiftless drunk Lamphere to work on his own forty acres to keep him away from Gunness and out of trouble.

But that was not enough to appease Belle. With tears welling in her eyes, she begged the court to issue a peace bond (the posting of money in court, as required by a judge or magistrate, by a person who has threatened to commit a breach of the peace or threaten to harm or commit bodily injury against another person) against Lamphere, claiming that he was following her all over town night and day, threatening her life. In desperation Belle sought out her lawyer, Melvin E. Leliter, to draw up a will in the event that this "madman" succeeded in murdering her in her bed one night. She was hysterical with anger and worry. The lawyer advised that her best course of action might be to "get a gun and shoot him" the next time he annoyed her, but Belle said that she "would rather die than do that."

During his brief time working at Brookside Farm, Joe Maxson noted nothing unusual or out of the ordinary and didn't believe that Belle, as he observed her circulating among the people downtown, was as paranoid about Lamphere as she intimated to the police and her attorneys. "I never saw Lamphere here except once," Maxson said, "and that was in the evening when he came out on the lawn but didn't go to the house. I saw him standing near the house when I came up from the barn that night and several other times. At these times, all Mrs. Gunness said was 'There's Lamphere again,' or something like that and didn't get excited although she always locked the doors carefully."[7]

As if her troubles with Lamphere were not enough, Belle had to fend off the prying Asle Helgelein. The walls were finally beginning to close in on her criminal operation. Asle was unconvinced that his brother had escaped LaPorte, and Asle demanded more information and immediate accountability from Belle, who fired back a lengthy reply on April 24. This letter was her final written correspondence. In it, she accused the treacherous Ray Lamphere of stealing letters presumably written by Andrew to his brother before they could be mailed to South Dakota. She suggested that Andrew, in these letters, had invited Asle to come down to the farm, where, in all likelihood, she intended to permanently silence this new adversary. Belle's final piece of correspondence read:

LaPorte, Indiana
April 24, 1908

Mr. Asle Helgelein,
Your welcome letter I have received for which I thank you. It is a wonder for me as well as for you as to where Andrew keeps himself. It is very strange that the man should go away with his belongings. However I will tell you all that I know and you can be sure that I am telling the truth. I cannot remember the accurate date he left LaPorte, but it was either the 15th or 16th of January. My little daughter, fourteen-years-old, took him to the street car station. He went by way of Michigan City as he had a

desire to see that little town about twelve miles from LaPorte. He didn't stay there more than a day and he left here at one o'clock in the afternoon. Two or three days afterward I had a letter from him from Chicago saying that he had hunted for his brother, but did not find him, and that next day he would look around the Board of Trade and see how it was, and also get in track of his brother. If he couldn't find him, he would go to New York and find out if he had gone to Norway. If such was the case, I think he would go to Norway too. As I said before he asked me not to answer his letter until I had one from him telling where he would stop for a little while so he could get an answer. This is all I can tell, and I haven't his letter; I got the letter in the morning and read it and laid it in a china closet in the kitchen and went to milk and when I came back the letter was gone. That Lamphere was here and he had probably taken it, but that part of a letter which I spoke of, we found in the barn door one evening when he was around. I will send it to you. I recognize Andrew's writing and think you do too and I believe that the letter was addressed to me as I do not think Andrew would write to any other woman. I have had it in my pocket book so long that it's about wore out. We found it the first of this month and Lamphere, he did not know anything about Andrew's trouble but he has lately found so much trouble to trouble us with. He has begun all over again. He is in jail now. You speak of sending me money with which to discover what has become of Andrew. If I thought this would be of any use I could not go and do the inquiring, so it would be useless for you to send any. However, he was not in any trouble here in LaPorte. This is a little town of about eight or ten thousand and they generally know just what is going on. However, he stayed in most of the time and it was not until he had gone that I heard all these stories, and I told you the truth. I think the Marshal wrote to Aberdeen to find out about this gabble. I do not know if he got an answer. If you will write to anyone here in LaPorte, I think that bank man is as accommodating as any and at the same time he is the only one whom I know of who talked with Andrew and he knows as well as so many others about Lamphere who has now been arrested so many times for the bother he has been. I assure you that I will do all I can if I only know something to do and if you will take a trip down here to see what you can do in this case I will be glad to see you. I don't know what we could do to find him and I don't understand what keeps him away so long, unless as you say he has gotten into some trouble and does not want any of us to know about it. I, for my part, thought it was strange I didn't hear from him, but I was pretty sure that Lamphere had in some way taken his letters but I don't see why he hasn't written to you. I thought after I found that part of that letter that he was coming back in May because he thinks of farming again in Dakota but this I don't believe. He kept things to himself. He didn't tell me that he had any papers up there. He had a few on him but I don't know what they contained. He told me a little about some, but as they were strange to me I have no clear idea of what they contain. I must now close for this time. Be very careful with that part of the letter I am sending you and send it back to me in your next letter if you please. Heartiest regards from all, Bella Gunness.[8]

As Belle contemplated her next move and the very real chance that her secrets were about to be revealed to the world, she could not resist the temptation to advertise in the *Skandinaven* for yet another husband. She found Carl Peterson in Waupaca, a rural town located in the middle of Wisconsin, and invited him to come down with much needed money to help her pay off the mortgage, which was her usual stated reason for checking the creditworthiness of a new suitor. Peterson wrote back to Gunness saying that while he could not meet her $1,000 financial requirement, he was "respectful and worthy in every way." He wished her well and hoped that she would soon meet up with her ideal mate.

On April 27, Belle filed her last will and testament with George Link, the clerk of the circuit court. She appointed Wesley Fogle, a farm implements dealer at 107 Main Street, where she had purchased her tools and equipment during the previous year, to serve as the executor of her estate. Gunness bequeathed the entire estate valued at $13,000 to the children— Phillip, Lucy, and Myrtle—but her will ignored poor Jennie Olsen, who, according to Belle's feeble explanation to Emil Greening, was sent to California in 1906 in the company of a "professor" to continue her education. "I was told that Jennie had gone," the youth said and sighed. "I wrote to her but I gave the two letters to Mrs. Gunness and I never received any answer. I don't believe there ever *was* a professor, for I did not hear any man's voice or see any strange man about the house."[9] Lamphere's attorney, Wirt Worden, never believed that Jennie had left LaPorte. "Before she was supposed to be sent to school Mrs. Gunness went to Chicago," he recalled later. "She bought the girl an entire new outfit. After she had the clothes she took particular pains to show them to the neighbors. Then a short time after that Jennie disappeared."[10]

John Widener, another aspiring sweetheart of Jennie's, was given two addresses in Los Angeles to try to contact the girl, but his letters came back as undeliverable. "In October 1907, I met Mrs. Gunness again and she told me that she had just sent Jennie $100," Widener said. "I told her that I had written several letters and had received no reply. She laughed and said, 'That's alright. I wrote and told Jennie that you were married.' I told her that I had not been married and that it was my brother and asked her to write and tell Jennie I was still single. She said she would. Jennie never wrote me."[11]

Jennie's sister Minnie Olander was given an entirely different explanation by Joe Maxson, who said he believed that the girl had gone off to Fergus Falls and was attending a Lutheran school there. But Jennie Olsen was already dead—murdered by Belle because she had discovered the woman's secrets. Fearing that the girl would go to the authorities, Gunness ended the girl's life. With Jennie no longer in the picture, Belle omitted Jennie's name from the will and specified that all her worldly goods would revert to the struggling Norwegian Lutheran Children's Home Society in Chicago if the other three children, Lucy, Myrtle, and Phillip, were to suddenly expire.[12]

On the night of April 27, 1908, the Gunness household was in a festive mood. There was nothing to suggest that Belle's will had been drawn up earlier in the day and was about to become a self-fulfilling prophecy. No one was aware of the horrifying climax that was soon to follow. The house was brightly lit, and Joe Maxson, who slept on the second floor, vividly recalled "a happy family gathering." The little ones laughed and giggled as they played a game of "Little Red Riding Hood and the Fox" in the parlor. Belle reprised her role as the devoted and caring mother one last time. She sprawled out on the floor, laughed, and sang along with the children. "Mrs. Gunness almost cried when the bad fox chanced to catch Little Red Riding Hood," he said. Maxson retired shortly before half past eight, but he couldn't remember what time Gunness put the children down for the evening. Eventually the house grew quiet as everyone bedded down for the night.

At four the next morning, Maxson awakened and sat up in bed. His room stood directly above the kitchen and was full of smoke, and for a moment he believed that Belle was downstairs cooking breakfast and that the stove might have caught fire. He arose, glanced at his watch, and quickly dressed. It was much too early for breakfast. Then the sickening realization set in that the entire house was on fire. He called out to Belle, but there was no answer. He tried to kick in the locked doors to her private apartment but failed. Maxson, choking from the smoke, raced down the stairs, clutching his valise and a pair of overalls. These he left in a carriage shed fifty feet from the property after he escaped from the burning house. He ran back seconds later attempting to rouse Belle and the children, but there was no response from inside. In the thick smoke, and from what he could see of it, the entire building seemed to be on lockdown as the flames spread wildly. Maxson ran about the property calling out for help. "I was yelling to attract the attention of Mrs. Gunness and the children," Maxson explained, "But I did not hear any sound except the roaring of the fire. I picked up bricks and threw them in the windows but no one showed up."[13]

William Clifford, who lived an eighth of a mile from the Gunness farm, was the first neighbor to arrive. The two men smashed windows but dared not enter the inferno. William Humphrey, who lived on the Russell Farm, which was due north, placed a ladder underneath the upstairs window, climbed to the second floor on the west side of the house, and said that the bed in one of the rooms appeared as if it had been occupied. Maxson believed that this was the room in which Belle usually slept at night. Soon other families from neighboring farms— the Nicholsons, Laphams, and Hutsons—arrived to lend Maxson some assistance. They did what they could to try to wake the occupants of the burning house—provided anyone had survived. Maxson wasn't sure, but he thought it was shortly before five when he hitched a horse to a buggy and drove to the LaPorte jail to notify Sheriff Smutzer, his deputies LeRoy Marr and William E. Anstiss, and the volunteer fire brigade. Maxson said he was convinced that one of Belle Gunness's enemies had deliberately set fire to the place.

Ray Lamphere was up and about at the same time as well. He had spent the previous afternoon in LaPorte and had bedded down for the night in the hovel belonging to "Nigger Liz," a suspected "voodoo woman" and one of the town's strangest characters, out on the south shore of Clear Lake.[14] He said that shortly after four in the morning, he left her dingy abode and set out on foot for the Wheatbrook farm, a distance of six miles away. He just happened to be passing by the Gunness farm and noticed fire and billowing smoke coming from the roof. Lamphere did not stop to help, nor did he attempt to notify the neighbors, but kept walking because, as he said, "I was afraid I might be suspected of having set it on fire."[15]

Within minutes the Gunness farmhouse and outbuildings were reduced to rubble and heaps of charred debris; the floor had collapsed, and only uneven portions of the brick walls were left standing. The devastation was absolute. By daylight, teams of men led by Sheriff Smutzer sifted through the smoldering, blackened ruins searching for the bodies of Mrs. Gunness and the children.

For the next twenty-four hours, volunteers removed debris that had fallen into the basement. The work was nearly three-quarters completed when searchers came upon the headless remains of an adult female and the body of Phillip Gunness wrapped in a blanket and lying on her breast in the northeast corner of the cellar. The bodies of the other two children lay on either side of the headless corpse. The positioning of the scorched fire victims immediately suggested that they had been deliberately arranged in that fashion before the house caught fire; however, the *Argus-Bulletin* saw nothing sinister in the positioning of the corpses: "It looked as though the mother in a desperate effort to save her children had gathered them to her side with the youngest clasped in her arms and met death bravely."[16] By May 5, however, Belle was branded a murderess by the press. By that time the questions everyone wanted to know were: Who was responsible for the outrage? And was the adult female skeleton the remains of Belle Gunness?

Sheriff Smutzer, who was most industrious in trying to unravel the mystery, thought that the skeleton was Belle's and surmised that the ferocity of the flames had burned off her skull; however, this opinion was easily dismissed because Belle was known to have had gold fillings in her teeth, and teeth are nearly impossible to destroy except perhaps in a blast furnace. No teeth or gold fillings were found in the first dig—apparently someone had carefully removed the head. A score of men dug deeper into the rubble but failed to find the skull. Frustrated by the lack of progress, Smutzer called in Alaskan gold miner and prospector Louis Schultz to set up sluicing equipment and take charge of the washing of the ashes in search of the gold in Belle's teeth said to be worth $300. On May 19, to the complete satisfaction of Sheriff Smutzer, the miner Louis Schultz declared that he had found the teeth containing the fillings. But what if Belle had covered her crime by throwing her porcelain teeth into the conflagration before fleeing from the scene of the crime?

Smutzer thought that the fire was started by someone who had gone through the front doorway. Joe Maxson pointed out that an oil-can that usually stood in the outside hallway in the same part of the house was missing. The crime was deliberate—four bodies found—and the remains were taken to the morgue where Coroner Charles Mack directed the postmortem. The four-man coroner's jury issued their findings based on the Schultz discovery of the teeth. They said they were confident in the belief that the headless body was Mrs. Gunness and other remains were her children. Death, they ruled, was caused by suffocation followed by burning. There was no evidence of gunshot wounds. The mutilation of the woman's body (severed at the neck) the jury said, was due to the fire.

Dr. Harry Long, who assisted in the postmortem, disagreed. He said that the body in the morgue was five inches shorter than Belle and weighed a full fifty pounds less than Belle did. "It is not correctly proportioned," he said. "It is that of a rather plump woman of the same contour of Mrs. Gunness but weighing between 150–160 pounds. Mrs. Gunness weighed fully 225 pounds. The fingers show evidence of careful manicuring and that was something Mrs. Gunness knew nothing about."[17]

As the physicians debated their findings, Sheriff Smutzer focused on Ray Lamphere. He was aware of the difficulties existing between Lamphere and Gunness. Their strained relations were confirmed by her lawyer, Melvin Leliter, and the finger of blame pointed squarely at Lamphere after John Solyom, a local youth, swore that he saw the farmhand running away from the house shortly after the first burst of flame shot from the roof. Lamphere was questioned by Deputies Anstiss and Marr on April 29 at the Wheatbrook farm in Springfield Township, quickly arrested, and taken back to town. "I found Lamphere standing on the stairs and said: 'Get on your coat and come to town[,] Ray," Marr said. "Lamphere's reply was 'Did those three children and that woman get out of the fire alright?' 'What fire do you mean?' I answered. 'The little fire at the edge of town?' Lamphere answered yes."[18]

Gunness's former hired man was arraigned on charges of arson and murder. With no attorney to represent him at that stage of the investigation, he was bound over to the LaPorte County circuit grand jury. But there were those in LaPorte of a sympathetic mind to the most obvious suspect. The Reverend Dr. E.A. Schell, pastor of the First Methodist Church, visited Ray Lamphere in his cell. Schell tried to make the prisoner at ease and get him to embrace the old-time country religion. He convinced Lamphere that salvation was attainable and advised him to read his Bible every day. Schell succeeded in getting him to open up in a way that law enforcement could not. "He is a toper [a drunk] and his relations with women are open to criticism," Schell told reporters, "but he is not a bad man. He told me he was jealous of [Andrew] Helgelein and that after he came Mrs. Gunness would not tolerate him but there are a great many citizens of LaPorte who feel that he is not guilty. He is not a vicious man, just a farmhand who has picked up a little knowledge of the carpenter's trade and of course cannot be expected to rate high mentally. But there is little in his past life to lead one to believe that he would be guilty of the crime of firing a house containing four people."[19]

At the time of his arrest, Lamphere was wearing an overcoat that had been the property of the missing John O. Moe and a watch that had belonged to another prospective Gunness suitor. "She gave me these things," he said. Chewing on his tobacco wad, Lamphere nervously added: "Five bodies? That woman—I knew she was bad, but that's awful! I always suspected that she killed Helgelein, but now I am sure of it. Once she wanted me to buy Rough on Rats [a poison for rodents] for her, and another time she wanted chloroform. I would not get them for her."[20]

The case took a horrifying turn when Asle Helgelein, brother of the missing Andrew, arrived at the farm on May 1 to begin digging in the soft portions of the ground 35 feet from the ruins of the house. In disturbing detail Joe Maxson explained that he had been directed by the widow to dig postholes at this location. This was the logical place to begin, Helgelein reasoned, if his hunch was correct, but provincial LaPorte officials initially opposed the action and accused him of "stirring up trouble." Self-serving, small-town politics and narrow, special interests threatened to compromise his efforts to strike at the truth. "I went to State's Attorney [Ralph] Smith and laid my case before him. The State's Attorney laughed at me," Helgelein declared. "He scoffed at my story. He said I was a dreamer and did [not] know what I was talking about. Then he accused me of trying to give the locality a black eye. I told him all I wanted was justice and that I had come for it. At first the officials of the County would do nothing and I went ahead with my own investigation until the evidence appeared overwhelming even to prejudiced eyes. Then the officials took action."[21]

Smith, a Republican, was facing a tough reelection campaign. The last thing he wanted on his record was political embarrassment brought on by an outsider who was asking questions and making dangerous accusations. Smutzer was retiring after four years in office as sheriff, and his deputy, William Anstiss, wanted his job. Anstiss was out to make his name. Smutzer, another Republican in a heavily Democratic district, just wanted to pin down the case, convict Lamphere, and let the matter be forgotten about. The sheriff traveled to Chicago to confer with detectives from the Pinkerton National Detective Agency and solicited the help of Assistant Police Chief Schuettler, who sent down one of his detectives, C.J. Smith, to aid in the investigation.

To a man, the Democrats, eager to discredit and thwart the Republicans at every turn, saw the Gunness case as the means to salt away the next countywide election for their state's attorney candidate by pushing the theory that the diabolical Belle had murdered her children, burned the house down, and escaped the conflagration. Lamphere, they were convinced, was a patsy—cleverly set up by Gunness to take the fall. Mayor Lemuel Darrow and his police chief, Clinton Cochrane, were in agreement on this point. Mayor Darrow, an important Democrat wheelhorse and wealthy landowner who controlled 50,000 fertile acres in northwest Indiana, was a distant relative of Chicago's famed

Clarence Darrow, the "attorney for the damned." Mayor Darrow's law partner, Wirt Worden, again agreed to represent Lamphere as defense counsel—likely as a sop to the defendant's father, the long-serving justice of the peace in Springfield Township. Everyone in LaPorte, it seemed, was related.

"Lem" Darrow, who had a financial stake in a Porter, Indiana, racetrack run by a gambling syndicate headed by the notorious South Side Chicago bookmaker "Big" Jim O'Leary, was in the middle of his five-term run as mayor.[22] The Democrats had controlled the political landscape for over two decades but were feeling vulnerable. The *Argus-Bulletin* was the mouthpiece of their organization. The newspaper called for a broader Gunness investigation as a means of building party credibility and was at constant odds with the town's Republican journal, the *Daily Herald*, whose editors pounded away at the hapless Lamphere.

These larger conflicts were of no particular concern to Asle Helgelein, whose singular determination to find his missing brother was the linchpin that revealed the horrors that lay buried four feet under the earth. Working side by side with McClung Road neighbors, Helgelein turned the hard clay bed of the chicken yard. At first the usual scattered debris was unearthed—cans, bottles, and broken glass—until Asle turned up a piece of gunnysack four feet under the surface. Sheriff Smutzer was called over as hundreds of curiosity seekers peered intently at the proceedings from behind the woven wire netting that circled the yard and Belle's personal garbage dump. Within minutes came a grisly find: the body of the missing Andrew was pulled out of the ground. Asle made the positive identification. Before sundown, the putrefied remains of four more victims were unearthed, but none was in the same state of preservation as Helgelein. Individual body parts wrapped in gunnysack cloth were badly deteriorated by the lime.

The skeletal remains of the missing Jennie Olsen were finally unearthed, and the mystery of her disappearance was solved. Anton Olsen and the dead girl's sisters were immediately notified and asked to come down to LaPorte; their heartache was monumental. Ole Budsberg's and John Moe's bodies were the next to be found. Their relatives were summoned, and, upon arrival, Deputy Anstiss accompanied them all to the temporary morgue—a carriage shed on the Gunness property—to make positive identification.

Dr. J.H. William Meyer, who had formerly been attached to the Cook County Hospital in Chicago, took personal charge of the postmortem examinations. He expressed astonishment and horror at the conditions of the corpses. "It is horrible," he said. "I am at a loss to express an opinion on the whole case. I believe that nothing like it was ever encountered before. No jury of the foremost physicians of the country could say how long ago and just how these different people were killed."[23]

By the third day, the remains of ten more victims had been unearthed from the Gunness graveyard. It had become a significant national story, and reporters from every large newspaper in the U.S. descended on the tiny hamlet of LaPorte, overwhelming residents and those who were officially charged with leading the investigation. The rush of visitors was so great that liverymen established a regular bus line from downtown LaPorte to the farm. The roads were clogged with automobiles and pedestrian traffic coming from every direction.

An estimated 15,000 people from all over northwest Indiana, Chicago, and Indianapolis stampeded their way onto the grounds. The mood was weirdly festive as the crowd was soon serviced by vendors selling lemonade and sandwiches at roadside stands. Picture postcards of the studio portrait of Belle and her children were produced by a local printing house and sold for ten cents each or three for a quarter to souvenir hunters. Ghastly, macabre images of the unearthed remains of Andrew Helgelein were quickly made into postcards and sold even faster than the Gunness family portrait. Picnickers who had packed a light lunch spread blankets on the grounds and took in the sights. Baseball games were played within 500 feet of the crime scene, and pickpockets were said to have conducted a lively business by roaming through the crowds on the train platform as visitors made their way home. "Awful isn't it?" sighed Sheriff Smutzer. "There does not seem to be any horror in it to these people. I never saw folks having a better time."

Big city reporters intruded on the investigation in such a manner as to alter police procedurals and influence the "conventional" thinking about the final fate of Mrs. Gunness. As was the custom established during the Johann Hoch manhunt, the *Chicago American* assigned a full battery of reporters to cover all the lurid angles in the evolving Belle Gunness murder mystery. The Hearst team was led by their editorial star, Arthur James Pegler, the father of the future Pulitzer Prize–winning columnist Francis James "Westbrook" Pegler (1894–1969), whose syndicated column was read by millions of Americans in the 1940s and 1950s. Arthur James Pegler was sent to stoke the fires of sensationalism. According to Smutzer, it was Art Pegler who was really the first to implant the notion in the public mind that Belle had plotted the crime, substituted a "body double," and vanished into the night.

"There were forty-five correspondents in LaPorte at the time of the case and not one of them believed that Mrs. Gunness escaped," recalled

Smutzer, who, in a 1934 interview, shied away from analyzing too closely the strong evidence of Belle's flight from LaPorte. "Then one night Art Pegler of the *Chicago American* came to me and said, 'Sheriff, I know Mrs. Gunness is dead, but I'm going to send in a story saying she didn't die in the fire, just to give the case a new angle.' When I protested he said I was a good sheriff but a poor newspaperman. The next day the story was spread over the entire front page of the *American*, and it was then that talk of Mrs. Gunness' escaping started. It had its origins in the mind of one newspaperman."[24]

On May 6, 1908, the *Evening American* quoted LaPorte County Coroner Charles Mack and ran the provocative headline that firmly planted the seed of doubt: "Woman Bluebeard Alive Says Coroner." "That woman is *not* dead," insisted Coroner Mack, who had nevertheless escorted the caskets of the "supposed" Belle and her children to Forest Home Cemetery in Forest Park, located west of Chicago, for interment following the results of the autopsies. "That was not the body we found in the ruins when her house was burned. She has fled and may be on her way to Europe. She used another body for a ruse after she murdered her own children and set fire to the house."[25]

Criminal forensics, as primitive as they were in 1908, tended to disprove Smutzer's contentions, but were those the actual spoken words of the coroner or merely Art Pegler's editorial license? Amid the roiling political controversies and the excesses of yellow journalism there seemed to only one absolute as the investigation moved forward—Belle Gunness. The seemingly loving mother who delighted in playing a simple child's game of "Little Red Riding Hood" the night before she chloroformed the little ones and burned them to death was a predator of the worst stripe who had hacked her way into infamy, eclipsing the frontier murderess Kate Bender, the bigamist Johann Hoch, and even H.H. Holmes in her wickedness.

The May 10th *Chicago Sunday Record-Herald* echoed that feeling. "In the palmist days of the Holmes investigation, the "Castle" murderer never was accused of killing more than thirty-five people. Johann Hoch's victims were variously estimated up to the neighborhood of thirty but the actual killings laid at his door, all of which were done with a certain nicety that did not disturb the sensibilities of an aesthetic lady killer, numbered probably eight. It is safe to say however that in the light of the disclosures of the past few days, Mrs. Belle Gunness, the LaPorte widow has eclipsed the record of the prairie vixen of Kansas [Kate Bender] and that she undoubtedly holds the palm as the most extensive slayer, man or woman, of the age."[26]

Chapter Eleven

Imperious and ruggedly handsome, Chief of Detectives George M. Shippy was, by his own estimation, hired and fired from the Chicago Police Department more times than any other officer in the city. Before meaningful civil service laws were enacted in 1895, every police officer and city employee identified with the losing party following a mayoral election would be discharged and replaced with political partisans loyal to the victorious candidate.

Shippy, a Republican and a second generation policeman who had served as a fireman for ten years before donning the policeman's blue tunic, had been dismissed four times by incoming Democratic mayors between 1889 and 1903. Each time he was put off the force, Shippy cheerfully accepted his fate and launched new ventures, all the while knowing that the political winds would eventually blow in his favor, as they did in 1903. At that time he was moved out of the Des Plaines Street Station on the West Side, where he commanded the Third Division, for a plum assignment as Captain of the Englewood Station, and then, within months, he was promoted to Inspector in the East Chicago Avenue detective bureau. He was promoted despite his fervent opposition to the common practice of Edward Dunne, the incumbent Democratic Mayor, of demanding political donations from the rank-and-file patrolmen to finance his election campaigning.[1]

An avowed enemy of the anarchist fringe that had threatened the peace of the large cities with such things as the national railroad strikes of 1877 and Chicago's Haymarket Riot of 1886 and the other social agitators, Shippy pledged to clear out the "slacker element" in his own precinct house. He was the eternal optimist, something of a wishful thinker, and an old-time copper with good street instincts. And his instincts told him that the beleaguered, sad-faced German woman standing before him struggling to make him understand her broken English was the victim of a dangerous criminal. This man Hoch, he was convinced, had escaped detection only because of the gross negligence of Captain Colleran, the "political cop" with the lack of polish, and the plainclothes men who saw Hoch as a harmless little poseur unworthy of their attention. "I had $750 in the bank and withdrew it out and gave it to him to pay the mortgage with," Amelia stammered. "Thursday afternoon he went out the back door and I haven't seen him since."[2] Shippy nodded thoughtfully and ordered Detectives Michael Loftus and Charles F. O'Donnell to the Union Avenue address to investigate, but Hoch had indeed vanished. The neighbors told police that they had observed a large number of women coming and going from the building all during the time that Hoch was in residence. They believed the peculiar little German was running a marriage bureau, but Shippy sensed there was more to it than that. "I believe the circumstances surrounding this case are so suspicious that they warrant the strictest kind of investigation," he said. "I am going to the bottom of it."

He ordered Coroner Peter M. Hoffman—a querulous, medically untrained buffoon who was brilliantly satirized as the bumbling, incompetent Sheriff Peter Hartman by Ben Hecht in his famous Broadway stage play *The Front Page*—to produce all available records.[3] Hoffman was one of the county officials on the *American's* list of "friendly and cooperative" politicians who knew to call City Editor Moe Koenigsberg or Andrew "Long Green" Lawrence before anyone else. As coroner, he was often bitterly assailed for delegating his physician to conduct needless autopsies that mutilated human remains. The coroner system in Chicago was fraught with incompetence and political drag until it was finally abolished in 1976.

Shippy and Hoffman summoned Dr. Reese at Englewood Union Hospital, but Reese was closemouthed and defensive. "There was nothing suspicious about the death!" he snapped. "I never heard any question until an hour ago from the Coroner's office." When asked by reporters assigned to the station house by the *American* to reveal the cause of Marie Walcker's death, Reese retorted: "I won't tell you! Find out from the health office!"[4] Once the medical records were examined in detail, Shippy asked Hoffman to procure the necessary court order from Judge Willard McEwen to allow Coroner's Physician Dr. Otto Lewke to exhume the body and conduct a postmortem.

The detective bureau acted with uncharacteristic dispatch—bitter irony given the indifference they had shown Reverend Haas six years earlier. Cablegrams were sent to German police requesting additional information, and the steamship lines and passenger railroads were put on alert that the suspect might try to flee the country. "Hoch in my opinion is a greater scoundrel than H.H. Holmes ever was," Shippy declared, raising the eyebrows of the press. "Judging from the evidence I have already at hand, he married more than twenty women—widows with money and property for the most part."[5] The inspector now believed that Johann Hoch was responsible for more crimes than were committed by Holmes, whose very mention caused quite a stir in the yellow press and among the bluecoats in Englewood under the command of Lieutenant James O'Donnell Storen.

In a serious breach of protocol, Storen leaked his suspicions that Hoch just might have been the slippery Jake Hatch, janitor at the 63rd Street "Murder Castle," to Evelyn Campbell, who presented the sensational revelation to Koenigsberg, the 26-year-old city editor who supplied the Hearst paper with its gaudiest yellow hue in the earliest years of the titillating front page exposes. Koenigsberg was one of two dozen city editors hired and fired at the whim of Hearst in the first four years of the paper's operation, but the young man had good instincts, and his suspicions were roused after he had noticed Hoch's name in a list of burial permits issued by the city. Koenigsberg, who routinely scanned the daily lists of vital statistics, seemed to remember running across the name of this man Hoch before. Now he was certain there was more to it than the run-of-the-mill crime story.

Andy "Long Green" Lawrence saw wonderful circulation possibilities and assigned reporter George Shoaf to secure the cooperation of the Cook County coroner and the state's attorney's office and work the angles inside the precinct stations in Englewood and East Chicago and lend assistance to Campbell.[6] In return for "exclusives," the paper would agree to share its findings and would guarantee these Democratic officeholders valuable publicity; in contentious election years, a powerful ally in the press was critical to currying favorable public opinion and winning votes.

Campbell probed Lieutenant Storen for additional details. Storen, not one of the department's most trusted or honest line officers, believed that Hoch may have played a critical role in the grisly murders a decade earlier. Storen fully cooperated with the *American*.[7] "I feel certain that Hoch was the janitor of Holmes' castle," Storen stated for the record, "and that if he did not actually operate with Holmes he learned the latter's methods pretty well." On January 24, 1905, the *American* played up Storen's hunch and blasted a screaming headline across the front page—"Police Call Hoch Aide To Famous Murderer

Holmes"—just as Campbell inserted herself directly into the investigation with the hope of producing the evidence to support such a bold and exaggerated claim.[8]

Every Hearst newspaper in America advertised and promoted crime stories to the public as a kind of narcotic for the senses. Salacious, bloodcurdling prose and unverifiable rumors were the sizzle that sold the paper, after all, and the *American* "serialized" the progress of the Hoch manhunt through newsstand placards and newspaper headlines that suggested this was a thrilling mystery story well beyond the normal routines of news reporting. Under a *Chicago American* headline asking "Are You Following Miss Campbell's Hock Clews? The Detectives Are," readers were informed of the case's progress:

> Are you reading Evelyn Campbell's wonderful analysis of the Hock [sic] case? Her comments on this baffling Chicago police case appears [sic] every day in this edition. Miss Campbell in the role of a detective has been following all the important clews and her work has been a great aid to the police. The story of Johann Hoch's countless marriages, his power over women, his ubiquity, his mischievous disguises, his successful efforts for a score of years to cover up his crimes reads like the pages of a French novel. It is stranger in some of its ramifications than any of the tales of Conan Doyle or Gaboriau.[9] Watch these pages daily. Follow the links of evidence supplied by Miss Campbell.
> —Chicago American, January 29, 1905

With the gossip firmly planted in the public mind that Johann Hoch had to be the missing sidekick of H.H. Holmes (through dubious headlines and the paper's acceptance of questionable police speculation as fact), it was not all that difficult for Campbell to secure eyewitnesses to attest that Hoch and Jake Hatch were the same man. William A. Slyter, a carpenter, was a resident of the apartment house infamously known as the Holmes Castle in 1892–1893. He was absolutely certain in his belief that Hoch was the man to whom he paid his monthly rent. "I lived in a flat on the second floor overlooking Stewart Avenue, and I remember one time I went up to the office to pay my rent," he recalled. "The office was in the tower at the northeast corner of the building and was reached by a winding stair. Jake was there and introduced me to Minnie Williams. Jake took my rent money—$8—and put it in his pocket, telling Miss Williams to make out a receipt and he would sign it. In fact, he gave every evidence of being always deep in the confidence of his employer."

Standing before Shippy and Bailiff William F. Feller in the Inspector's private office on East Chicago Avenue, Slyter stated that Hoch (or Hatch) had moved the unpaid furniture from the Tobey Company into a hiding place through a trapdoor in the bathroom floor of Holmes's apartment. Slyter said that he had complained to Holmes many times about the disruptive and annoying tactics of the Chicago police during their search of the castle for the missing furniture. He said that Jake Hatch had placed an oil cover made of canvass over the trapdoor in the bathroom floor to conceal it from police. On many occassions Slyter had observed Hatch in the basement tinkering with the stationary boiler used by Holmes in his ruse to convince the gas company that the machine could convert Lake Michigan water into natural gas. Johann Hoch was a chemist and machinist by trade, which lent credence to what Slyter reported. Slyter described the man:

> "My wife used to call him 'that sneaky old Jake.' When I first met Jake, he was rather under medium stature and of stocky build," Slyter continued. "He wore a slight moustache. He spoke with a broken accent that, without regard for his heavy Teutonic cast of features, revealed at once his German descent. He was then a man about 160 pounds in weight. At that time he was always dabbling with drugs—that he, when he was not tearing down doors and building up partition walls, closet walls, and other portions of the dark rooms and dark passageways that honeycomb the Castle he claimed to have knowledge of drug mixing. And all the time I knew this man Jake [he was] meeting Holmes almost daily."[10]

M.G. Chappell, the bone articulator, was equally certain that Hoch was Jake Hatch. "I have seen the photograph of Hoch in the *American*. These photographs are pictures of Jake, Holmes' lieutenant[,] and I believe the two men are the same. During the time I worked for Holmes, I saw Jake repeatedly." Anna Boyd, an Englewood neighbor, agreed. "I was very familiar with the Holmes Castle," she said.

> My home was right across from the alley from the Castle. The two basement doors were very close together. I used to sew for some of the women Holmes brought to the house. This man Hoch whom I only knew as 'Jake' was Holmes' right hand man. A relative of mine who lived in my house was a friend of Holmes I am ashamed and sorry to say. The three men were inseparable. My relative was a veterinary surgeon. The three men used to insure valuable horses and then poisoned them so

they could collect the insurance. Many and many a time I have seen this man Hoch, as you call him, mixing, mixing different poisons together. Two or three days before the arrest of Holmes my relative and Jake disappeared. I have never seen either of them since until today until I looked on the face of Hoch.[11]

Were these eyewitnesses credible or just publicity seekers egged on by the yellow press and perhaps provided with some "cash inducement" by the *American,* as the druggist E.H. Robinson, who ran the apothecary on the ground floor of the castle from 1892 to 1894, suggested? The evidence was compelling but circumstantial and mostly hearsay. "I never saw Hoch before," Robinson said. "Mrs. Boyd has come forward now, I believe, to gain notoriety. I do not believe Slyter ever paid his rent to anyone but Holmes or Pat Quinlan. Quinlan was Holmes's right hand man. He collected all the money that Holmes did not collect himself. I never heard of a Jake until Holmes confessed just before he was hanged. I believe with the police that Jake Hatch was a figment of Holmes [sic] imagination. As for Chappell I regard him as a seeker after cheap notoriety."[12]

What were the police to make of all this? Personally, Shippy did not believe for a second that Hoch was Jake Hatch or vise versa, but there was no other choice than to keep quiet about the matter until Hoch was apprehended and brought back to Chicago. Then he would have him face his accusers, and, based on whatever else could be learned, only then would a determination be made to prosecute Hoch as an accomplice to the Holmes murders.

Gustav Strelow, a Wabash Avenue pitchman who paired up widows with eligible men in his newspaper *Fortune,* volunteered to become one of Shippy's informants—if only to save himself from being named an accessory after the fact and possibly charged with aiding and abetting murder. Strelow supplied the names of earlier victims and the various aliases Hoch had used, while Shippy learned from an expressman that Hoch had shipped his belongings to the Atlantic coast. Armed with this information and the approval of Chicago Police Superintendent Francis O'Neill to proceed, the Inspector, bound for points east, set out by train on January 26 in the teeth of a winter storm. Heavily disguised, and with his movements kept secret, Shippy was reported to be only "within a few miles" of Hoch and closing in. Arrests were imminent, the *American* breathlessly predicted. Readers were kept at the edge of their easy chairs awaiting news of his capture—or so Andy Lawrence hoped as he cranked out extra editions of the paper.

Meanwhile, customs officials in New York, Hoboken, Weehauken, and Bayonne, New Jersey, where the tank docks of the Standard Oil Company were situated, were alerted that Hoch might try to book passage on a tramp steamer bound for Europe, possibly securing his passage as a cook or a steward. Among his other skills was a flair for the culinary arts. East Coast police agencies were put on high alert, and by now the story of the Chicago bigamist was widely reported in newspapers across the land. With his photograph displayed so prominently in the press, police counted on an eyewitness coming forward to provide them with a tip. It was only a matter of time, they reasoned.

The *American* added to the frenzy with more wildly speculative stories that had no basis in fact. In a sizzling front page "exclusive," the paper concluded that Johann Hoch was the brother of Louis J. Thombs, a convicted killer executed in 1902 for the murder of a young servant girl named Carrie Larson aboard the steamer ship *Peerless*, as it moored in the Burlington slip of the Chicago River on December 30, 1901.[13] Because of strong physical similarities between the two men, Editor Koenigsberg ran front page side-by-side drawings of Hoch and Thombs, listing their weight, height, and hair color. There had to be no doubt, the *American* decided. The penchant for murder was hereditary, after all. Unsubstantiated rumors that Lewis Thombs had entered into a bigamous marriage and had killed a woman in Ceder Lake, Indiana, several years prior to the Carrie Larson murder suggested that the two men were linked by birth, and Hoch had contrived with Thombs, a "man of ungovernable temper," to murder this poor girl who had been hired to work as a cook on the vessel. The rumors flew thick and fast and were accepted by many readers as fact. But pure sensation driven by speculation in order to sell newspapers did not build a reliable case. The real evidence against Hoch was produced by a battery of pathologists.

In Chicago, medical science operated at a far less frantic pace. The body of Mrs. Walcker was exhumed from Oakwoods Cemetery and taken by patrol wagon to O'Donnell's undertaking parlor at 6328 Cottage Grove Avenue on the South Side where Dr. Lewke, accompanied by Dr. Reese, conducted the autopsy. Amelia Fischer and Bertha Sohn were on hand to identify the corpse. Lewke dealt a temporary setback to the prosecution's case against Hoch with a statement to the press that during their microscopic examination of the external organs, no evidence of poison could be found. Rather: "There were evidences the woman had a chronic endocarditis and arterial sclerosis or hardening of the arteries and blood vessels. There were no traces of any poisons of any sort which would cause death. The microscope showed no foreign substances that would cause death," he confidently declared.[14]

Before the findings could be given over to the coroner's jury for a verdict, Professor Walter S. Haines, a distinguished Chicago chemist and toxicologist who held a chair at Rush Medical College continuously from 1876 until his death in 1923, agreed to take a second look.[15] Under more stringent scientific analysis, Haines's examination of the internal organs revealed the presence of 7 6/10 grains of arsenic in the stomach and 1 1/4 arsenic in the liver. Two grains constituted a lethal dose. Because there was no arsenic present in the embalming fluid after it had been separated from the tissue, evidence of foul play pointing to Hoch in the death of Mrs. Walcker was now clear.

Professor Ludwig Hektoen, a co-lecturer with Haines at Rush College, agreed with the second diagnosis: Mrs. Walcker had died as a result of arsenic poisoning. Dr. Reese, who signed the death certificate, listing the cause of death as nephritis and cystitis (inflammation) of the bladder, was now forced to admit that he had been wrong. Arsenic had claimed the woman's life. It was an embarrassing moment for Reese and the coroner. That Hoch was able to deceive the attending physicians to this degree further demonstrated his expert knowledge of the uses of poison—and the institutional incompetence of the heavily politicized coroner system that continued to plague the Cook County criminal justice system for the next 71 years.

With evidence of murder about to be turned over to the Cook County state's attorney, George Shippy returned to Chicago—minus Hoch. Shippy's real mission had him headed not to New York but to New Orleans, where he nabbed Vincent Briscoe, a fugitive cop killer. After so many false starts and wild rumors and so much fanfare and overheated, minute-by-minute coverage, the arrest of Johann Hoch, bigamist and murderer, turned out to be a rather low-key and anticlimactic affair. It was carried out effortlessly on the night of January 30, 1905, in a furnished rooming house belonging to Mrs. Catherine Kimmerle, a buxom widow living at 546 West Forty-Seventh Street in Manhattan. This time, Hoch was the agent of his own undoing.

Not two hours after arriving in New York, Hoch had picked up a copy of a German-language newspaper, *Das Morgen Journal*—a publication of the Hearst chain—and spied Mrs. Kimmerle's notice for a lodger. At 2 o'clock that afternoon, Hoch, identifying himself as Mr. Henry Bartels, called on Mrs. Kimmerle and rented a hall room. His clothes were new, and he had an untroubled air about him. After settling in to comfortable surroundings, he joined her in the kitchen and offered to help peel the potatoes for the evening dinner. "I'm a good cook. I'll cook your dinner for you," he offered, but the woman declined. That evening Hoch positioned himself at the dinner table nearest to Kimmerle in order to ply her with a full measure of his charm, either unaware or unconcerned that he was fast becoming a national crime celebrity.

The next morning, as the widow washed the breakfast dishes, Hoch popped the inevitable question. "How would you like to marry me? I'm a rich man—the son of a count. Don't you think I'd make you a good husband?"[16]

"Isn't this all rather sudden[,] Mr. Bartels?" The blushing Catherine then explained that she'd had a husband once and wasn't in the market for another one, at least not yet. Besides, there was another German man living in the boardinghouse who seemed to fancy her and had in fact already staked a claim for her affections.

But it was the tidy sum of $2,000 that Kimmerle had on deposit in the Chemical Bank that Hoch was after, and he wouldn't take no for an answer. "If you marry me we can go to Germany on our honeymoon; you can give up this boardinghouse and need never bother with it any more."

Mrs. Kimmerle resisted. "I hated the man for his effrontery," she said later. "But there was something about his manner that forbade me telling him. I could never forget the way he smiled at me. He seemed to leer like the character in *Faust*—what do you call him? Mephistopheles?"[17] After hearing the second no from Catherine's lips, Hoch broke into tears and related the tragic story of his dearly departed first wife—killed, he said, by a streetcar in Chicago three years earlier—and his quest to find a good woman of fine moral character to relieve the aching loneliness and years of suffering. Kimmerle wavered but ultimately held her ground. She was practical and refused to be swayed by sympathy; she had heard sob stories before from deadbeat lodgers with a plethora of excuses for not paying their rent on time.

Later that afternoon, Hoch stepped out to make his rounds. After he left, Kimmerle went downtown. She picked up a newspaper, scanned the front page, and let out a scream. A photo of the short, broad-shouldered lodger who had just proposed marriage to her was prominently displayed. She showed the likeness to her neighbors and was quickly convinced that the Chicago fugitive was her newest lodger. Kimmerle made her way to the West Forty-Seventh Street Police Station to make her report. After hearing the story, four detectives hurried to the boardinghouse, where they waited until 10 o'clock that night when the fugitive finally returned. "Hello, Hoch!" greeted Detective Sergeants

Edward B. Frye, Harry Foye, and Sergeant W.J. Fogarty of the New York City Police Department.

"My name ain't Hoch! I am a salesman for a wine house at Frankfort-on-the-Main!" he snapped as police frisked him, removing $600 in currency, a pocket watch, perfumed handkerchiefs, and a memorandum book.[18] Frye's search of Hoch's trunk turned up a newspaper dated December 4, 1904, a wedding ring, a loaded revolver, and a fountain pen with a barrel filled with 58 grains of commercial white arsenic. The pen was the device he most often used to discharge the poison into the coffee or food of his victims, but to Officer Fogarty, Hoch claimed the substance was just harmless tooth powder.

Hoch was taken to the precinct station and "sweated" by detectives until he finally admitted to Acting Inspector Stephen O'Brien at the Detective Bureau that his name was not Bartels—and in point of fact he was the same man wanted in Chicago who answered to the name Johann Hoch.[19] "Yes, I am the man wanted in Chicago," Hoch said and sighed. "But they are mistaken as to the charges. I am wanted for some trouble I had with my sister-in-law about some furniture. Do you think I'm a Mormon? I know the stories about me. But look at me! Would I be fat and happy if I had a hundred wives?"[20]

Hoch was arraigned on a charge of bigamy and swindling but not murder—before Magistrate Crane in the Jefferson Market Court after mug shot photos were taken and copies were dispatched to Chicago. Placed in a lineup hours later, Hoch was readily identified by John Schappe of Jersey City, who claimed to have known the prisoner back in Germany.

In Chicago, Evelyn Campbell of the *American* arranged with her editors to pay the necessary travel expenses for her to escort Anna Hendrickson to New York to pick the archbigamist out of a lineup of 12 men. Hendrickson had married Hoch on January 2, 1904, and was abandoned three weeks later. She told Campbell that she had spent the previous year and a considerable amount of money trying to locate this man. "Would she mock him as I felt she would be perfectly justified in doing?" the reporter wondered. As Hendrickson approached the raised platform inside the detention room at 300 Mulberry Street with Evelyn Campbell at her side offering encouragement, she pointed to Hoch. In a startled tone, she told the police inspector that there was no doubt in her mind. The little German lowered his gaze. His face was flushed from embarrassment, and his chalky complexion and sagging shoulders suggested that he was thoroughly beaten. Hoch simply said: "I'm sorry, Anna."

"Why the man has actually the grace to be ashamed of himself!" gasped Hendrickson, who had been warned not to engage in conversation with Hoch, who was quickly led away.[21]

Later, after regaining a measure of his customary bravado, Hoch joked to the guard: "Her eyesight was always poor!" Then he said he was only married twice—to the Walcker woman and her sister.

Hoch was put on suicide watch and imprisoned in "the Tombs," the notorious Manhattan Detention Complex at 125 White Street, an austere stone fortress that was an imposing example of Egyptian Revival architecture. In 1842, during his stateside visit, Charles Dickens described the original Tombs prison, which was demolished and rebuilt in 1902, as a "dismal fronted pile of bastard Egyptian." Turning to Campbell and a swarm of reporters as he was being led across the "Bridge of Sighs" separating the jail from the Tombs Police Court, Hoch snarled: "Dogs of the press! You are hounding me now but I will get even with all of you!"[22] The next day the *American* published a front-page exclusive with the headline "Hock Confesses to Evelyn Campbell That He is a Bigamist." The confession, if it could be called that, was hardly a revelation. Hoch also had spoken candidly about the charges against him with the *Tribune*'s Arthur Sears Henning, one of the great newspaper men of the twentieth century.

"Was your fountain pen found in your room?" Henning asked.

He ignored the question, but he understood what he was really asking. "No, it doesn't!" Hoch screeched, his anger rising. "It ain't poison—its headache powders!"

"Oh, then you *do* know something about it?" Henning asked. He also recalled that Hoch's response was a convulsion of laughter, and that he said the joke "was too good to keep."[23]

The younger, less experienced Evelyn Campbell managed to secure a few minutes of interview time with Hoch, and he told her that he had been a bachelor for the first forty-four years of his life. "He chuckled," Campbell wrote. "This chuckle of his is characteristic. That he has a strong sense of humor I could tell from his face as well as his matrimonial record."[24]

In Chicago, Chief O'Neill prepared extradition papers and sent then on to New York Governor Frank W. Higgins in Albany. As the wheels of justice turned, Detectives Loftus and O'Donnell were sent east to pick up Hoch and return him to the Midwest to be booked on murder charges—this coming after the New York Police indicated that they would not surrender the prisoner until after they had investigated reports that Hoch had married and swindled two women in Brooklyn and Manhattan. Inspector Shippy forwarded Captain James Langan of the New York Police an anonymous letter he had received from a woman living in the Belvedere Hotel in Manhattan; the letter revealed the existence of the two wives. However, the registrar of vital statistics in the Brooklyn Health Bureau could not provide any death certificate for a woman named Bartels living in the borough. The registrar did not bother to cross-check any of the dozen aliases used by Hoch in the course of his bigamous career.

Hoch declared that he would not oppose his extradition back to Chicago. "What's the use of all this red tape this extradition business?" he asked Magistrate Crane. "I'll go to Chicago with you if you want to take me."[25] There he would plead guilty to bigamy and take his chances, he said.

The compliant prisoner was told by Loftus that "at least 14 wives would be waiting for him" at the train station back in Chicago. "That's nice. I would like to see them altogether [sic]—poor deserted women. Do you think they can all agree on me?" he sneered. As Hoch was escorted by Detective Fogarty from the Tombs back to the Jefferson Market Police Court—a distance of 10 blocks—women crowded the doorways and windows of buildings and all along the street corners hoping to catch a glimpse of the modern Bluebeard. They were disappointed by his ordinary appearance. "Well of all things—you don't say so," said one. "Looks like an old clothes man, don't he?"[26]

Another 500 curious women showed up at the Lackawanna Railroad ferry at the foot of Barclay Street as Detective Loftus led his handcuffed prisoner to the boat. Hoch was allowed to don a new red-and-black necktie and groom himself immaculately prior to his departure from New York. Loftus was most accommodating. "Let all these women who think they married me come around and look at me," Hoch said. "I am ready for them. I don't need any help from lawyers or newspapers or anyone." One indignant woman armed with a horsewhip and loudly cursing his name elbowed her way to the front of the crowd to take the full measure of Hoch. Claiming that she had married him in a Lutheran Church at 100th and 9th Streets in Manhattan on May 4, 1904, Mrs. Mary Steinert was at the point of hysterics and had to be forcibly restrained by police.

Hoch was unfazed by the dramatic scenes unfolding before him and continued to deny his guilt. As to the accusation that he was a hypnotist and a poisoner, he dismissed the whole thing as "chew the rag talk." "All this poison talk is a lie. The powder they found is tooth powder."[27] During the trip back to Chicago, Hoch was put at ease by Detective Loftus. Hoch was full of good humor and willing to talk—even in the presence of the pushy Miss Campbell. In an unguarded moment, he confessed that the white powder was indeed arsenic that he had purchased for the sum of ten cents along with the incriminating fountain pen from the Frederick O. Collins drugstore on Broadway near 3rd Avenue in Manhattan.

Hoch said that by that time he had read the newspaper dispatches identifying him as a wanted man—at which point he realized that the game was about over and his time was short—he intended to ingest the arsenic and do away with himself. However, a subsequent search of the druggist's records failed to turn up evidence of a sale of commercial arsenic on the day in question. But the discovery of a glass vial (the ink barrel matching the fountain pen in Hoch's possession) later found in a desk drawer at 6430 S. Union Avenue by Chicago detectives established that Hoch had owned the device for a longer period of time than he had reported to Loftus.

The Nickel Plate train conveying Hoch and the detectives rolled through Midwestern towns. Spectators lined the platform at each stop to glimpse the famous murderer. At first his notoriety seemed to cheer Hoch. Campbell noted:

> Toward the end of the journey Hoch became visibly nervous. He had joked and laughed and whistled incessantly all the way to Chicago. He had enjoyed the crowds who came to each village railroad platform to see him. He had waved to the women and shouted greetings to the men and laughed in pleased vanity at the attention he received. But at Knox, Indiana a crowd of school children thronged the tracks. 'Get a rope! String him up!' shouted a boy. It was the idlest boyhood bravado. But Hoch's face paled. His hands twitched. He shrank back into his seat. 'Why do we not hurry up out of a place like this?' he demanded irritably. From that moment he became gloomy and thoughtful. He went with Sergeant Loftus into an empty Pullman where they remained barricaded until the end of the journey.[28]

The train steamed into Union Station the morning of February 9. None of the 14 or so wives were present, but a crowd estimated to be 2,000 strong—most of them women—waited for hours by the gates for a glimpse of Hoch. Inspector Shippy and his men hustled the prisoner past the excited spectators and into a patrol wagon and conveyed him to the Armory Station on Harrison Street in the South Loop—Chicago's equivalent of the Tombs. From there Hoch was transferred to East Chicago Avenue on the North Side where the elite cadre of the city's criminal justice system awaited him—Chief Francis O'Neill with Assistant State's Attorneys Harry Olson and Thomas J. Healy.[29]

Hoch confronted his accusers one by one before the dreaded "sweating process" commenced. Old and familiar faces were on hand to greet him: the saloon keeper Benno Lechner; F.J. Magerstadt, the furniture man; Emma Rankan, victim and fellow bigamist; and others who swore to have seen him lurking about the Holmes Castle a decade earlier. "He looks a bit stouter and more prosperous than formerly, but otherwise he is the same," opined William Slyter. "I know a dozen more persons living near Holmes' Castle who could identify him. Pat Quinlan could say positively whether Hoch is Jake, if Quinlan could be found."

"Who is Quinlan?" Hoch asked, puzzled. "I know nothing about Holmes. All such talk is foolish! I have read about him in the papers but that is all! I thought until Inspector Shippy told me Holmes was hanged in Philadelphia, that he was hanged in Chicago."[30]

Anna Boyd looked Hoch square in the eye and said she had no doubts. Hoch stared back at her and glared at the assembled throng with contempt, his famous composure and glib manner cracking under the stress. "You mean to say I was around the Holmes place? You are a liar!" he screamed, inching forward in a threatening manner.[31] Shippy placed a restraining hand on Hoch's shoulders and warned him that he had better steady himself.

Following the identification, Shippy announced to the press that Hoch had prepared a statement recounting his movements from 1895, the year he claimed to have arrived on American shores aboard the Bremen steamer *Stuttgart*. "Hoch has made a full statement to me of his actions since coming to this country and I believe him," Shippy stated. "I have been unable to find any evidence which would lead me to believe that he was in Chicago prior to 1895, while Holmes was in the heyday of his career in 1892–1893."[32]

The evidence of Hoch's involvement with H.H. Holmes was circumstantial—but nevertheless the word of the Englewood witnesses could not be easily dismissed. They were certain that Johann Hoch was the man seen lurking about the castle. There could be no doubt, they said. Shippy chalked it up to the idle talk of publicity hounds and the excitement and hysteria of the moment. That Hoch was in Chicago prior to 1895 seems more certain, although through cunning and lies, the accused murderer managed to convince Shippy that his arrival in the city in 1895 coincided with the purchase of a saloon at 1908 Western Avenue from Louis Witte. "I closed that deal on July 15, 1895," Hoch insisted. "I have been back to the old country twice since then."[33]

Hoch was bound over to the Cook County Coroner's Jury on a charge of murder. "I will plead guilty to bigamy because the police have the goods on me on that charge," Hoch admitted. "But I will not plead guilty to any murder charge they bring against me because I never have killed anyone in my life! I deserted my wives and took their money because what was theirs was mine, but otherwise I was invariably kind to them."[34]

An indictment based upon the chemical analysis conducted by Walter Haines, Professor Hektoen, and Dr. Lewke was handed down on February 23, but the other victims of Hoch's cunning were not mentioned when the grand jury indictment was returned in Judge McEwen's courtroom on March 4, and the Holmes connection was dropped for want of evidence. The defendant was tried solely for the crime of murdering Marie Walcker. "I'm just looking forward to a triumphant acquittal," Hoch said, beaming, after the indictment was read aloud. "Just watch us. We'll show up a few things that will surprise the police and everybody else. Do I look worried?"[35]

Assistant State's Attorney Harry Olson expressed the solemn belief that although no one had actually witnessed Hoch administering his poison to Marie, Hoch could still be convicted by the legal process of exclusion—that is, excluding the probability of anyone else committing the crime by proving that Hoch was the only person with motive and opportunity. This view was challenged by Isadore Plotke, an undistinguished, one-term Illinois State Representative from the Sixth District whom Hoch had retained as his defense counsel. Plotke was a rather cartoonish, excitable character principally remembered by Dr. Francis W. McNamara, physician at the county jail, as a man with a "Charlie Chaplin personality and a Weber & Fields dialect." He had no training or background in analytic chemistry and was a poor choice for defense counsel in a capital murder case.[36] It was Plotke's German ethnicity and involvement with Chicago's various German fraternal societies that appealed to Hoch, whose unconcern about his pending trial was astonishing, given the gravity of evidence mounting against him.

But then again, the prisoner had every reason to believe that his situation was only a minor irritation. He was being accorded every possible consideration by police and treated more like a visiting celebrity than a fiendish wife killer. His face wreathed in smiles, Hoch relaxed in comfort inside his jail cell at the Chicago Avenue Police Station, where he dined on choice cut porterhouse steaks catered by a nearby restaurant and delivered to his basement cell by an obliging Chicago police officer. The prisoner reclined on a soft couch ordered in at his own expense. He lasciviously ogled female prisoners in the nearby women's department, calling them "sweetheart" or "*mein liebe*" as they were led past his cell. Twice a day he was permitted to stroll around the grounds unfettered and was a frequent visitor to the barbershop. Keeping up appearances was important to him.

"He's got money and he pays for his nice meals," explained one of the commanding officers to an inquiring *Tribune* reporter who was more accustomed to seeing detainees in the lockup subsisting on the usual fare of bread and water in sparse, often inhumane surroundings.[37] As Valentine's Day approached, female admirers mailed cheerful greetings and missives of affection to him in care of "the gentleman in charge of the Chicago Avenue Police Station." An offer of marriage came in from one hopeful spinster who asked if he "would care to win the heart and hand of a girl 40 years old who has money to use in an endeavor to free you." Turning to Detective Loftus, Hoch expressed the solemn belief to his warden that "Marriage is a funny thing. . . . It is a lottery. Before marriage a man swears to love—afterward he loves to swear. Many a time I have told these women I would gladly die for them. And now if I weren't contented I would wish I had kept my word."[38]

Chapter Twelve

As the grim task of digging up the Gunness graveyard was temporarily halted because of a soaking rain in LaPorte, the search for the fugitive Belle was already in high gear despite fervent insistence from the sheriff and Republicans that the case was closed and the woman dead. Within five days of the fire there were reported sightings of her in Chicago and across the country. In Syracuse, New York, Cora Belle Herron, the widow of a chemical salesman from Chicago, who was en route from Franklin, Pennsylvania, to New York City, where she planned to visit her sister, was rudely accosted, removed from a Pullman sleeping car, and dragged off to jail on suspicion of being Belle Gunness. The matter was straightened out, but the indignant woman filed a lawsuit against the police.

Andre W. Thompson of Paulina Street in Chicago furnished the police with a photo of Belle and swore that she was hiding in plain sight in his neighborhood. Thompson could not be easily dismissed as a fool—he had been a boyhood friend of the late Mads Sorensen and was the best man at Mads and Belle's wedding. Thousands of copies of the Gunness photo were reproduced and sent to police agencies in the U.S. and Europe by order of Assistant Chief Schuettler, but a search of Thompson's neighborhood failed to produce Belle. Wild rumors were printed in the national press and accepted as fact. One far-fetched story out of Louisville claimed that Belle was the sister of Kansas murderess Kate Bender, who was officially missing and presumed to be dead by 1908.

From across the country, relatives of missing persons held out faint hope that the Gunness farm might yield up clues to a score of unsolved disappearances of loved ones. In Elkhart, Indiana, Jacob Hoeckle announced that he was on his way to LaPorte to see if there was any chance that his missing cousin Justina Loeffler—believed to be one of the vanished wives of Johann Hoch—might somehow be connected to this latest tragedy. Loeffler had disappeared from Chicago in 1902 after marrying a mysterious stranger named Robert Schmidt whom her family members said they never had met. The discovery of Jennie Olsen's remains suggested that there might be other female victims on the property, and the chance for a final resolution to this long nightmarish ordeal seemed to be at hand. But sadly for the Loeffler kin, their loved one remained missing.

Other horrifying reports simply defied imagination. From Warsaw, Indiana, came word that 70-year-old Jacob Pouch committed suicide on May 10 while "temporarily deranged" after reading newspaper accounts of the Gunness crimes.

In Chicago U.S. Attorney Edwin W. Sims ordered the arrest of every shady keeper of matrimonial agencies—the notorious "cupid masters" who led young girls into disorderly houses; middle-aged widows and spinsters into the arms of bigamists, cads, and sharpers; and lonely bachelors to their deaths in murder traps like LaPorte. The fallout from the Belle Gunness case sparked a wave of political action and a long overdue crackdown against these shady storefront operators first urged by Representative William Martin back in 1899. "I believe the managers of the bureaus will go to any depth in order to wring a few pennies from these poor persons who answer their alluring advertisements. The persons who answer these advertisements are an un-intellectual set and could be murdered and put out of the way without much danger of exposure," commented Assistant U.S. Attorney Seward S. Shirer. "While I do not mean to say all matrimonial agencies do this class of work—I insist all are illegal and there is no telling how far each manager will go. I am confident all will be arrested before the end of the month."[1] But even after the arrest and prosecution of Johann Hoch in 1905, nothing was done to end this business.

The Gunness murders encouraged tipsters in Chicago to alert the police to old rumors swirling about the house on Alma Street and the West Side candy store Belle once owned. Lieutenant Matthew Zimmer of the Austin district led a fruitless search for a druggist named Cramer who allegedly sold the poisons to Belle. On a separate front, the post office inspector conducted a rigid search for matrimonial bureaus that it was believed Belle engaged to lure her victims. But in truth, no one really needed to look any further than the personals section of the *Skandinaven*.

Coroner Hoffman called for an excavation of the former candy store address at 313 Grand Avenue in order to determine if Belle had buried a little girl named Lucy whom he believed was adopted by Gunness back in 1894. No such excavation was ever conducted, and Assistant Chief Schuettler doubted that the backyard of the Alma Street property was a burial ground either. "I'm satisfied that the woman didn't run any baby farm there," he said. "Our records don't show the disappearance of any local people at that particular point."[2] David Nellis, the owner of the old Gunness home in Austin, was not anxious to see his yard torn up and the possible structural damage to the foundation of the home that such an action might cause, despite assurances from Hoffman that he would help defray any associated costs of a dig. Nellis and his brother pleaded with Schuettler directly, saying that the house represented the sum value of their entire life savings. The assistant chief, a practical thinking man, sympathized and declared the dig off—unless something more tangible than idle neighborhood gossip turned up.

In LaPorte, where the normal rules of small town living were temporarily suspended, digging at the Gunness farm continued as known victims (whose remains had been identified by family members) were processed through the carriage shed where body parts, disarticulated bones, and gunnysacks of human remains were piled up like cordwood. The stark horror of the scene inside the shed and the human drama of the townsmen who had bravely and gamely volunteered to excavate the grounds in the belief that it was their duty as neighbors and LaPortians were quite a contrast to the merriment, baseball games, picnics, pony rides, and souvenir sales going on in the ghoulish carnival sideshow outside the gates.

In time, LaPortians came to view their most famous resident in more benign terms; Belle became a twisted but fascinating example celebrated in community folklore. In the coming years citizens tried to outdo one another by eulogizing her in satirical theatrical performances and a musical ballad, produced locally. One verse well known to the location populace went like this:

> When Andrew Helgelein came,
> His check he first cashed in–
> And then that night
> She caught him right
> And he was soon bashed in.[3]

What other inappropriate limericks, wisecracks, and doggerel were the rubbernecking spectators saying to one another during those long, tedious afternoons of making merry at the "Gunness picnic grove" while the serious police work was going on?

Inside the fenced-in area of the farm, Sheriff Smutzer was encouraged by the miner Louis Schultz's surprising discovery of three engraved gold rings in the sluice boxes. The inscriptions on two of them read: "PG to JS Aug - 23, 94" and "PS to JS, 5-3-96." Smutzer and Ralph Smith, the prosecuting attorney, believed that the rings belonged to Belle. They were found near the remains of the torso of the adult female that was located after the fire, and this stunning new evidence seemed to close the case to the satisfaction of Ralph Smith.

But the initials were not Belle's, and no one could figure out the identity of the people who might have matched the inscriptions on the inside of the rings. Did Belle plant them in her hasty escape, knowing that they would confuse law enforcement? Or did they belong to the mysterious female victim whom Ray Lamphere contended had been lured to the farm from Chicago and murdered? Many believed it was the torso of this unknown woman's body—not Belle—that was recovered from the basement.

The hottest summer in LaPorte history quickly passed. Lamphere had made a partial confession to Reverend Schell shortly following his arrest, but on the advice of his attorney, Herman "Wirt" Worden, he retracted it and said nothing further in the weeks following the tragedy as he languished in the recently opened LaPorte County Jail.[4] He was a living portrait of anxiety and was in a state of nervous collapse as his trial for arson and murder approached. The trial was to be held in the LaPorte County Courthouse, a somber Richardsonian Romanesque red sandstone structure in the downtown center designed by Brentwood S. Tolan of Fort Wayne and completed in 1894 at a cost of $300,000.

In the oak paneled, stained glass–windowed courtroom of Judge John Carl Richter on the afternoon of November 9, 1908, jury selection for the Lamphere trial began. The actual trial commenced four days later. By remarkable coincidence it was Friday the thirteenth, Ray Lamphere's birthday.

In a larger sense, this was shaping up to be not so much a criminal trial as it was a bitter test of wills between Democratic and Republican rivals, each determined to destroy the reputation and standing of the other. The Republicans had prevailed in the 1908 fall election. William E. Anstiss replaced his former boss, Albert Smutzer, as sheriff. Charles Mack was defeated for renomination as coroner in the LaPorte County Democratic Convention because he believed that the remains of the woman in the cellar was Belle Gunness, which ran counter to the case that Mayor Darrow and his law partner, Wirt Worden, were building for Ray Lamphere as his defense counsel. Mack was unceremoniously dumped by the Democrats because he had betrayed the interests of his party. Prosecutor Ralph Smith sent challenger Philo Q. Doran, supported by the LaPorte saloon keepers, down to defeat following a blistering campaign in which the handling of the Belle Gunness case was called to account by the Democrats and friends of Lamphere.

Attorney Worden continued to push hard on the theory that most people came to accept as truth that Gunness had escaped from the firetrap, and backed his arguments with convincing proof.[5] "The main question was whether the body in the fire was Mrs. Gunness," Worden recounted in a classroom lecture years later. "It was the theory of the State that when the house was set on fire they were all in bed on the second floor and had fallen in the basement. But the piano case was on the first floor and the bodies were under the piano. If this theory of the state was true, the bodies beat the piano to the basement."[6]

Ralph Smith was equally confident in his strategy of pinning the murders of Gunness and her children on Lamphere after scrapping his initial plan to try the accused man for the murder of Andrew Helgelein. "I am tired of this silly rot that she is alive! I am going to put a stop to all this talk about her being seen in forty different places in the country by every Tom, Dick and Harry who thinks he is a detective!" Regarding Lamphere, Smith expressed confidence of the outcome. "There is no possibility in my mind that the verdict will be other than guilty," he declared on the first day of jury selection. "I anticipate a good deal of trouble in securing a jury owing to the wide publicity that has been given the case but a special venire of seventy-five men have been drawn. That the dead woman found in the house was Mrs. Gunness we have conclusive proof. I have the evidence to hang the man in my office! The effort to make political capital of the case failed."[7]

District Attorney Smith would have to first overcome the compelling findings of Dr. Walter Haines, the eminent Chicago toxicologist who had produced the damning evidence against Johann Hoch three years earlier. Haines was once again called in to a major criminal trial and was summoned to LaPorte to conduct an analysis of the three bodies dug out of the basement. Professor Haines identified sufficient quantities of arsenic and strychnine in the stomachs of the victims to cause death. Based on what Haines told the court, it would be very difficult for the state to establish that Lamphere first poisoned the victims and then torched the entire house.

As a result of strong feeling for and against Lamphere locally and the widespread publicity given to the case across the region, an estimated 500 people jammed into the courthouse square trying to gain admission to a room that seated only 300. In an action unusual for the time, numbered tickets were distributed to spectators in the order they applied in an effort to prevent overcrowding. The trial proceedings were of special interest to women, who had come from South Bend, Terre Haute, Michigan City, and other northern Indiana locales to witness the unfolding drama.

Ray Lamphere, the town drunk, ne'er-do-well, and jack-of-all-trades had no assets to speak of or the means to pay the considerable legal expenses of Wirt Worden, Worden's law partner, Mayor Darrow, and Worden and Darrow's co-counsel, Ellsworth E. Weir, a distinguished lawyer from the Indiana bar whose appearance at the defense table on the opening day of the trial came as a surprise to court observers. Asked later where he thought the money had come from to pay his legal fees, Lamphere shrugged his shoulders and said he didn't know. It was evident from the moment of the judge's banging of the gavel to open the trial that extraordinary measures had been taken to ensure an acquittal. Lamphere was cleaned up, dressed in a suit, and looked more like a respectable bank clerk than a farmhand with questionable associations and a poor reputation. His elderly mother—estranged for years from his father—made a tearful plea on her son's behalf. She evoked strong sympathy when she told of his early circumstances and the grinding poverty that compelled her to hand sew his clothes up until his tenth birthday.

The daily courtroom proceedings were full of unpredictability— evidenced by the flamboyant Weir, who asked George Link, the clerk of the circuit court, to issue a summons for Belle Gunness to appear on the fourteenth of November, an action that provoked anger from the prosecution and loud guffaws from the public. But Weir was dead serious, saying: "In my opinion the woman is not so far away that she could not answer the subpoena and her coming into court or otherwise will depend largely on the advice of her counsel. It might not be so easy of a matter to convict Mrs. Gunness of a crime as many people seem to suppose."[8]

Eyewitnesses recounted startling tales of the strange goings-on at the Gunness place. On the fifth day of testimony, jurors were told of a midnight visit to the farmhouse by one Addie Landis, a young woman who was to meet up with Belle about securing possible employment. The hackman, Leo Wade, said he had driven Miss Landis to the house. She alighted from the carriage, ran up to the back door of the place, and peered into the window. The girl let out a loud, bloodcurdling scream, stumbled back to the carriage—falling down several times on the way—and demanded that Wade drive her to the residence of Pearl Corey, another prospective employer. "I've seen the most awful thing I ever expect to see!" she said almost incoherently. According to the solemn word of the carriage driver, Corey refused to admit Landis to her home, so he let her off downtown. He found out the next day that she had taken the train to Valparaiso. Within a week Addie went stark, raving mad and had to be institutionalized at the Logansport State Hospital for the insane.

Corey verified the truth of the driver's story. She said that Landis was to have come out that night to see her about a job as well. "I would have kept her but she was raving like a maniac about the sight she had seen at the Gunness house. I could not make much sense out of what she said except that it was about cutting up a body and I believe[d] the girl a lunatic. In light of other developments I am inclined to think that what she saw that night drove her crazy."[9]

Joe Maxson provided important testimony about events in the house on the night of the fire. He claimed to have spotted Lamphere lurking in the evergreens near the house and then racing across the fields. He recalled Belle's apparent nervousness and Maxson's belief that she had injected dope—possibly choral—into a Florida orange she gave Maxson in order to put him to sleep. A strange feeling of drowsiness came over him after ingesting the fruit, he testified. He said he went to bed at 8:30 and never could have heard any sounds emanating from downstairs in that deep state of sleep. Poisoning the fruit was Belle's favorite method of subduing a victim before removing him to the basement for butchering.

Grocer's clerk George Wrase recalled selling Mrs. Gunness her supplies in town the day before the fire, including two gallons of kerosene in a five-gallon oilcan. As she completed the transaction, Ray Lamphere came into the store to purchase a five-cent plug of chewing tobacco, and for a minute the two had stared at each other contemptuously. Was this an expression of mutual hatred or a means of silent communication? It was very disturbing, he recalled. The oilcan was later found in the ruins of the cellar under a pile of brick debris a few yards from the four bodies.

Peter Colson, who worked on the death farm for two years, told of Lamphere's obsession with and fears of Mrs. Gunness. Colson also admitted to his own sexual adventuring with the LaPorte murderess. "She made such love to me!" he exclaimed as loud murmurs from the women spectators in the gallery interrupted proceedings. "Mrs. Gunness purred like a cat. She was soft and gentle in her ways. I never saw such a woman! She attracted and repelled me at the same time. I finally had to run away from that place. For six months I slept in a haymow on a farm a half mile away."[10]

The state was momentarily encouraged by Judge Richter's ruling to admit Coroner Mack's verdict that Gunness had perished in the fire, but Richter reconsidered the matter and then reversed his own ruling. It was a setback for the prosecution, but a grisly display of jars filled with human bones, fragments of flesh, bits of cloth, and other evidentiary material pulled from the charnel house sat on a table directly in front of the downcast Lamphere. The jury could not help but connect in their minds the crime of arson to the defendant by viewing these items.

Forty prosecution witnesses were summoned, but only one—miner Louis Schultz, reportedly in Little Rock, Arkansas—failed to show. Ex-sheriff Smutzer, the linchpin to the state's case, identified the three rings found in the ruins as the same rings he had observed Mrs. Gunness wearing when she came to his office shortly before the day of the fire to complain about Lamphere. Smutzer hotly denied an allegation put forth by Wirt Worden than he had any "special interest" in the case, other than a strong sense of duty to the community. Smutzer said he had no special desire to prove or disprove any particular theory for personal or political reasons. LaPorte dentist Dr. Ira P. Norton testified that the teeth found in the burned house were without doubt those of Mrs. Gunness as he had attended to her dental needs and knew the woman well. The teeth seemed to provide the physical evidence necessary to convict Lamphere. The hired man's jealous anger, Belle's broken promise to share Helgelein's money with him, and his thirst for revenge provided the motive. The disgruntled handyman not only fired the house but had witnessed the killing of Andrew Helgelein.

These main points were at the heart of the state's case underscoring the belief in Lamphere's guilt, but the partisan Democratic newspaper was unmoved. "Prosecutor Smith is now playing the part of the great Jupiter who rolls the balls down the bowling alleys of the heavens," sniffed the *Argus-Bulletin*, [and he] "scored a clean strike." But with a high degree of skepticism, the reporter cautioned that "since then several spares have been recorded to his credit but withal it will be necessary to land several more strikes to anywhere near approach a 300 score."[11] After defense counsel Worden wrapped up his address to the jury, the *Argus-Bulletin* reported in more flattering prose that "several of the jurymen edged over to the front of their seats as if drawn toward the speaker like a needle attracted by a magnet. When he had finished there was a profound quiet. The spectators realized that Worden had made assertions and made them in such a masterly manner that if he proved able to back them up by the testimony of witnesses, Ray Lamphere's neck would be saved from the noose that William Anstiss, sheriff-elect of LaPorte County, placed around it yesterday afternoon."[12]

All of the circumstantial evidence tended to prove that Belle had faked her own death and substituted a body double. "We will prove by testimony that on the afternoon of April 27th, Mrs. Gunness had a conversation in front of the First National Bank building with a certain man in which she said 'It must be done tonight and you must do it!' Something *was* done that night," Worden continued. "A torch was applied to the Gunness house and the bodies of three Gunness children were found in the ruins. We will produce a witness who saw Mrs. Gunness drive out to her house on the Saturday preceding the fire in company with a woman who had never been seen since unless it was her body that was found in the ruins of the fire."[13]

In his closing remarks, Smith warned the jury not to be sidetracked by the crimes of Belle Gunness as they deliberated over the guilt or innocence of the defendant. "The badness of Mrs. Gunness is no defense for Lamphere," he said. "She was as bad as hell. Lamphere was associated with her. Lamphere was going to marry her. It was Lamphere who came upon her the night she was killing Helgelein and helped her dispose of the body." Shaking his fist, Smith's face was red with rage and his voice was rising. "The defense wants to know where the miner Schultz who found the teeth is. I ask: Where is 'Nigger Liz'? Why don't the defense bring her here and prove their alibi by her?"[14]

Elizabeth Smith had a lot to tell the court, but she was never summoned to testify. The intolerant racial attitudes of the day and her reputation as an addled eccentric precluded the defense from bringing her to the stand. Without Liz Smith to account for his presence at her shack on the night in question, the case for Lamphere's acquittal was shaky when the jury retired to consider its verdict on November 25. Each side was confident in a favorable outcome—but the outcome was unforeseen and it did not represent a clear victory for either the Democrats or Republicans in this politically charged trial. On Thanksgiving evening, after twenty-four hours and nineteen ballots, the jury compromised and decided that Lamphere was guilty of the crime of arson but not murder. Two jurors, Charles P. Nelson and W.A. Glasgow, favored a reduced sentence and held out against the other ten, who pushed for a life sentence. Judge Richter read the sentence and pronounced an indeterminate sentence of two to twenty-one years in the penitentiary. The prosecution team appeared to be satisfied by the outcome.

Worden, Darrow, and Weir, however, took the verdict harder than Lamphere, who seemed strangely unconcerned. "I have no particular complaint to make," the prisoner said afterward. "The evidence was pretty strong against me and I am willing to take my medicine but my own conscience is clear and that helps some," he said.[15] Was this a self-conscious admission of guilt? That night Lamphere slept much better than he had at any time in the previous five months now that the suspense was finally over. His mood was decidedly upbeat the next morning following a reunion with his mother and two sisters inside his cell in the county jail.

Later that week he was escorted to the state penitentiary at Michigan City by Albert Smutzer in an "inter-urban" automobile, a rare accommodation for prisoners in those days.[16] Throughout the thirteen-mile drive, Lamphere was glib and seemingly resigned to his fate. "I'm lucky to be here," he murmured. "Why? I might have been chopped up and put in a hole in old woman Gunness' chicken yard. I'm going to prison with a clear conscience. I didn't do any more than hundreds of others in my place would have done."[17] Asked by a reporter if he would make a clean breast of things and reveal what he had witnessed the night he bored a hole into the Gunness parlor in order to spy on Belle and Helgelein, he was defiant. "No I don't think I ever will."

Lamphere remained closemouthed right up until the end of his days. He died on December 30, 1909, in the prison hospital ward of consumption as eleventh-hour efforts to obtain an official pardon from Indiana Governor Thomas R. Marshall failed.

Opinions were divided about the so-called "Lamphere deathbed confession" given to fellow convict Harry Myers on January 6, 1909. Myers, whom the warden of the Michigan penitentiary dismissed as a crank, described Lamphere's account of Belle's escape from LaPorte in a two-seated rig drawn by a pony nine miles from town, where Gunness was met by another man who escorted her on to Chicago. With only a few hours left to live, Lamphere purportedly told Myers that he drove the widow to the predetermined rendezvous point. She carried two large valises and a small tin box containing a stack of one-hundred dollar bills, expensive items of jewelry, and other valuables necessary to begin a new life.

As to the identity of the woman who perished in the flames, the unfortunate soul was thought to be a Chicago woman whom Belle had met up with on State Street during one of her frequent shopping expeditions to the Windy City. The unknown woman had been seated on the stairway of a building and looked rather downcast when Gunness struck up a cheerful conversation. She promised to improve the woman's lot in life with a good paying job and invited her to work as her housekeeper in LaPorte. The woman agreed and traveled with Belle to her death.

Myers related a conversation he had with Lamphere about what happened next. The ex-farmhand remembered that Gunness had asked him to build a wooden box measuring two or three feet square—large enough to hold the severed head of the Chicago woman. When the task was complete, Belle brought out the head, which was wrapped inside a rug, and placed it in the box. She nailed the lid shut and ordered Lamphere to take the box out to the orchard and bury it. Myers said that Lamphere could not recall the exact spot where he had buried the object, which of coursed raised more doubt about the validity of the entire story.[18] "I arranged for the parole of Harry Myers and employed him and some other men to dig in the orchard for the box," recalled Wirt Worden. "Although considerable time was spent on the farm in digging for it, the box was never located. It was a difficult task to begin with and merely a matter of guess work."[19]

Prison Warden James Reid disavowed Myers's claim that he was present with Myers when the dubious confession was given by Lamphere. Reid also expressed the opinion that he had little confidence in the words of a convicted burglar and thief. At the same time, Reverend E.A. Schell of Iowa Wesleyan University broke his vow of silence. He told of receiving Lamphere's confession on the eve of the trial, and his account reached the newspapers in January 1910 when he agreed to an interview with the *Chicago Tribune*. According to Schell's recollections, the liquored-up Lamphere and his boon companion "Nigger Liz" had entered the Gunness household in their cups and were intent upon stealing the woman's valuables. Together, they chloroformed Belle and the three children although Lamphere denied having set the fire. He wasn't sure how the fire had started, but he believed it was possibly caused by the tipping over of the candle that they had carried into the house to illuminate their path. Despite Lamphere's penchant for lying, Albert Smutzer accepted the story as true—following the Republican Party line, of course.

Wirt Worden and the physicians whom Worden consulted wondered how it was possible that a woman of Belle's large size and physical prowess could be so easily subdued by her attacker. She would certainly have awakened from her sleep, alerted the children by her screams, and fiercely resisted. The story was simply not believable, and Liz Smith emphatically denied the charge. She was taken into custody for questioning and released on a $500 bond.

The version of events that has been accepted as the truth by most people in the intervening years tends to follow the story told in court by Daniel Hutson, the Gunness neighbor who had briefly worked for Belle before buying his own farm on adjoining land. As darkness set in during the early evening hours of July 9, 1908—two months and eleven days after Belle was supposedly consumed in the flames—Hutson was making his way home in his rig when he spied a man and a woman walking on a hill. The couple was plainly exposed from the road near the ruined farmhouse. "I was within fifty feet of them at that time," Hutson remembered and continued:

> As soon as the woman saw me she said something to the man and they both got into the buggy. It was a side-bar buggy and the horse the woman was driving was a dapple gray weighing, I should say, 1,250 pounds. They seemed in a hurry to get away and were whipping the horse. As they passed out of the gate they were very close to me and I saw at once that the woman was Mrs. Gunness. I tried to shout to her but I was so taken aback by the sight of her that I was unable to say a word. They drove on down the road to Michigan City as hard as they could drive and I made all the haste I could after them but I was driving a hayrack and it was difficult to keep up. I noticed that the man sitting with Mrs. Gunness in the rig had streaks of gray hair under his hat on the sides. Mrs. Gunness was dressed in black and wore two veils, both of black net. The one veil was rolled up so the other did not conceal her features. I should have known the woman anywhere because of her odd physical characteristics. She is as broad as a man and has an odd way of turning her head. It is a furtive way, as if she had to fear something from behind. They kept whipping that horse until they were a good distance ahead of me and had passed the gate entering my farm. I knew it was no good to pursue in the dark so I turned into my farm and for fear of frightening my wife I said nothing. Later the child of one of my neighbors, Martha Scheffer, came over and without knowing I had seen the Gunness woman, told of meeting her driving along the road with a man and described the same horse and buggy.[20]

Hutson reported that his daughters Eldora and Evaline also saw Gunness and many years later as elderly women they stuck to their original story.

Farmhand Frederick Lambright backed Hutson's story. He too said that he had spotted Belle on the night in question and provided aditional details. Lambright said that the woman and her male companion had parked their buggy near the southeast corner of the house. The man stood next to the buggy and held a hitching strap in his hand as he talked to the woman Lambright believed to be Belle. "I distinctly heard her say 'That money ain't there.' I saw Mrs. Gunness as she bent over feeling for something on the ground. I told of my experience a few nights later to William Humphrey."[21]

Sheriff Smutzer ridiculed Hutson and refused to take his statement. The farmer wondered why local law enforcement was acting so close-minded about the matter, but as time passed, Hutson began to suspect that the whole thing was a cover-up—or worse. He considered the very real possibility that the police were in league with the murderess. "Belle Gunness is dead," the sheriff told Hutson with finality. "And she ain't coming back! You sure you didn't just see a ghost[,] Daniel?" Smutzer threw back his head and laughed.

Chapter Thirteen

On the eve of his trial, Johann Hoch was transferred to less hospitable surroundings in the Cook County Jail, which was attached to the Cook County Criminal Courts building at Hubbard and Dearborn Streets, the setting for many important and historic trials down through the years. He occupied cell 611 on the sixth tier up against the roof and slept in a narrow iron bunk with a bare mattress and a thin blanket. Gone were the comforters, soft linens, his bottles of Budweiser, and catered meals permitted by Inspector Shippy, who had fallen victim to Hoch's persuasive charm and willingly accommodated Hoch with all the comforts of home. "I wish I were back at East Chicago," Hoch said, sighing, after that first night in the cold, dank lockup.

With jury selection set to begin during the third week of April 1905, Attorney Plotke announced his strategy. He planned to plead that his client was insane with the confident hope of sparing Hoch an appointment with the gallows, but Johann Hoch did not take kindly to the idea of being branded a lunatic in open court before his many female admirers. "I have nothing to say," Hoch said with a scornful sneer as he drank a sip of frothy lager beer from his glass. "I have an attorney but I may have something to say about my defense. Am I crazy? If you ask me I say that everybody is crazy. Only some more than others."[1]

On the surface of things, the selection of Judge George Kersten of the Cook County Circuit Court seemed to Plotke to bode well for Hoch. A change of venue had been granted from Judge Richard S. Tuthill to Judge Kersten after Plotke argued that Tuthill had presided over the trial of a villainous German immigrant accused of committing a grisly murder eight years earlier: sausage maker Adolph Luetgert had boiled his wife in a vat of potash acid inside his North Side factory. Might Tuthill be predisposed against another German defendant accused of taking the life of a woman?[2] Plotke thought so. Granting Hoch the widest latitude, the circuit court agreed to the request and assigned Kersten, an experienced, liberal-thinking Democratic jurist of German descent who came up from the streets and was presumably sympathetic to the common man caught up in the web of the judicial system. But Johann Hoch was not a "common man," nor was he a poor wretch from the back alleys who had turned to crime as a means of survival.

The judge was born in 1853 in the tough Smoky Hollow section of the city just north of the Chicago River. The presence of the gasworks in a high crime area such as this and the ever present haze of industrial pollution choking the air made for tough circumstances, but the young man persevered and was recognized early on for his ambition and keenness of mind. Kersten was appointed justice of the peace by Mayor Carter Harrison I in 1883, a post he held continuously until 1903. In subsequent terms on the circuit court bench in a career spanning 47 years, he tried more than 100,000 criminal cases. It was widely accepted that no other jurist in the U.S. up to that time possessed more intimate knowledge of the ways of the habitual criminal than Judge Kersten.[3] He witnessed the daily maelstrom firsthand in the justice of the peace courts, which were noisy, unclean, chaotic "justice mills" housed in police stations and presided over by politically connected jurists confronting the pathetic dregs of the street: criminal panders, prostitutes, fences, second-story men, rapists, con artists, gamblers, swindlers of the worst stripe, and their shady bail bondsmen on hand to spring them from the lockup. Discipline was lax. The "motion to fix"—a term of derision among defense attorneys accustomed to the corruption of the Cook County system of justice—was most always "in" through the contrivance of politicians and people of influence, that is, a pre-determined verdict through bribery and the exchange of influence.

That Kersten understood the criminal mind after twenty years of laboring in this ragged underbelly of the corrupt judicial system in Cook County was no exaggeration. Despite Plotke's optimism that he could plant a seed of reasonable doubt in the minds of the jurors, the hope of an acquittal was a long shot. Hoch was an outsider, a rogue unlikely to engender any degree of sympathy from Kersten, nor did he have any important local "sponsors" to speak up on his behalf.

The indictment on which Hoch was called to judgment was drawn on April 18, 1905, less than an hour before the case was scheduled to be called following one of the quickest actions by a Cook County grand jury on record—too quick, as a matter of fact. Assistant State's Attorney

Olson's trained eye noted with alarm a spelling error of the decedent's last name in the original true bill. On February 15, the original grand jury had erroneously recorded the victim's name as Marie Welker-Hoch, not Walcker-Hoch. Such an error, however technical and minute as it may have seemed, would have likely proven fatal to the prosecution's case if it were to be detected and acted upon by Attorney Plotke. Harry Olson wasn't taking any chances in the matter. He rushed back into the grand jury room demanding that a new indictment be issued forthwith. After the defense counsel learned of this peremptory action, Plotke was incensed. "I will protest the action of the Prosecution in making the grand jury to vote an indictment without evidence!" thundered Plotke, but the judge was unsympathetic.

"I can show that I never killed that woman no matter *how* she spelled her name!" Hoch murmured under his breath.[4]

In anticipation of the hard fight that Plotke was likely to put up against the selection of potential jurors adversely influenced by press coverage of the case, bailiffs from Judge Kersten's court scoured the Criminal Courts Building to borrow jurors from other courtrooms to stand ready in case they were needed. On April 19, 1905, the prisoner was formally arraigned and the indictment read aloud by Clerk Thomas Cerny. "Johann Hoch, alias John Hoch, alias John Schmidt, you are charged with the murder of Marie Walcker-Hoch. Are you guilty or not guilty?"

"Not guilty," the defendant stammered.[5] In that one revealing moment, Hoch appeared nervous and ill at ease—his mask of bravado withering as he comprehended the gravity of the charge laid against him.

As expected, jury selection in the case of *The People v. Hoch* was slow going. It was also complicated by Hoch's incessant demand for the impanelling of German jurors and Plotke's rapid-fire dismissal of dozens of men on the grounds that he believed them to be prejudiced against the defendant and unlikely to buy into defense arguments that Walcker was murdered by another person. As Plotke and Olson sparred with the potential jurors, it was noted in the courtroom that Hoch had trained his "baffling, steely eyes" on each and every potential venire man as if he were attempting to hypnotize them. Leaning back in his chair, he peered at them intently. A reporter noted that his gaze was "weird and uncanny." Not the least bit perturbed by Plotke's failure to procure his release on the grounds that Marie's name was misspelled, Hoch had regained his confidence and was his usual merry self.

The chamber was filled to overflowing. The majority of the curiosity seekers were women, many of them richly clad in the bright finery of their new spring attire. "Johann, you ought to be allowed to pick your own jury from the women here," quipped Inspector Shippy, now on a friendly, first-name basis with the prisoner.[6] "Judge Kersten seems a nice man," Hoch replied, "and, with Germans on the jury, I have no fear of the result. I know the men I want! Let them give me all Germans!"[7]

The presence of so many female spectators in the courtroom during jury selection, the dilatory tactics of Isadore Plotke, and the flirtatious smiles and leering side glances made by Hoch to the women so irked Judge Kersten that he ordered Deputy Sheriff Cornelius Mahoney to move the ladies into the corridors and warned counsel that unless the exhausting process was concluded forthwith, he would force them to continue all night and not be permitted to leave, if necessary. Among the milling throng, three of Hoch's revenge-seeking ex-wives were spotted sitting together outside the courtroom, commiserating, anticipating, and delighting in their coming revenge.

The process of securing a jury dragged on for nearly 11 days before wrapping up on the same day the trial began—the afternoon of May 1, 1905. At the onset of deliberations, the state stunned Hoch and his attorney with the revelation that the body of Marie Walcker had been exhumed and a substantial presence of arsenic was detected. Why hadn't this been revealed to the defense prior to the trial? Plotke demanded to know. Hoch reclined in his chair, his humor temporarily gone.

Amelia Fischer, both outraged and despondent, was the state's star witness, although Plotke tried unsuccessfully to block her testimony on the grounds that a wife cannot testify against her husband. Judge Kersten overruled the defense after Olson reminded the court that no legal marriage had actually existed between Hoch and Fischer because Hoch was already married. Amelia's story was straightforward and contained no embellishments. "Mr. Hoch spoke about the expense of the funeral and did not get a minister because he said, one could be buried in the cemetery we were going to without a minister," she testified. "So we did not have any. It was just after we were married that Mr. Hoch asked me for my money. He said his debts had been so much and that he needed to pay all that he owed on his house and that if I would give it to him he would pay me cent for cent when we returned from Germany. He was to start a big hotel then and I could help run it and there would be lots of money."[8] Amelia said she was 52 years old and in the business of renting and subletting apartments in Chicago. Casting a withering look at Hoch, she said that her life savings were dissipated—the bank account cleaned out by this untrustworthy man whom she had given her hand in marriage.

In a highly unusual legal maneuver, Plotke as counsel for the defense asked for and was granted permission by the court to take the witness stand to denounce Fischer for what she had been saying about him. Harry Olson did not object, although, in a low tone of voice easily overheard by several courtroom spectators, Olson called his opponent a "four flusher." Plotke ignored the insult and was sworn in. He told the court that Amelia had repeatedly "annoyed" him with visits to his office, soliciting his opinion about Hoch's guilt or innocence. She was beginning to have second thoughts and was looking for Plotke's affirmation that the man she married had been wrongfully accused. He told the woman that the doctors said Marie Walcker suffered nephritis.

"Did you not also tell her that medicine given Mrs. Walcker-Hoch was bitter?" Olson asked Plotke.

"I don't think I did. I don't know whether it was or not."

"Did you caution her not to tell the jury her sister's throat burned?" The volume of Olson's voice rose.

"No," Plotke answered. "She talked to me several times at my office, at this building and in the jail and several times I told her 'Woman[,] I don't want to talk to you.' But it was no use: she would talk."[9]

Next, Coroner's Physician Dr. Otto Lewke told the court how, in two tests, he found a large quantity of arsenic in the stomach and kidneys. "That person [Walcker] died of arsenical poisoning," he concluded. Then the undertaker, Frank M. Spreyne, who, along with his son Anthony and their assistant David Probolsky, had prepared the body of Marie for final burial, dealt a crippling blow to the defense when, under cross-examination, Frank Spreyne recounted his earlier conversation with Hoch inside the rented house on Union Street. "Looking into the casket he [Hoch] exclaimed, 'there she lies now. If she hadn't deceived me into marrying her she would be alive today.'"[10]

Johanna Reichel, one of Hoch's jilted wives, was the chief witness for the prosecution on the twelfth day of the trial. She told the court how the defendant turned up at her residence at 458 N. Milwaukee Avenue the night before he fled to New York and asked if she would take a little trip with him to the east. He flashed a railroad timetable and a thick wad of bills she estimated to be well over $1,000. After she refused the offer, Hoch bedded down for the night and proceeded to the train station the next morning.[11]

A battery of impressive witnesses for the prosecution—seventy in all—was summoned to the stand, including the New York druggist who had sold a quantity of arsenic to Hoch. The words of the medical experts and the testimony of Inspector Shippy, who read aloud from

Hoch's verbal confession, which were given to him on February 9 and 11 and signed by the defendant after two revisions, established a strong chain of evidence and a firm basis for a conviction. After examining three additional but minor witnesses, Harry Olson rested the case for the state on May 13.

Knowing that a plea of insanity would be instantly rejected by Hoch, defense counsel was left with only one shaky option: disproving the findings of the coroner and the pathologist or pinning the murder on someone else. The tactic was destined to fail.

Even more fraudulent and damaging for the defense was the testimony of Plotke's only witness, Austrian surgeon Dr. Gustave Kolischer, who for 13 years had been a member of the Vienna University Hospital (*Allgemeines Krankenhaus der Stadt Wien*).[12] Kolischer testified that the arsenic found in the body of Mrs. Walcker probably came from the soil of the graveyard and had entered her system *after* her burial. Cemeteries, he explained, are saturated with arsenic-laden embalming fluid, and a small quantity of the substance had undoubtedly seeped into the casket. It was a specious argument, and Kolischer was easily refuted by the state's expert, Dr. Walter Haines, who said there was no arsenic in the letheform embalming fluid used by Spreyne and Probolsky. The arsenic had indeed been ingested by the deceased. Additional experts for the prosecution—Dr. Ludwig Hektoen, Dr. Harold Moyer, and Professor Mark Delafontaine—all agreed that arsenic is not soluble to the extent of penetrating a corpse in the ground. Kolischer was easily discredited on the witness stand.[13]

And so, on May 17, after Plotke was finished criticizing the police for their coercive tactics and the doctors and the state's attorney for heaping malicious criminal intent upon a man who did his level best to save his wife from the agonies of death, the attorney injected an element of high drama into the proceedings when, in his closing address to the jury, he accused Amelia Fischer and Bertha Sohn of conspiring to poison their sister Marie Walcker because of the bitter antagonism that had existed for many years between Amelia and Marie. Pale with rage, Mrs. Fischer laughed at the absurdity of the accusation. "No one but that man is guilty!" she solemnly asserted through a translator. "A thousand times would I swear before God that I am not guilty of the murder of my sister!"[14]

Marie had displayed her jealousy of Amelia's attentions to Hoch even as she lay dying in her bed, Plotke told the jury in an agitated tone of voice. "If the State will turn to the right path, there, they will reach the real culprit. That woman ought to be the defendant, not Johann Hoch!"

he screamed. "Instead of going on the witness stand for the State she should be in the defendant's chair!"[15] The evidence to support such a charge hinged on conjecture and gossip. It was a desperate ploy.

In a dramatic flourish, Isadore Plotke closed by declaring that the presence of arsenic in Johann Hoch's pen was intended to be used by Hoch as a final exit from this "veil of tears." Suicide was his true aim, not murder. But in a moment of reflection, Plotke said, Hoch had stiffened his resolve to fight the charges against him rather than taking the coward's way out. Then, in his closing address to the jury on May 18, Plotke recited three verses of Cardinal John Henry Newman's immortal hymn "Lead Kindly Light" in an impassioned plea to the jurors to spare Hoch's life.[16]

> Lead, Kindly Light, amid the encircling gloom,
> Lead Thou me on!
> The night is dark, and I am far from home—
> Lead Thou me on!
> Keep Thou my feet; I do not ask to see
> The distant scene; one step enough for me.
>
> I was not ever thus, nor pray'd that Thou
> Shouldst lead me on.
> I loved to choose and see my path; but now
> Lead Thou me on!
> I loved the garish day, and, spite of fears,
> Pride ruled my will; remember not past years.
>
> So long Thy power hath blest me, sure it still
> Will lead me on,
> O'er moor and fen, o'er crag and torrent, till
> The night is gone;
> And with the morn those angel faces smile
> Which I have loved long since, and lost awhile.

"I ask you to take with you into the jury room the remembrance of that song that our dying President William McKinley repeated," Plotke exhorted, evoking the memory of the martyred president who had been felled by an assassin's bullet in September 1901. "In the last moments allotted to me I make a last appeal for the life, the liberty of this defendant! Entirely circumstantial is the evidence which the state has woven around this man until they will ask at last for the severest penalty." Hoarse from his many hours of courtroom elocution, Plotke ended his plea, saying, "I beg of you do not make a mistake now, something you will regret to the end of your days! Are you going to crush out a life for the sophistries and theories of the state? I beg you do not make a mistake now."[17]

Harry Olson arose from his chair. Low-key and understated, he argued that "Every man should hope that the beautiful words of Newman had been recited at the grave of Marie Walcker with the fervor and feeling that Mr. Plotke put into them, instead of the mock sorrow that desecrated that grave of the dead woman, coming as it did from Johann Hoch!"[18] Hoch fidgeted uneasily as Olson flayed the defendant, but in striking contrast to the closing argument from the emotional, overheated Plotke, Olson's modulated tone was careful and measured. "The dead are for the dead, the living are for the living. That is this man's moral," exhorted the prosecutor, shooting a menacing glance at Hoch who twiddled his thumbs impatiently.

The jury received its instructions and retired to consider its verdict on the afternoon of May 19. Everyone, it seemed, was worn out and exhausted by the ordeal except Hoch, who maintained his confident, smug air all along. Turning to Attorney John Manchester, who had assisted Plotke throughout the trial, Hoch whispered: "I bet you I will be acquitted." The lawyer frowned. Although assigned to the defense team, Manchester did not buy into Hoch's claim of innocence and viewed him with cold disdain. "I would not bet on a man's life" was all he had to say to his client.[19] Throughout the trial Hoch appeared detached and unafraid, and he stoically maintained his composure even as the jury came back with a verdict on May 19.

At 2:45 p.m.—barely half an hour since the jury had retired—Johann Hoch was pronounced guilty of murder on the first ballot and sentenced to death on the second ballot. In the spectators' gallery, one woman wept hysterically and another fainted. The overall reaction seemed to be one of surprise and dismay. Hoch sprung to his feet, looked about the room, and collapsed back into his chair. The jury was polled, and a motion for a new trial was entered, but neither Plotke nor his co-counsel, Manchester, so much as uttered a word of consolation to Hoch who sat transfixed. For the defense counsel, the sting of losing the case in the legal arena was their greatest setback—not the ultimate fate awaiting their client, although Isadore Plotke seemed much more committed to the cause of his client than Manchester. "I believe Hoch is guilty and I believe he will hang," Manchester said later. "I am convinced that it is just that he should."[20]

It wasn't until he was led away by two deputy sheriffs that Hoch finally spoke. "It's all over with[,] Johann," he whispered, shaking his head. "I told you so." Then, incredibly, his mood changed. He flashed a smile and placed his hands around his throat, mimicking strangulation on the gallows.[21] In an interview in his cell just 30 minutes later, he said to Plotke, "It served me right. I would rather hang in a half an hour rather than allow my lawyer to go to Governor [Charles] Deneen and plead for a life sentence." But just as quickly as he admitted guilt, he again asserted his innocence. "I am more willing to die an innocent man than live with a cloud of guilt over me."[22] Hoch was transferred to a cell in the murderers' row section of the Cook County Jail, where he shared narrow quarters with Joseph "Jocko" Briggs, who had been sentenced to die for the robbery and murder of a cigar store owner at Damen and Lake Street in 1904.[23]

In a published editorial two days after the verdict, the *Tribune* applauded the work of the 12 jurists and reminded the public of the gravity of Hoch's crimes. "Hoch's victims were all poor women. Most of them were widows. Their money was the savings of years of hard work. When he did not murder them he left them penniless and miserable. Since his arrest he has been sometimes a braggart, sometimes a cringing coward. Hypocritical, pitiless, murderously avaricious, he seems to have long had a heart devoid, as legal phraseology has it, of social duty and fatally bent on mischief and a good day's work will be done when he is removed from his field of maleficent labors."[24]

On June 3, Judge Kersten overruled the defense motion for a new trial and fixed the date of execution for June 23. Hoch said he was "a man of common sense—and innocent of the crime," but Kersten saw no compelling reason to delay. "I will say nothing to harrow up your feelings or dwell unnecessarily on the details of your awful crime. You deserve the punishment about to be inflicted upon you. Undoubtedly you can comprehend fully that the crime you committed is of such atrocity that it does not present one solitary mitigating circumstance."[25]

Visited by F.L. Frenke, the owner of a nearby tailor shop and a jailhouse hanger-on known as the "Good Samaritan of the County Jail," Johann Hoch consented to his plea that he should warmly receive Reverend William Schlechte and accept spiritual devotions and forgiveness. Over the next few weeks Johann became a willing convert to old-fashioned religion as he passed his time on murderers' row penning the opening chapters of his unpublished autobiography, *The Life, Travel and Experiences of Johann Hoch*, a rambling discourse that he hoped would interest a publisher enough to help him defray the cost of his State Supreme Court appeal. Though under the sentence of death, he feverishly worked to complete 25,000 words—three chapters —in one day and promised the guards and jailer, John Whitman, that the treatise would be "lively and full of incident and romance."[26]

As the days and hours before his date with the gallows melted away, Hoch maintained an air of cheerful unconcern. His composure was remarkable even after John Dorinjanovich aka John Mueller, convicted of murdering his wife and two infant children in a moment of madness, and Robert Newcomb, an African-American man who killed a policeman and two others, were marched past his cell and to the scaffold where they were executed within minutes of each other. This morbid scene played out just seven days before Hoch was scheduled to die. Horrified attorneys for the two condemned men went before Judge Kersten hoping for a stay, but he refused to interfere with the executions.[27]

Hoch said his good-byes and went about his business. He was allowed to freely roam outside of his cell and was even summoned by Whitman to lead a delegation of Norwegian penal officials on a tour of the Cook County Jail. Hoch's language skills proved invaluable, because the Norwegian criminologists were able to communicate in German but not English. They visited the death chamber, the dungeons, the boys' department, and other areas of interest. When the entourage reached Hoch's cell block, they asked him if there were any condemned prisoners residing on this tier. "Yes, we have one on this floor," Hoch answered laconically. "It is *me*[,] Johann Hoch. I expect to be hanged next Friday." The astonished visitors filed their report and expressed their surprise at the freedom that death row inmates enjoyed.[28]

Meanwhile, Isadore Plotke was busy in Springfield petitioning Governor Deneen for an eleventh-hour reprieve in the hope of allowing Hoch sufficient time to raise enough money to pay for his appeal. The governor said he was willing to delay the hanging only if Harry Olson agreed. When reached by telephone, Olson said he did not believe there had been any trial irregularities that would overturn the verdict but promised that he would not stand in the way of an appeal.

Five frantic weeks passed. Hoch managed to raise only $500 of the $1,100 needed to prepare the records for the appeal. At 3 o'clock on the afternoon of July 27, the governor informed Plotke that all further hope for another stay was useless. The law did not provide a remedy, he said, and he was sorry about that but he must enforce it. "Hoch must die because he is too poor to appeal his case. It is a sad commentary on our laws," Plotke sermonized.

Three hours before Hoch was scheduled to receive his last meal, Plotke admitted that it was "useless to fight any more." They could not raise the money for the appeal. "It is *not* useless!" Hoch retorted. "I will not be hanged until 10:00 tomorrow morning! You get out of here and get that money before that time and I'll not die. Rob someone! Kill a millionaire!" Hoch laughed aloud at his unintentional gallows humor.[29]

On July 28, the eve of Hoch's execution, several hysterical women visited the lockup to beg for his life. Even the grizzled and hardened assistant jailer, J.F. Jenks, who had led a dozen men to the drop over the years, protested to Whitman that he was just not up to it. "I can't lead Hoch to the gallows, you'll have to find somebody else to do it," he said.[30]

Albert H. Thompson, a wealthy Chicago lawyer who had been following the case in the newspapers with more than the usual interest, pitied Hoch and offered to provide the $500. On August 22, a bill of exceptions was filed in Springfield and a writ of superseades was taken. "The familiar symptoms of sentimentalism toward condemned murderers began to appear," Francis McNamara, chief physician of the Cook County Jail at the time of the Hoch case, remembered. Looking back on the Hoch case, he recalled that a group of spiritualists convened a séance to contact the spirit of the departed Marie Walcker. Claiming to have reached the great beyond, they had it on the highest authority that the deceased woman wished no harm to befall Johann Hoch: he was an innocent man.[31]

With the minutes to Hoch's execution ticking down, Deneen granted a temporary reprieve after the check was cashed at the Hibernian Bank and word was received from Plotke from his suite at the Sherman House Hotel. The governor instructed the lawyer to place the bills in the hands of State's Attorney John J. Healy and then promised that the stay would be granted forthwith. Plotke rushed back to the jail to convey the happy news to his client. "I am much obliged!" gushed Hoch as he fervently shook Plotke's hand. "I am the happiest man living!"

But just days after Isadore Plotke's tireless efforts to save his client's life, Hoch unexpectedly discharged him from his duties and chose as his new counsel Frank D. Comerford, "boy orator" of the state legislature who made headlines by denouncing certain Illinois General Assembly members as bribe takers and "a pack of crooks" after serving just four weeks of his first term from the Second Senatorial District of Cook County. Comerford was a young and impetuous reformer with big ideas who was bent on exposing an entrenched and corrosive system of payoffs made to state representatives within his own party to influence the passage of legislation within the 44th General Assembly. By a vote of 121–13, the House unceremoniously expelled him as a member of their body on February 8, 1905, for slandering the reputation of two downstate Democratic legislators who probably deserved to be pilloried in the court of public opinion. But the old guard rallied to protect its good name from this shaggy-haired do-gooder from the West Side of Chicago who threatened to expose the "great public auction" he estimated to be worth $250,000 to lawmakers during each session of the legislature.[32]

Thereafter Comerford became intensely interested in taking up the case of Johann Hoch, and he made it his own personal mission to save this "poor, innocent victim of wrongful justice" from the gallows. He presented his credentials to Hoch, who had decided that Isadore Plotke was no longer up to the task before him. Understandably angered by these desultory actions, Plotke branded Hoch an ingrate and a "mean man."

Attorney Comerford jumped into the fray with vigor and determination by filing an affidavit with Governor Deneen on behalf of Amelia Fischer to say that she had perjured herself on the witness stand and her testimony was the result of threats made against her by the prosecution. Mrs. Fischer, whose thirst for vengeance landed Hoch on death row, had by now become a sympathetic convert to his cause and had renounced the prosecutors for their high-handed tactics in barring her from visiting Hoch during his confinement and "keeping her a virtual prisoner" in her own home. She signed an affidavit confessing to perjury while testifying for the state, saying that Assistant State's Attorney Olson compelled her to state that her sister had never been sick a day in her life until she met Hoch. This, Amelia declared, was not true. Marie suffered various kidney ailments long before she sailed to America. "I have no fear of death," Hoch said stoically. "But it is horrible when one thinks that a man's life can be sacrificed on perjured testimony.[33]

"Oh, Johann! I have done something terrible," Amelia sobbed as she spoke to Hoch through the bars of his cell. "But if they hang you, I too will go to my death! I want your permission to kill myself after you have also given me forgiveness for having done what I did! I would be willing to go to prison if only I could right the wrong that I have done you. I could not help it though. They hounded me for months. Please forgive me!"[34] To help raise money for Hoch's appeals, Amelia traveled to New York to exhibit herself in a dime museum as the wife of the "Infamous Chicago Bluebeard." The murder case had turned farcical.

Calling Hoch's crime a "money making murder," the Supreme Court ignored the pleas of the repentant wife and the "Young Lochinvar"[35] of the Cook County criminal bar and denied the appeal on December 15. "The verdict of the jury should be upheld," wrote Illinois Attorney General William H. Stead. "Hoch had a fair and impartial trial and no reversible error has been assigned. About his guilt there can be no doubt whatsoever. When he was asked by the Court if he had anything to say why the sentence of death should not be pronounced against him, he said, 'I will say now that the crime was committed. I am a man of commono [sic] sense. I think poisoning was done.' And yet the defense made for him at the trial and to this Court is that this was not a case of arsenical poisoning!"[36]

The date of execution was set for February 23, 1906, between the hours of 10:00 a.m. and 2:00 p.m., by prior agreement with the press. This was an extraordinary accommodation given to the *Chicago American,* but it was granted so that the Hearst editorial staff would have enough time to issue a special edition of the morning paper and an expanded edition of the late afternoon sheet.[37]

As Hoch lounged in the visitor's section in short sleeves smoking his cigar, the news traveled fast through the cell blocks of the Cook County Jail. To a man the inmates expressed their sympathy to Hoch, but he joked and kidded with them that he was not yet dead and that the case would be taken all the way to the U.S. Supreme Court. "Well that's alright. I expected it. There's nothing to it now," Hoch said.[38]

Hoch's last hope for a reprieve hinged on the State Board of Pardons and the compassion of Governor Charles Deneen, who had it in his power to grant executive clemency. On February 20, the board agreed to hear a final plea in Springfield from Attorney Comerford, who was accompanied by Professor F. Robert Zeit of the pathology department of Northwestern University. After examining the kidney, liver, and spleen of the deceased, Zeit was convinced that Mrs. Walcker had suffered from a terrible affliction of Bright's disease that resulted in death.[39] But under cross-examination Zeit conceded that he could not rule out the possibility that the subject had been poisoned with arsenic, and thus the condemned man's fate was sealed. "Evidence that the deceased came to her death from arsenical poison was sufficient for a jury to find the petitioner guilty," the pardon board concluded.

> And this view was fully sustained by the Supreme Court. The fact that she was afflicted with Bright's Disease would not have prevented the consummation of the crime of which the petitioner has been convicted.

There could be no justification of our disturbing the verdict unless we were satisfied that the new evidence presented to us is of such a nature that it raises a doubt as to the guilt of the petitioner. No such doubt can be entertained upon the testimony of Dr. Zeit who admits he knows nothing as to the causes of death of the deceased except she was afflicted with a disease which might have resulted fatally at any time. We see no reason for disturbing the verdict and recommend the denial of the petition.[40]

Acting on the recommendation of the board, Governor Deneen denied the plea for commutation. Hoch, nervous and depressed for much of the time as he awaited word from Springfield, became enraged upon hearing the news that all hope was now gone. "I will not hang!" he shouted. "I've been closer than this to the gallows before and yet I am alive today. Wait till I see my lawyer! I'll disappoint them all yet. I never killed my wife and I never will hang for her death!" Then he added somewhat wistfully as a guard lit up his cigar for him: "I may die to satisfy the state's attorney but the people of Illinois do not pay for murder. They pay money for justice."[41]

The next day, Hoch was taken from his cell and transferred into the most comfortable room in the county jail, the library. It was furnished with writing tables, chairs, and shelves of books—but to the condemned of murderers' row, it was simply known as the "death chamber."

Shortly before his last day on earth, Hoch was visited by a spiritualist who offered to hypnotize him, but he laughed at the man and sent him on his way. A 30-year-old woman with her two little girls in tow appeared at the front desk of the jail demanding to meet with Hoch, saying she was destined to become his "future wife," but John Whitman sent her off, deciding that she was demented. Frank Comerford expressed his sorrow but vowed that he would continue the fight up until the last second. In the evening of the day prior to his execution the female inmates of the jail gathered around the organ and joined in a chorus to sing "Jesus, Lover of My Soul" and "Nearer My God to Thee." In this most bizarre *tableau vivant*, Jailer Whitman, his eyes moist with tears, dropped to his knees and recited a prayer while Hoch patted him on the shoulder in an assuring manner and told him not to fret. One would have thought it was Whitman who was marching off to the gallows rather than Johann Hoch.[42]

On the morning of the execution, the gallows were made ready in the north corridor of the jail as 100 spectators gathered to witness the hanging. The doors of the death chamber swung open shortly after 10:00

a.m. Hoch said an emotional farewell to his five guards: Harry Kerin, Harry Donnelly, Thomas Butter, George Neeley, and Gene Hugelet. He had struck up a warm friendship with each of them in his ingratiating way and fought back tears as he stepped out of his cell.

Escorted by Deputy Sheriff Charles W. Peters, Jailer John Whitman, and two Lutheran ministers, Hoch, calming himself, began the final walk to the gibbet when a sudden commotion was heard from outside. On the sidewalk along Hubbard Street, a sudden cheer went up among the throngs of idly curious after watching Frank Comerford rush into the building with a determined expression on his face. "You'll save him yet!" one man called out. Breathless and perspiring, his hair unkempt, and his tie hanging loose around his neck, Comerford bolted up the stairs and emerged from the hallway shouting excitedly, "Send Whitman here! I've got a stay!" A *Chicago American* reporter described the chaotic scenes unfolding outside:

> A crowd surpassing any gathering at an execution in Chicago since the anarchists were hanged in 1887, and so large as that of 1887 surrounding the jail today. So demonstrative were the spectators that twenty-five policemen had to be called from the Chicago Avenue Station to keep order. With drawn clubs the police charged the crowd and drove them from the sidewalks surrounding the jail. Women and children were conspicuous in the gathering. They pushed, fought and struggled in efforts to reach the door of the jail. The police were masters however, and the people had to content themselves with standing at a distance. The sidewalks at Dearborn Avenue and Illinois Street opposite the jail were jammed with people as the hour of execution arrived. Each arrival of a person interested in Hoch's defense was the signal for a craning of necks and pushing forward which compelled the police to fight.[43]

A guard examined Comerford's document and whispered to Peters and Whitman, whom they left hurriedly after issuing an order to return Hoch to his cell for the moment. "Well boys, I'm hungry!" beamed Hoch. "Let's have dinner!" With the stay accepted and the death march temporarily halted, Hoch was all smiles. He asked for a thick sirloin steak with German potatoes to be prepared in celebration. But State's Attorney Healy said the bond that Comerford had displayed wasn't worth the paper it was written on. Nevertheless, Peters and Healy agreed to grant a delay until 2:00 p.m., by which time the writ of habeas corpus would have to be granted or Hoch would hang. With only a couple of hours left until Hoch's execution, Comerford and his law partner,

J. Julius Neiger, climbed into a carriage and raced downtown to apply for a writ of habeas corpus with federal judge Kenesaw Mountain Landis, the flinty-eyed, white-haired despot of the United States District Court, on the grounds that his client's execution would be in violation of the Constitutional clause providing that no person shall be deprived of life, liberty, or property without due process of law.

At the "Madhouse on Madison Street," *Chicago American* Editor Koenigsberg was beside himself after Assistant City Editor Jim Bickett tipped him off about this stunning development. A special edition of 75,000 copies with a screaming page-one banner announcing Hoch's execution had already hit the streets of Chicago and was being hawked by newsboys on every corner in the Loop. The headlines—"Hoch hanged! Read all about it!"—were looking very bad for the Hearst reporters as Hoch was *not* hanged, at least not yet. Koenigsberg placed frantic telephone calls to the friendly Democratic politicians and the warden of the jail wanting to know "what could be done" to speed the execution along. He was told by the state's attorney that Landis was a Federal judge appointed by a Republican president and was therefore wily and utterly unpredictable. The usual Cook County political "influence" did not reach into his courtroom.

At 10:30 a.m. Comerford appeared before Landis, who was destined to become professional baseball's first appointed commissioner following the Black Sox scandal of 1919–1920.[44] Comerford pleaded that the execution should not be allowed to proceed because of three key points: (1) the judgment was given by a court not of competent jurisdiction; (2) it was a violation of the Fourteenth Amendment to the Constitution in that Amelia Fischer had testified against her lawful husband; (3) and Hoch was arrested on a charge of bigamy in New York but prosecuted on a charge of murder in Chicago.

Judge Landis was neither sympathetic nor patient—traits he repeatedly exhibited throughout his judicial career and as the upholder of the integrity of baseball, America's national pastime, in later years. At 11:45 that morning Landis denied the petition and scolded Comerford for not utilizing the proper remedy—a writ of error from the decision of the state Supreme Court to the U.S. Supreme Court. Landis said the writ of habeas corpus was fatally defective, but as he walked to the elevator, anxious to make his lunch appointment, he promised Comerford and his team: "Later in the day I will enter such an order as will enable you to have this case reviewed by the Supreme Court in the absence of your client. I will not now complicate matters further by delaying the execution. It would be much easier for me to grant this man ten days time in which to have this case reviewed by the United States Supreme Court, but respect for orderly procedure compels me to do what I have done."[45]

"My God[,] Judge! Don't leave the building! Please don't do it! Give this man the right of appeal," begged Attorney Edward Maher, another member of Comerford's defense team.[46] Landis said he would be back in court at 2:00 p.m. to enter the order—but by then Hoch would already be dead, Maher reminded him. "There will be murder on your hands[,] Judge! We will push for a criminal indictment if that is the case!" But Landis was unfazed by threats. During his brief time on the bench, he had been threatened by members of the Black Hand extortionist ring from the Near West Side Italian ghetto and other criminal malefactors. Turning to Maher, he calmly reiterated that he was on his way to lunch, and that was that. The judge exited the building promptly at 1:00 p.m., hailed a hackney cab, and was driven to a downtown location to make his appointment.

As the hands of the clock ticked past 1:30 p.m., Comerford, Maher, and Neiger raced frantically through the private club rooms of the city to the Great Northern Hotel in an effort to catch up with Landis in the dining rooms where they suspected he might be gorging on his filet, but it was useless trying to track him down. By the time he returned to his courtroom to grant the appeal at 2:15 p.m. to the trio of lawyers pleading for a temporary stay, Johann Hoch was already dead.

The desperate battle to save the life of the murderer whom one Chicago newspaper dubbed "The Hardest Man to Hang in the History of the Cook County Jail" ended unceremoniously at 1:33 p.m. when Hoch was dropped to eternity after uttering his final words. He invoked the words of Jesus Christ in a firm denial of his guilt. There was no sign of trembling or hesitation in his voice as he stared blankly at the assembled reporters and jail personnel who had come to witness the execution. "Oh Lord, forgive them. They know not what they do. I must die an innocent man. Goodbye!" The cowl was placed over his head as his spiritual advisor, the Revered J.R. Birkelund, read aloud the Twenty-third Psalm. The door sprung open, and the sound of death punctured the quiet of the chamber. A jury of physicians found Hoch's neck broken at the second vertebrae and pronounced him dead at 1:52 p.m. The corpse was placed in a rough wooden coffin.

Amelia Fischer asked for and received all of Hoch's correspondence and personal effects in a suitcase. She left the Cook County Jail without opening the contents, but, turning to Whitman, the grief-stricken woman reaffirmed that she would kill herself. Without her beloved Johann, she said that death was preferable to living.

Hoch's remains were delivered to a West Side undertaker's parlor where the body was placed in Amelia's custody. The next day, in the cold and driving rain, Reverend August Schlechte, who had counseled Hoch during much of his time in jail, mounted the hearse as it began its delivery of the plain pine box coffin to the cemetery. But Waldheim and Forest Home Cemetery, located west of the city, turned the wagon away at the entrance gates. Johann Hoch was unwelcome and would not be received.

The only other option was to cart the remains out to the burial ground at Dunning, where the county poorhouse and insane asylum were situated well northwest of downtown and far from populated areas. It was here at Dunning that the miserable poor, the mentally impaired, and the criminal classes of Chicago were buried anonymously in the craggy, weed-strewn potter's field. It was to be the final resting place for the scoundrel Johann Hoch, whose ironic request to jailers was that he be buried with dignity in a Christian cemetery.

In the driving rain, a small gathering of Dunning officials, including the business manager of the asylum, watched silently as inmates lowered the casket into the soaked earth on a bluff overlooking the rear of the hospital. A simple Bible passage was read aloud, and the grave was covered over. Amelia Fischer-Hoch said she was too ill to attend the graveside service.

Chapter Fourteen

The trial of Johann Hoch, heard before the State Supreme Court, established the Doctrine of Exclusion—an important legal precedent in Illinois jurisprudence. Essentially, evidence had been introduced by the prosecution team to show that facts and circumstances that preceded the death of Marie Walcker excluded the guilt of everyone else who might have known or attended to the woman. Moreover, the case of *Johann Hoch v. the People of Illinois* also marked the first time in a state criminal proceeding in which the testimony of a pathologist—in this case, Dr. Ludwig Hektoen, who provided evidence based on an *indisputable* conclusion of exact science—was admitted into the record. Before this time, experts from the field of chemistry were the only scientists whom lawyers summoned to testify during Illinois poison trials.

The same week that Johann Hoch was put to death on the gallows of the Cook County Jail, a congress of Protestant ministers, reform-minded politicians, and ecumenical leaders decried the moral turpitude of Chicago and its intolerable crime conditions. They took their crusade to city hall and out into the neighborhoods. "The events of Chicago show that this city is a paradise for criminals," complained North Side Alderman Winfield P. Dunn. "In a decade the city of which we are so proud has gone through a woeful change. How we love to recall the Chicago of 1893, the Chicago of the White City. And what an alteration in 10 years or more! Chicago is no longer the White City of 1893, but the *black city* of 1906; a city of lawlessness and of our civic shame."[1] Dunn called for the establishment of neighborhood law and order leagues, additional police officers, the closing of disreputable dance halls, and increased licensing fees for saloons but ignored the problem of crooked matrimonial bureaus, lonely hearts swindles, and the rogue confidence men preying on the good nature of desperate, unattached women.

The Klio Association, one of the largest and most influential women's organizations in the city, traced the blame for rising crime to the press for the amount of space devoted to the coverage of revolting crimes and hangings. Harriet Thomas cited the Johann Hoch case as an example of the "glorification of crime and criminals" by the press—singling out two Hearst papers, the *American* and the *Examiner*, for censure. "It would have the effect of checking crime if the newspapers would devote less space to details of crime," Thomas asserted. "Everyone was interested in the Hoch case because the papers made him famous. But why should columns have been devoted to the last hours of a wretched man who had been found guilty of murder? Why should the public be told that he had a good breakfast of ham and eggs?"[2]

Nine daily newspapers were circulated in Chicago in 1906. The number of column inches given over to the Hoch execution by each of these news journals was proportionate to their established reputations and editorial policy. The *Tribune, Chronicle, Inter-Ocean, Post,* and *Daily News* were considered "serious" news publications because of their intense coverage of politics, foreign affairs, finance, and the commercial life of the city. The morning *Tribune* proudly noted that it had given the story a scant 20 column inches while the *Record-Herald* and the *Examiner* each devoted 81 inches of space, the *Inter-Ocean* allotted 60, and the *Chronicle* a mere 21.5. Among the afternoon newspapers, the *American* devoted 250 column inches to the case; the *Journal,* 169.5; the *Daily News,* 102; and the *Post* just 61.

The *Record-Herald, American, Examiner,* and *Journal* appealed to more prurient reading tastes (and became part of future playwright Ben Hecht's early success). Not surprisingly their "yellow" standards of journalism did not survive the merger and consolidation frenzy occurring within the newspaper industry over the next 50 years. The Chicago *American* newspaper—an intrusive, often unwelcome presence during the Hoch and Gunness investigations—carried on until 1969 but only because the Tribune Company had acquired the holdings of the former "Madhouse on Madison Street" five years after William Randolph Hearst's death in 1951.[3] However, the disappearance of the "yellows" from the scene did not forestall the fundamental changes overtaking American journalism at this time, which was primarily the inevitable shift from reporting of hard news with minimal photographs and illustrations toward a greater investment of time and resources dedicated to crime coverage, sports, and entertainment news with splashy headlines and graphic images.

Conservative upholders of the standards of virtue and decency opposed to an unfettered press argued that salacious details of morbid crimes published by the scandal sheets inspired copycats, i.e., feeble-minded people who duplicated the patterns of behavior of celebrated criminals. These incidents are isolated, and there is no evidence to suggest that Johann Hoch spawned a new generation of bigamist wife killers—although a rash of stories appeared in the newspapers in the months and years following Hoch's execution in 1906. Published dispatches from around the country inevitably resurrected and compared the Johann Hoch case to the latest celebrity bigamist.

Frederick E. Carlton, the "Brooklyn Bluebeard," was described by police agencies as the "second Johann Hoch" with a record of crime "as black as night" following his conviction in October 1905 for bigamy and insurance fraud. Carlton blazed a trail of fraud and murder from New York to the gold mining camps of Colorado with the aid and assistance of his "fiancée," a female confederate named Elenor Vandeventer, who helped him identify the women he would victimize and then posed for daring nude photographs. Carlton, an amateur studio photographer, would then transpose the image of his intended victim's face over Vandeventer for blackmail purposes if his marriage offer was rejected. However, prosecutors could never make a homicide charge stick although the woman was arrested and incarcerated on obscenity charges.

Carlton was a man of a certain suave and debonair charm, not unlike Hoch—equally vain and boastful. Describing his opinions of women to a *Washington Times* reporter on July 31, 1905, he said: "They are too confiding, too prone to be led, but we couldn't get along without them," adding: "if the police will go about their business without so much foolishness they will find I'm not a bad man. I don't drink. I don't swear, and well, about the only thing I have ever done was to innocently . . . yes . . . I say innocently, make love to a few women. Isn't it a man's privilege to win the heart of a woman? And if she falls in love with him, can he help it?"[4]

Brooklyn detectives and the local coroner could not produce the necessary physical evidence to convict Carlton on a murder charge. His first wife, Jennie Smyth of East New York, died from lockjaw. The second wife, Mary Carlton, expired from tetanus resulting from a cat scratch. In the case of Smyth, death was said to have resulted from a pin scratch, although one Henry J.B. Schaub, who lived in a Brooklyn boarding house with Carlton, swore that he had observed the suspect mixing suspicious white powders in his room. Arsenic perhaps, or did he apply a different kind of poison to the fatal pin? The police and the coroner could not prove it. This bluntly efficient killer was held in the

Adams Street Court and sentenced to nineteen years in prison by a New York judge on three counts of grand larceny.[5]

In 1908, the remarkable George A. Witzhoff, an unlicensed Swiss dentist, was arrested in Bristol, England, and accused of marrying 500 women in the U.S. and Europe during a ten-year period, an astonishing record. He studied hypnotism, traveled from city to city under assumed names and clever disguises, whispered missives of love to female patients in his dentist chair, and arranged hasty nuptials through a crooked marriage bureau in the fashion of Hoch. Unlike Hoch, who mostly acted alone or with his one confederate, Gustav Strelow, Dr. Witzhoff organized a ring of 27 young sharpers to woo impressionable women with plunder deposited in New York City banks. Secret Service agents infiltrated this "Syndicate of Bigamists" and arrested a number of its low-level promoters.

Witzhoff was active in Chicago, New York, Philadelphia, Boston, Kansas City, Minneapolis, Menlo Park, Newark, and Long Island City before fleeing to Europe after a grand jury indicted him in New York in August 1905.[6] The fugitive was convicted by a British court in February 1908 and sentenced to 12 years in prison for bigamy and fraud. Answering to the name of Arthur Hyne, the defendant denied that he was Witzhoff the famous bigamist, and there were many who believed that he was not the same man.[7] "Compared with his slippery methods, the lovemaking of the unlamented Johann Hoch was a cumbersome and awkward affair," wrote one East Coast journalist who was convinced that Hyne and Witzhoff were one and the same.[8] According to Amelia Jaeger, the Chicago wife of the "most married man in the world," George Witzhoff and Johann Hoch were well acquainted with one another, and Witzhoff was a frequent visitor to the Cook County Jail in the weeks leading up to Hoch's execution.[9]

Crimes of bigamy on so vast a scale as this no longer occur in the present day. It is simply not possible for a man or woman to escape detection for as long a time period as Johann Hoch or George Witzhoff did. Mass communications, the social security number as a means of instant personal identification, improved methods of police detection, and emerging technology have doomed the serial bigamist to oblivion. Storefront matrimonial bureaus, considered a benign nuisance by law enforcement up until the murders at the Belle Gunness farm in La-Porte, finally led to arrests and a crackdown in 1908 and had all but vanished by the 1930s. The changing role of women in society, women's entry into the workforce in large numbers during World War II, and the safety net of the monthly social security check to help safeguard a person against insolvency and the economic infirmities of old age eliminated the urgency for a widow or single woman to "shop" for a husband during her advancing years.

With the gradual assimilation of immigrant groups into the mainstream of American life, much of the traditional ethnic, foreign language press in the United States disappeared and with it the opportunity for skillful con men to prey upon women of their own heritage and national background through the placement of classified ads. Sadly, with the rise of the Internet in our modern age, predators of a different stripe abound in the online world, and their crimes remind us that the old days of grab and greed are far from over.

Dramatis Personae

The principal players in the trial, conviction, and dramatic execution of the ubiquitous Johann Hoch lived out the remainder of their lives in varying degrees of contentment and tragedy. Amelia Fischer Hoch decided to choose life over suicide despite repeated threats to do herself in. There were no reports of her tragic, grief-stricken, guilt-ridden demise by her own hand following Johann's death. Nor does it appear that she made the necessary arrangements to transfer his remains from the potter's field in Dunning to a more respectful resting place, as she said she intended to do.

Bigamist Emma Rankan-Warneke, who married Hoch and drove him off at the point of a gun, was an important witness during the murder trial. She died of pneumonia and starvation in the Cook County Hospital on November 30, 1915, after she was found subsisting in two bare rooms at 658 Race Street. The self-annihilating woman was believed to be indigent until police searched the premises and were stunned to find furs, silk gowns, and expensive articles of women's wear locked in a trunk; however, she had only $1.03 in cash, and without relatives to claim the body, she was laid to rest at the county's expense— in the potter's field not far from Johann Hoch's grave.

Hoch's nemesis, Inspector George Shippy, was appointed superintendent of police in 1907 after Republican Fred Busse was swept into office as mayor. Ambitious and resolute, Shippy battled the entrenched gambling syndicates and attempted to clean out pockets of organized vice in the Levee District and on the south and west sides—as thankless a task as trying to cork up the Atlantic Ocean in a glass bottle. On his watch the first actions were taken against the crooked practices of the matrimonial bureaus. In an era of unchecked police graft and malfeasance, Superintendent Shippy was a cut above the pack and generally well thought of by the press.

His law enforcement career took an abrupt turn on March 2, 1908, when Lazarus Averbuch, a young Jew born in Kishiniff, Russia (the setting for bloody anti-Semitic rioting in 1903), and a recent émigré from Austria who had been in the U.S. for less than three months, attempted to assassinate Shippy and his son Harry in the foyer of their Lincoln Park brownstone. The thug Averbuch was a disciple of renowned anarchist Emma Goldman, a former hairdresser from Russia, and her lover, Ben Reitman, both of whom were leaders of the nihilist fringe who had been sponsoring a series of lectures at Brand's Hall and whipping up class hatred that over a period of weeks had turned increasingly volatile.

Shippy had heard rumors of a planned assassination attempt against him after he had dispatched undercover detectives into the meeting halls to infiltrate the group and gather intelligence. The recent murder of Denver priest Leo Heinrichs by an Italian anarchist opposed to the doctrines of the Catholic Church had put the police on edge. There were fears that Goldman and her followers would target the mayor, the police chief, and members of the clergy after scrawled notes sent to Shippy's residence warned of dire consequences unless his bluecoats desisted in their harassment of the group and allowed the anarchists to rent a hall, stage a rally, and parade through the downtown streets.[10]

Having materialized from out of nowhere, Lazarus Averbuch rapped on the door of the Shippy residence on Lincoln Place at 9:00 p.m. that Sunday night. He had not come to pay a social call or exchange pleas-antries with the superintendent: the young man was wielding a knife and concealing a gun in the pocket of his black overcoat although his fellow revolutionaries would fervently deny that he was carrying concealed weapons. Armed or unarmed, Averbuch was a menacing presence in view of recent threats that Shippy had been receiving in the mail coupled with the memory of the demented young man who shot and killed Chicago Mayor Carter Henry Harrison in 1893 in the hallway of his West Side residence under similar circumstances. Shippy confronted the ragged looking stranger and reacted quickly, determined not to become the next public official to be assassinated. There was a tussle, and shots were exchanged. Shippy's son sustained a near-fatal bullet wound in the chest as Averbuch collapsed to the floor, shot dead with a bullet to the heart. The entire struggle was witnessed by Shippy's wife, his daughter, and his niece—and it was all over in less than two minutes.

George Shippy had been stabbed below the armpit in a desperate fight for his life, but within 24-hours, sharp accusations were made by the dead man's sister and indignant members of the extreme political left that the police chief had slain an innocent, unarmed man—an absurd charge. No thinking person could possibly explain away the gunshot wounds suffered by Harry Shippy and James Foley, the family coachman, as a sinister police cover-up.[11] Enraged, Foley had pumped five unnecessary shots into Averbuch. Much was made of his actions by Goldman's supporters, but it was the adrenaline of the moment, nothing more, that guided Foley's hand to shoot in rapid-fire succession.

At the time of the altercation, George Shippy was an ailing man. He was granted a departmental furlough and medical leave not long after the jarring encounter with Averbuch. During his period of convalescence, doctors determined that the former chief was in the early stages of paralytic dementia—likely brought on by his unchecked syphilis. As he struggled to regain his health, intermittent murder threats mailed by anarchists and their sympathizers to his home further tormented the family and aggravated Shippy's delicate physical condition. Broken mentally, physically, and financially, Shippy was committed to a state hospital for the insane in Kankakee, Illinois, on February 6, 1913. Shippy died in his home at 6421 Monroe Street just two months later on April 13, 1913, and was eulogized by the press as a brave, honest, and honorable man who had been above the partisan political fray of Chicago.

Frank Comerford, Harry Olson, and Judge George Kersten enjoyed long and meritorious careers on the bench of the circuit court of Cook County. Olson went on to serve as its chief justice continuously from 1906 until 1930, and received credit for being the prime mover behind the implementation (in 1906) of the modern municipal court system that superseded a corrupt and inefficient system of politically connected, unqualified, and in many cases, untrained justices of the peace dispensing verdicts from crowded, chaotic courtrooms in the backrooms of police stations and satellite offices. He died in 1935. Isadore Plotke continued his law practice into the 1920s and was active in various Jewish fraternal societies and membership organizations. The fate of the surviving wives of Johann Hoch, apart from Emma Rankan Warneke, cannot be ascertained.

In March 1936, wrecking crews completed the demolition of the Cook County Jail in which 97 men were executed during its notorious history spanning the years 1873–1929.[12] The jail was emptied out and closed on April Fools' Day 1929 with all prisoners transferred to the spacious new $7,000,000 facility located on the West Side at 26th and California. During the worst years of the Depression, homeless men and women slept in the cell blocks on the murderers' row on which Johann Hoch, Adolph Luetgert (the North Side sausage maker who murdered his wife and dropped her corpse into a boiling sausage vat in May 1897), and the 1924 "thrill killers" Richard Loeb and Nathan Leopold (those who murdered the young Hyde Park boy Robert Franks in order to prove their intellectual superiority by outwitting the police) once roamed. "If those walls could only talk" murmured the cynical, old-time police reporters assigned to cover trials in the adjoining courthouse and executions at the jail during those rollicking times when the *Chicago American* and the *Examiner* were stirring the pot of journalistic sensationalism and newsmen kept their gin flasks handy in desk drawers beside them. The electric chair replaced the gallows as the preferred form of execution in Illinois in 1927. Cop killers Anthony Grecco and Charles Walz were the last men to be put to death in the old Cook County Jail before the building closed.[13]

Chapter Fifteen

A steady stream of reported sightings of the fugitive Belle Gunness arrived at the LaPorte Police Department and sheriff's office over the course of the next twenty years. Belle was seen here, there, everywhere—and nowhere. In April 1914, Sheriff Anstiss traveled to New York City to verify a report that police were holding a local woman they believed to be Belle, but there was nothing to it. Deputy Marshall Clinton Cochrane continued to pursue the most promising leads with resolve and determination, but at the end of each trail he found only bad information, rumors, tall tales, and cases of mistaken identity. At the same time that Anstiss was in New York, Cochrane had already arrived in Neville, Saskatchewan, to chase down rumors. With local newspapermen at his side, he rapped on the door of one Joseph Wisner to see if the occupant was harboring the fugitive murderess. The woman inside the house bore no resemblance to Belle. After many more baseless Gunness sightings, Cochrane, Anstiss, and their successors in office simply abandoned the chase and allowed the story to drift into the realm of superstition and folklore, a tale destined to forever be retold over a roaring campfire late at night out in the woods by spellbinding storytellers adding a flair of the supernatural and the macabre to achieve dramatic effect with their listeners.

LaPorte law enforcement had grown weary of the many false Gunness sightings. Their attitude was one of impatience and cynicism, and the public was informed that no more taxpayer appropriations would be allocated to dispatch detectives on wild goose chases across the country. Thus an official attitude of indifference permeated the town. But as the years passed, new information surfaced to suggest that just maybe the hard-bitten old soak Ray Lamphere had been right all along.

In the spring of 1931 Deputy District Attorney George Stahlman of

Los Angeles sent word back to LaPorte County Sheriff Tom McDonald advising the LaPorte police of the arrest and incarceration of two elderly women, Esther Carlson and Anna Erickson—the "Arsenic and Old Lace" killers—who had been recently arrested for the poisoning murder of Carl August Lindstrom, an 81-year-old lumberman. The Gunness modus operandi in this case was all too familiar to those who were still close to the case: the accused murderess, her accomplice, and the victim were all Scandinavian (Lindstrom and Erickson were both Swedes).

Mrs. Carlson, if that was in fact her real name, worked as a housekeeper for the wealthy old man. The Erickson woman was said to be a close friend of Carlson's. Suspicions were cast by the victim's son Peter Lindstrom who reported the disappearance of a $2,000 joint savings account that the old man had opened with his housekeeper. The day after Lindstrom's death, the savings account vanished. Peter opened an investigation that led police to a Long Beach druggist, where it was found that Carlson had attempted to purchase arsenic.

Arrested and indicted on a charge of murder, Carlson said she had lived in Hartford, Connecticut, from 1892 to 1909 and denied any connection to LaPorte. Her friends in Los Angeles said her words were true. They said she was born Esther Johnson—in Sweden, not Norway. Carlson fell ill during her incarceration; the diagnosis was tuberculosis, and her condition was terminal. She was hospitalized and fading fast when, at Wirt Worden's request, Los Angeles homicide investigators produced witnesses from Chicago and LaPorte to provide some possible identification. R.C. Ganiere, the former photographer from Austin who was now in the grocery business in California, was located and he told of taking studio portraits of Belle nearly 33 years earlier. He was positive that the facial features of the dying Carlson were remarkably similar to Gunness's.

This opinion was supported by L.E. Silvey of Monterey, formerly of LaPorte, and John "Dennis" Daly, a 70-year-old retired boilermaker who appeared at the county morgue at the behest of Sheriff McDonald. Daly claimed that he was "one of the few men alive" who had actually seen Belle flee the LaPorte crime scene in May 1908. "With me was a friend—neither of us knew the Gunness farmhouse had burned during the night—and we saw a heavily veiled woman dressed in black hurrying across the tracks toward the railroad station," Daly recalled. "I said to my friend, 'there goes Belle Gunness.' I had an impulse at that time to stop her but I didn't. When we went into town a few hours later, we learned that the farmhouse had been burned and it was believed that she burned with it."[1]

Could they really be sure the body lying in the casket was Belle's, or was the body Esther Johnson of Hartford? Published photos of the Carlson woman appearing in the LaPorte newspapers and the Chicago *American* bore a strong resemblance—although Carlson's face was much thinner and more withered than Belle's by the passing of the years. Carlson and Gunness shared the same forehead crease, the eyes were alike, and both had rather long earlobes. If indeed this was the real Belle Gunness, one of the most diabolical and fiendish serial killers of the twentieth century, the woman who tempted fate in life had succeeded in cheating the hangman in death.

On the blustery afternoon of November 5, 2007, a team of forensic anthropologist-researchers led by LaPorte native Andrea Simmons, a historian and an Indianapolis attorney, and Dr. Stephen Nawrocki, a board-certified forensic anthropologist and tenured professor of biology and anthropology at the University of Indianapolis, opened the grave of the supposed Belle Gunness lying next to the body of Mads Sorensen and Belle's children at Forest Home Cemetery to try to solve the 100-year-old riddle that has fascinated Simmons and so many LaPorte residents for years. Their purpose was to conduct scientific testing of the skeletal remains. They found that the zinc-lined, wooden caskets shipped by the Frank Cutler Funeral Home in LaPorte to Chicago had all but disintegrated, but bones from the headless adult female remained. The fragile remains were removed and taken to the University of Indianapolis Archeology and Forensics Laboratory where they were analyzed by a team of anthropologists. The commingled children's remains were exhumed the following spring. DNA from the adult remains and original envelopes from Belle's letters to Andrew Helgelein were sent to the State Police Forensics Laboratory in Indianapolis for analysis. Later additional samples were sent for DNA testing to a university laboratory in Texas. On hand to witness the exhumation of the adult remains was Suzanne McKay of Portland, Oregon, a great granddaughter of Nellie Larsen, Belle's estranged sister in Chicago.

Results of the testing have yet to be announced, but Nawrocki said he "leans toward it being Belle." The team pinned their hopes on extracting a sample of DNA from the sealed envelopes that Gunness had sent to one of her suitors and comparing them to the bone fragments.[2] The DNA analysis is being done pro bono, so they must continue to wait patiently because ongoing forensic investigation of evidence relating to current criminal cases takes precedent. Simmons reserves judgment and draws no conclusions or suppositions until science weighs in with a final verdict. "I would like to remain neutral," she said.

"The *null* hypothesis is that she died in the fire. But if it is her it raises many questions regarding the events of the night of April 8, 1908," Simmons adds. "Additional DNA testing is underway on the bones of the children to establish whether or not they are Belle's offspring, or if they were adopted. We hope to find that out, but it is more difficult to extract DNA from the bones of a child because there is less cortical mass. Bone material from adults is more robust, and in teeth for example, there is a bigger pulp chamber that is much more developed than what you will find in children. The integrity of the older bone material—even the remains that were charred in the fire—is much better to evaluate and more likely to hold up."[3] If the charred bones of the adult female in the grave are proven not to be Mrs. Gunness, Simmons and her team will seek family members' permission and funding to exhume a sample bone from Belle's sister, Nellie Larsen, in order to confirm the findings. Simmons would also like to exhume the remains of Esther Carlson in Los Angeles.

Dramatis Personae

"Nigger Liz" Smith, a daughter of Virginia slaves, Belle's friend, Lamphere's lover, and the worker of charms and incantations who fooled the townspeople of LaPorte into believing that she was a witch possessed by Satanic powers, died on March 17, 1916. Her tumbledown shack out on Railroad Street at the edge of town was filled to the rafters with worthless junk, including 980 pounds of carpeting and the riprap of her seventy-plus dissolute years, although no one was exactly sure just how old Liz really was. It was not an enviable task to clear away all of her curious paraphernalia and finally tear down the public eyesore. Found in the piles of junk were torn and soiled letters from men she had corresponded with through matrimonial bureaus, a manual on hypnotism, and recipes for spells and magical potions. The scavengers were shocked to find insurance policies, a bank account with a sizeable balance of cash on hand, and deeds to six other properties in LaPorte. In her failure-laden life, she had lived like a hermit, but it turned out that she was worth a small fortune. Her accumulation of wealth, it was said, came to her after the fire at the Belle Gunness place.

But what gave everyone a start was the discovery of a cobwebby skull pried loose from between two mattresses. At first it was believed to have some connection to Belle. Possibly it was Belle herself or, more likely, the long missing skull of the woman she had lured from Chicago. A.J. Harness, charged with closing out the Smith estate, brought the skull to police investigators, but they were unsure if it belonged to a man or a woman or whether it was ten or fifty years old. The lower jaw was missing, and only a few rotted roots marked where the missing upper teeth once were.

Liz took her secrets to the grave despite a promise made to Wirt Worden that she would one day reveal all she knew—but only when death was in plain sight. Unfortunately Worden was in Louisiana at the time of Smith's passing. He rushed back home as fast as he could, but by the time he arrived in town, old Liz was already gone. She steadfastly refused to divulge her secrets to anyone other than Worden.

The Chicago newspapers sent their reporters to file an update to this weird tale and its latest strange turn, but they left too soon and failed to bring back the rest of the story. The skull, as it turned out, predated Belle's arrival in LaPorte. The African-American community was just as fearful of Liz and her special "powers" as her white neighbors. "She used that skull to conjure with!" said one woman. "My mother, she's dead now, but she often told me about she see her sitting up at night with the light shining through the holes in the skull and 'Nigger Liz,' she sit and read to it out of the Bible!"[4] It was whispered that Liz scribbled the names of the victims of her spells on the skull.

Liz Smith had acquired the morbid relic from C.F. Russell, a traveling man who claimed to have dug it out of the prairie ground where the Seventh Cavalry met its demise at the Battle of the Little Big Horn in 1876. Russell claimed that it was the skull of an Indian chief, and he made off with his souvenir before passing it on to Liz for safekeeping in 1891.[5] Or Russell may have simply invented a colorful tall tale, but either way there was no connection to Belle Gunness—although it kept people talking and the story alive.

Liz Smith's friend and confidante Herman Wirt Worden left the defense bar to become a LaPorte County prosecutor. He was elected a judge of the circuit court in 1934 and served in this capacity until he was felled by a heart attack and died at age sixty-eight on January 3, 1943. Albert Smutzer quit law enforcement after his term of office was over and left LaPorte to take construction jobs in Chicago and other cities until he returned to live out his days with his daughter. That was in 1933—just four years after his deputy and successor, William E. Anstiss, passed away at the age of sixty. Smutzer died in October 1940, unable to crawl away from the notorious shadow of the Gunness case or the endless second-guessing he had to put up with until the end.

Belle's sprawling Victorian home on Alma Street (now Latrobe Avenue) in Austin was razed decades ago, and for a long while only an empty, weedy lot remained. It is an accepted fact that at locations in which a particular infamy occurred, the buildings and properties become cursed either by superstition, circumstance, or their very nature. In a practical business sense, realtors find it difficult, if not impossible, to sell a home where a murder was committed. Prospective buyers shy away—just as a person of a superstitious mind would not walk under a ladder or get married on Friday the thirteenth. But the empty lot on North Latrobe Avenue was finally redeveloped, and a new 1,560-square-foot, two-story, gated frame home was erected in 2003—sufficient time had passed to erase the memory of Belle Gunness in Chicago.

Down in LaPorte, the fire debris at Brookside Farm was cleared away, leaving behind only the stone foundation of Belle's home. Fifteen years passed. Moss covered the cement walls of the basement, and the land went to seed. Community superstition repelled prospective buyers from redeveloping the property. All of LaPorte was taken aback when John Nepsha built his new home atop the old foundation in June 1923. Bad luck followed—or so it has been said. Nepsha's wife later divorced him, claiming that she couldn't live there, and in 1936 an assistant surveyor dropped dead while surveying the private graveyard. Visitors kept coming from all over the U.S. and overseas. They made pests of themselves by calling on the Nepshas at odd hours, seeking information and asking for souvenirs. Many naturally wondered why anyone would want to live in that house and put up with the annoyance.

In preparation for her 2006 documentary about the Gunness case, *Only Belle: A Serial Killer From Selbu*, Norwegian filmmaker Anne Berit Vestby interviewed the current owners of the farm and discovered that their son "sees dead people" on the property. Such a revelation should not be surprising given the proliferation of vice and the unsavory character of the neighborhood well before Belle arrived. A drive down McClung Road today takes the visitor past rows of small single-family homes—modest looking wood-frame, vinyl-sided worker cottages flanking the street with small boats in the backyards and woodpiles awaiting fireplaces in winter.

Belle's 48-acre farm was subdivided many years ago, and a collection of homes was built on her former pastureland. It is doubtful that there are any unmarked graves left to discover that far away from Gunness's kitchen window where she surveyed her holdings and kept close watch on her help and on her graveyard. The adjacent neighborhood dwellings were built after the Gunness murders, and they reflect a sense of orderliness in the community that was absent in this part of LaPorte for so many years. The seedy gambling and vice dens lining McClung Road—those that had so enraged Belle that she had filed a report with

Mayor Darrow complaining that the area was no longer a "fit neighbor-hood" to raise a family in—vanished long ago. The backdrop of Clear Lake provides a quiet commune with nature. But in winter when the lake is frozen over it is almost too quiet, eerily quiet: observers can sense a modern still life as they struggle to come to terms with the disturbing past.

Belle Gunness and Her Enduring Legacy— the Collision of Community Folklore with Impropriety and Bad Taste

A rather shocking Belle Gunness "cottage industry" stretches from LaPorte, nicknamed the Maple City, to mainstream popular culture and raises serious ethical questions about values and attitudes toward certain criminals considered clever, quaint, and, by some standards, amusing when weighed against the depravity of modern-day serial killers. In her 1985 volume, author Janet Langlois discussed commu-nity values and reprinted a spate of rhymes set to folk music mocking the victims of Belle Gunness and the crimes of the murderess herself. The passage of a long period of time seems to have a peculiar way of mitigating the horrific acts of violent criminals, at least certain types of violent criminals. In Chicago, there is a serious attempt on the part of a handful of ardent Prohibition Era aficionados to cleanse the reputation of 1920s gangster and murderer Al Capone in order to recast him in the unfamiliar role as the misunderstood "Good Capone." Similarly, the city of LaPorte has elevated Belle Gunness to celebrity criminal status in the same fashion that Capone has practically become a favorite son of Chicago and the subject of an endless stream of books and cable television documentary programs.

The LaPorte County Historical Society Museum features a disturbing Belle Gunness exhibit in the lower level of their otherwise fascinating collection of artifacts spotlighting community achievement and area history through the years. While the Gunness case was an important, defining event in LaPorte history, the life-size papier-mâché manne-quin dressed to look like Belle and posed by a side panel from one of the wood sheds relocated from her property is strange and unsettling.[6] Opinions among staff members are divided equally concerning this is-sue. The museum also houses a large collection of artifacts, including a skull that is purported to be one of the unidentified victims. This object was analyzed and tested by Simmons and her team, but it likely does not belong to the headless female remains. It is not on public display, and it is unlikely that it will ever be interred because records identifying the precise location of the potter's field in the Davison Patton Cemetery where the remains of the victims were buried were never recorded.

With the exception of the four children who perished under her care and the anonymous woman, the victims were middle-aged men of Scandinavian descent. Most of the men were without families and were therefore destined to become anonymous in death. There was no period of bereavement when they were buried in unmarked graves in the pauper's section of the Patton Cemetery, where Jennie Olsen and many of LaPorte's "old settlers" are also interred.[7]

Andrew Helgelein, the last man to be slain at Brookside Farm, has been treated with derision in the folkloric Gunness ballads, published in the 1930s. One rhyme is especially concise:

> When Andrew Helgelein came–
> His check he first cashed in.
> And then that night
> She caught him right
> And he was soon bashed in.
> —"The Ballad of Belle Gunness," Little Theater Club, LaPorte[8]

Another verse from that same period makes light of the "Norska folk" who, by implication, are trusting but simpleminded hicks with distinctive, lilting Scandinavian drawls that were so prevalent on Minnesota farms and forests:

> Now all those men were Norska folk
> Who came to Belle from Minn-e-sota;
> They liked their coffee and their gin:
> They got it plus a Mickey Finn
> And now with cleaver poised so sure
> Belle neatly cut their jug-u-lar
> She put them in a bottle of lime; and left them there for quite some time."[9]

Does this verse suggest in an unintended way that our culture tends to treat the adult male victim of a serial killer as a "throwaway," the victim least deserving of honor and respect? Perversely, and by the same token, Belle could be considered by some to be an early feminist, running her farm and her business in a harsh, unyielding physical environment and doing the punishing "man's work"—though history remembers her only as a serial murderer.

One cannot conceive of a time now or in a hundred years when the thirty-three unfortunate teen-aged victims of John Wayne Gacy, the prostitutes slain by the Green River Killer, Ted Bundy's coed victims, or, for that matter, those who were killed by any other predators, lampooned in such a distasteful way as the men slain out on the Gunness farm. Nor can it simply be dismissed by saying that the separation of 100 years have blunted our sensibilities and allowed fiends like Belle Gunness, whose methods were very similar to Gacy's and whose body count of victims likely exceeded that of Gacy's, to creep into cultural folklore.

The argument for historical separation is plausible until considering the carnival-like festivities going on outside the farm at the time of the excavation of bodies in 1908 when the sale of grisly souvenirs, photos of a severed head, and other curios and notions by fast-buck artists circulated through the crowds. Even the throngs milling around outside the Cook County Jail awaiting news of Johann Hoch's execution in 1906 were not being solicited to purchase trinkets and photos of his victims, ten lonely and vulnerable women. In the final analysis, what it demonstrates is that no historical era can claim moral superiority over another, and the foibles of human nature are such that our fascination with the morbid, the grotesque, and the vulgar far too often outweigh sensitivity.

Andrea Simmons sensed a feeling of benign amusement toward the Gunness male victims from a number of women who came to hear her lecture on the case. "I have detected a dismissive, even light-hearted view toward the men that Belle murdered that is very callous," she said, "a feeling that perhaps they should have known better, or how could they have been so greedy and ignorant, or even that they might have deserved what they got. I have definitely observed a look of amusement on the faces of some of the women who have attended my talks. In my examination of contemporary news accounts of the case from 1908 I gained the sense that this attitude was common even back then."[10]

Chicago writer and historian Kay Henderson views the issue differently. "A cartoon about a cat who kills a mouse would hardly be fit for children, but when the mouse kills the cat we find it amusing as the traditional roles are reversed and the prey becomes the victor. It is unlikely that anyone applauds Belle or her actions, but historically we see this reaction whenever an underdog laughs at the expense of the usual bully," she said. "To the extent that women feel oppressed, or see themselves as a member of a group with limited protections and freedom, they may laugh when one of them is portrayed as being able to act with power even when the result is horrifying. The French philosopher A. Penjon has written: 'Laughter is nothing but an expression of the freedom which we experience or long for.'"[11]

What Would Have Happened if
Belle Gunness Had Met Johann Hoch?

Belle Gunness is the more complex and disturbing figure of the two Gaslight Era serial killers in deed and action. Her psychological motivations ran much deeper and were far more complex than the mere accumulation of wealth that guided the hand of Johann Hoch. The question of what would have happened if the two had met was put to Cook County Deputy Sheriff Charles Peters in 1908. Peters had no firsthand experience with Gunness, but he had gotten to know Hoch intimately inside the old jail before his execution, and from the viewpoint of the criminologist he offered this assessment: "If the paths of Johann Hoch and Mrs. Gunness had crossed and each had conspired to take the life and worldly possessions of the other, each ignorant of the other's plot[,] the psychological developments and result would have been of interest to criminologists. She was a woman Hoch and he was a man Gunness." Peters reflected:

It is an absorbing question. Which would have won had they met? It would have been a game of life and death, plot and counter plot and gold would have been the stakes. Hoch undoubtedly was criminally insane. She too was, in my opinion if the reports are true, criminally insane. Mrs. Gunness schemed deeper, took greater chances and played for greater stakes. Her goal was in the hundreds of thousands. She fell back on the old dodge—the matrimonial advertisement. They would have met first by a mere handclasp.

Each would have coldly calculated on the other's shrewdness. Each would have wondered just how long it would take to work out the idea. Human life would have meant nothing. Then perhaps there would be two smiles. Each would say to himself or herself, 'This one will be easy.'

The next day a discussion of finances probably would have arisen. Hoch would have told the widow he had thousands of dollars with him to put into the common fund. She would have smiled and answered that her acres belonged to him when they were married. Possibly right there, victory in sight for both. They would have set the date for the wedding. It would have beaten, I believe, any dreams of villainy ever produced on the stage. Who would have done the other?[12]

Acknowledgments

I am very grateful to the staff and archivists at the LaPorte County Historical Society Museum, including Curator James A. Rodgers, Susie Richter, Assistant Curator, and Fern Eddy Schultz, LaPorte County Historian, who provided access to the considerable Belle Gunness re sources, and to Arnold Bass, author of a locally published community history. The wide search for fragmentary information about the early life of Gunness brought me into contact with Torger Størseth of Selbu, Norway, who communicated valuable genealogical information to me via e-mail. Torger's interest in this case took him from Norway to La-Porte to view the Gunness sites as they look today, including the nearby graveyard where Andrew Helgelein is interred. To mark the anniversary of this case, the LaPorte museum invited the Gunness relatives and the descendents of the victims to the town that drew the attention of the world in 1908. I also extend appreciation to Andrea Simmons of the Pollack Law Firm in Indianapolis and Dr. Stephen Nawrocki of the University of Indianapolis whose interest and historical curiosity led them on a quest to solve the "mystery of the bones" and bring some final closure to the Belle Gunness riddle.

In contrast to the Belle Gunness case, little has been written of Johann Hoch, with few primary sources to turn to and little in the way of reliable secondary source information. Hoch has been mentioned in a cursory way in several true crime anthologies published over the years, and the rudimentary, well-established facts of his criminal career can be found on a handful of Web sites devoted to serial murderers, but there is not much else left to the serious historian and researcher. The Chicago History Museum has archived the transcript of Hoch's appeal to the Illinois State Supreme Court, and Linda Cunningham Fluharty has researched aspects of Hoch's marital adventure in

Wheeling, West Virginia—information she generously shared with me. But the cupboard is mostly bare, and that was surprising given the ever growing public fascination with this type of criminal as evidenced by the proliferation of documentaries airing on *truTV*, *48 Hours Mystery*, *Forensic Files*, *Investigation Discovery*, *The History Channel*, and other cable programming spotlighting true crime.

Many thanks to J. Alex Schwartz, Julia Fauci, and Sara Hoerdeman of Northern Illinois University Press, who encouraged this project from its inception and offered helpful suggestions as my research progressed; to Tracy Schoenle for her fine and detailed editing;, and to Rose Keefe, the author of *The Starker* and other notable work within the genre of historical crime, who read the manuscript and commented helpfully. I am lucky to have supportive family, friends, and colleagues who have valued my work, including my wife, Denise; my colleagues and friends from the Chicago real estate world, John Wickes and Janine O'Brien; Ellen and Frank Deckert; Bob Deckert; Daniel Kelley; Tamara Schafer; Dr. Bernard Brommel; Dr. Joseph Morton and President Sharon Hahs of Northeastern Illinois University; Faro Vitale; Augie Aleksy, proprietor of Centuries & Sleuths Bookstore; Bill Sawisch of the Suburban Chicago Sherlockian group Hugo's Companions; William J. Helmer; Arthur Bilek of the Chicago Crime Commission; Biart Williams; Anne Lunde; and Val Gobos. And finally my deep gratitude goes out to Kay Henderson, who has faithfully championed my work and generously devoted her time and resources to bringing my stories to life through several projects.

Appendix I

Johann Hoch's Known Victims, 1897–1905

Name of Victim	Year	Residence/ Location	Amount of Embezzlement	Victim's Fate
Callie Charlotte Andrews	1897? –1898	Chicago, IL	$500	Survived
Minnie Westpahl	1898	Jersey City, NJ	N/A	Survived
Mary Schultz	1900	Argos, IN	$2,400	Disappeared along with her daughter Nettie in Chicago
Elizabeth Marie Goerke	1901	Chicago, IL	Failed to secure her money	Survived
Mary Becker Schultz	1901	St. Louis, MO	$400	Murdered
Justina Loeffler	1902	Elkhart, IN	$1,700	Murdered
Nathalie Peterson-Irgang	1902	Chicago, IL	Failed to secure her money	Survived
Mrs. H.L. Rick	1902	Chicago, IL	N/A	Murdered

Name of Victim	Year	Residence/ Location	Amount of Embezzlement	Victim's Fate
Mrs. A. Kelley	1902	Appleton, WI	$3,600	Murdered
Hulda Nagel	1902	St. Paul, MN	$2,500	Survived
Mabel Leichsman -Hart	1903	Minneapolis, MN	Failed to secure her money	Survived Hoch's murder attempt
Mrs. Mary T. O'Connor	1903	Milwaukee, WI	$200	Survived
Ida Zazuil	1903	Milwaukee, WI	N/A	Survived
Wilhelmina Rummier	1903	West Nyack, NY	$400	Survived
Regina Miller Curtis	1903	Dayton, OH	$1,756	Survived
Ada Dodd	1903	Dayton, OH	N/A	Survived
Alice S. Hauk	1903	Peoria, IL	N/A	Survived
Sophia Fink-Pahnke	1903	Aurora, IL	$700	Survived
[first name unknown] Loughran	1904	San Francisco, CA	N/A	Murdered
Susan Maynard	1904	San Francisco, CA	N/A	Murdered
Lena Hoch[a]	1904	Milwaukee, WI	$1,500	Murdered
Gretchen Hoch[b]	1904	Milwaukee, WI	N/A	Murdered
Catherine Wilson	1904	Mazomonie, WI	$1,650	Survived
Emma J. Kleneke	1904	Baltimore, MD	$100	Survived
Anna Hendrickson[c]	1904	Chicago, IL	$1,000	Survived

Name of Victim	Year	Residence/ Location	Amount of Embezzlement	Victim's Fate
Johanna Reichel	1904	Chicago, IL	N/A	Survived
Caroline Streicker	1904	Philadelphia, PA	$1,800	Survived
Marie Shippnick Walcker	1904	Chicago, IL	$250	Murdered
Amelia Fischer	1905	Chicago, IL	$750	Survived

Note: This table is as accurate a listing of Johann Hoch's movements prior to and following his release from the Cook County Jail—through all of the known deceptions and frauds up until his final sham marriage—as is possible to reconstruct after more than 100 years.

[a] Maiden name never revealed
[b] Sister of Lena Hoch
[c] Married in Hammond, IN

Aliases Used by Johann Hoch

John Joseph Hoch	Henry Bartels
Jacob Hock	Dewitt C. Cudney
Alfred Busteberg	Jacob Schultz
Alfred Buschberg	John Huff
Alfred Hoecht	H. Irick
George Schmidt	Johann Heh
Martin Dotz	Adolph Hoh
Joseph A. Brunn	Jacob Huff
John Hoeshe	Count Otto von Kern
N.H. Chalfont	Edward Gerald James
Frank Lucas	Robert Cable
Jacob Huss	Jacob Adolph
C.A. Mayer	

Appendix II

Belle Gunness's Victims

Name of Victim	Year of Murder or Disappearance	Residence
Caroline Sorensen	1896	Chicago, IL
Axel Sorensen	1898	Chicago, IL
Mads A. Sorensen	1900	Chicago, IL
Peter Gunness	1902	LaPorte, IN
T.J. McJenkins	n.d.	Carsopolis, PA
Andrew Anderson	n.d.	Lawrence, KS
Johann Sorensen	n.d.	St. Joseph, MO
Andrew Schwindler	n.d.	Cincinnati, OH
Charles Edmonds	n.d.	Newcastle, IN
Linder Mikkelsen	n.d.	Huron, SD
Ole Olson	n.d.	Battle Creek, MI
Axel Gunderson	n.d.	Green Lake, WS

Name of Victim	Year of Murder or Disappearance	Residence
Lee Porter	n.d.	Edinburg, IL
Emil Tell	n.d.	Osage City, KS
Sam Hopping	n.d.	Harrison, OH
Olaf Svenherud	n.d.	Chicago, IL
Frank Brodright	n.d.	Medina, ND
James Kane	n.d.	Tunnell, NY
William Mingay	n.d.	New York, NY
Olaf Edman	n.d.	Neutral Isle, PA
Gustav Thuns	n.d.	Castle Shannon, PA
Charles Ermond	n.d.	Newcastle, PA
Frank Riedinger	n.d.	Delafield, WI
Willy Buntain	c.1905	Clymers, IN
Olaf Jensen	c.1905	Carroll County, IN
Gustav Tgus	1905	Washington, PA
George Berry	1905	Tuscola, IL
Henry Gurholt	1905	Scandinavia, WI
Olaf Lindboe	1905	Rockefeller, IL
Edward Canary*	1906	Pink Lake, IN
John O. Moe	1906	Elbow Lake, MN
Herman Konitzer	1906	Chicago, IL
Jennie Olsen	1906	LaPorte, IN
Ole B. Budsberg	1907	Iola, WI

Name of Victim	Year of Murder or Disappearance	Residence
Andrew K. Helgelein	1908	Aberdeen, SD
Myrtle Adolphine Sorensen	1908	LaPorte, IN
Phillip Alexander Gunness	1908	LaPorte, IN
Lucy Bergliot Sorensen	1908	LaPorte, IN
Unknown female, possibly Esther Worchowski	1908 †	Chicago, IL

Sources: The above list of Belle Gunness's victims was published in various media outlets, including "The Mrs. Gunness Mystery" (undated pamphlet. La Porte, Indiana County Historical Society), 177–78; *Chicago Tribune,* December 31, 1909; *Chicago Record Herald,* May 19, 1908; and *Journal,* May 8, 1908, but no identification of the remains was ever made to prove conclusively that all of these individuals had actually perished at Brookside Farm or if there were additional unknown victims.

Note: This table of known and supposed victims of Belle Gunness is based on positive identifications made at the crime scenes and reports filed by relatives of men from around the country who were known to have traveled to LaPorte to meet a "farm woman with a large estate" but went missing afterward.

n.d.= No date available

* Eighteen-year-old Edward Canary went missing and was believed to have worked on the farm and was *presumed* to have been slain. However it was never conclusively proven that he was killed by Belle or buried on the farm.

† Location uncertain. Esther Worchowski of 507 W. 14th St. in Chicago is the only other female victim (apart from Jennie Olsen) listed in the "Mrs. Gunness Mystery" pamphlet. No other explanation is provided.

Notes

Introduction

1. Robert Ressler was instrumental in setting up Vi-CAP" (Violent Criminal Apprehension Program), was its program manager, and contributed to the formation of the National Center for the Analysis of Violent Crime. The Center maintains a centralized computer database of information on unsolved homicides. Information is gathered from local police agencies and cross-referenced with other unsolved killings that are tracked across the United States. Ressler, now retired from the Bureau, is the author of several books, including *Whoever Fights Monsters: My Twenty Years Tracking Serial Killers for the FBI.* He is the co-founder of Forensic Behavioral Services International, a private firm. He was one of the first, along with fellow profiler John Douglas, to conduct clinical research into the minds of serial killers and study their motivations through a series of prison interviews with the nation's worst offenders.

2. French poet and author Charles Perrault (1623–1703) wrote *Sleeping Beauty, Cinderella,* and *Mother Goose.* Historians believe that the Bluebeard character was a hybrid of Gilles de Rais seigneur et baron de Rais (1404–1440), and Comorre the Cursed, a Breton chief of the 6th century married to the noblewoman Triphine.

3. *Hartford Courant,* January 11, 1873.

4. In an episode of *Deadly Women,* it is asserted that the Bender family members escaped justice and were never located.

5. "Scores Being Slain by Poison, Charges Coroner Hoffman," *Chicago Examiner,* June 22, 1912

6. "The End of the Holmes Case," *Chicago Tribune,* May 8, 1896.

7. For a good account of the evolution of the *National Police Gazette,* see Gene Smith, "The National Police Gazette: A Visit to the Lower Depths," *American Heritage Magazine,* 23, no. 6 (October 1972).

Chapter One

1. Born in Clinton Junction, Wisconsin, Nana B. Springer was a former Milwaukee schoolteacher and assistant Sunday editor of the *Milwaukee Sentinel* before moving over to a feature writing and reporting assignment for the *Chicago Examiner* and *Chicago American.* Springer (aka Adele Garrison) attained her greatest fame as the

author of the serialized melodrama "Revelations of a Wife," published in the Hearst papers beginning in 1915. Without interruption, it continued for 35 years and ran in 200 newspapers, bringing the problems of Dicky Graham, temperamental artist, and his wife, Madge, to a million readers in increments of 800 words per day.

2. See Susan E. Lederer, "Political Animals: The Shaping of Bio-Medical Research in Twentieth Century America." *Isis*, 83, no. 1 (March 1992): 62–63.

3. *Chicago Tribune*, November 8, 1901.

4. *Chicago Tribune*, December 8, 1901. The *American* was the only newspaper in Chicago to support Edward Fitzsimmons Dunne's bid for mayor in 1905. With strong editorial backing, Dunne was swept into office by 24, 248 votes. He went on to become Governor of Illinois from 1913 to 1917.

5. Harold Schechter, *The Devil's Gentleman: Privilege, Poison, and the Trial That Ushered in the Twentieth Century* (New York: Ballantine Books, 2007), 98–103. Also *Chicago American*, various dates, January 1904–March 1907.

6. Andy Lawrence began his newspaper career as a *San Francisco Examiner* reporter in 1884 at age 23. Backed by George Hearst, father of William Randolph Hearst, Lawrence served one term in the California State Assembly but was accused of extorting $10,000 from a widow in return for helping pass a bill in which she was interested. When Hearst moved to New York, he took Lawrence with him. Then it was on to Chicago at the request of Arthur Brisbane, the nominal "chief" of the *American*. For years Lawrence exploited his position on the newspaper for material gain. In 1913 he demanded a $105,000 payoff for introducing the Empire Voting Machine Company of Syracuse, NY, to city officials. Contemptuously regarded as an annoying gadfly by the journalistic establishment, Lawrence was eventually "run out" of Chicago by Attorney Weymouth Kirkland of the Chicago Tribune Company. Dumped by Hearst and mostly washed up in the business, Lawrence ended up with the *San Francisco Journal*. See the *New York Times*, August 15, 1913. See also John Boessenecker, *Lawman: the Life and Times of Harry Morse, 1835–1912* (Norman: University of Oklahoma Press, 1998), 288–93; and Ferdinand Lundberg, *Imperial Hearst: A Social Biography* (Equinox Cooperative Press, 1936), 150–56; and a retrospective on city journalism by Arthur Sears Henning found in "A Newspaper Era Comes to Life," *Chicago Tribune*, September 8, 1953.

7. *Chicago Inter-Ocean*, January 27, 1905.

8. The Roskosz story was reported in the *American,* April 19–21, 1905.

9. "Hock Clews Weighed Ounce by Ounce," *American,* January 26, 1905.

10. *Chicago Tribune*, January 29, 1905.

11. *Chicago Journal*, February 15, 1905. Hoch moved into Pullman in December 1903 and took a job as an assembly line foreman in the sleeping car factory shop for $50 per week. He later told police that when he was the foreman, he fired all the men who were liars.

12. There were four popular German-language newspapers circulated in Chicago at this time: the Illinois *Staats-Zeitung*, the Chicago *Arbeiter-Zeitung*, the *Chicagoer Freie Presse*, and the *Abendpost*. Each appealed to a different demographic segment of the German community and was widely read across the Midwest. The *Abendpost,* under the direction of editor Fritz Glogauer, was a liberal paper resolutely opposed to temperance laws and Prohibition.

13. See *The Tribune* for November 8, 1902, and an account of the Standard Correspondence Club at 408 Avers Ave. run by one J.W. Schlosser, a 250-pound poseur whose inventory included portraits of unidentified men and women, instruction

pamphlets on the proper techniques of courtship, mailing lists of intended victims, and standard love letters used to entice hopeful correspondents. See also *The Tribune* for February 13 and March 21, 1903. Two men and one woman who operated The Edna Directory, The Martin Directory, and the Globe Directory Company—three sham marriage bureaus run out of one address at 161 Michigan Street and offering happy testimonials from women worth $120,000 who had married "kind and loving coachmen" and daughters of millionaires who wedded farmers, "preferring home life to society,"—were bound over to a federal grand jury for mail fraud with the resulting conviction of one of the three agents. State Representative William Martin, the sponsor of the bill, was the only African-American to serve in the Illinois House in 1899 and was only 30 years old at the time.

14. *Chicago Tribune*, March 4, 1899.

15. "Bigamy as Business," *Chicago Tribune*, September 5, 1905.

16. *Chicago American*, February 5, 1905.

Chapter Two

1. In 1877 the townsfolk of Drammen, Wisconsin, named their village after the place of their ancestors in Norway.

2. Named for real estate developer Henry Austin, the suburb was annexed into the city of Chicago in 1899.

3. *LaPorte Daily Herald*, May 7, 1908. Founded in 1840 by Joseph Lomax, the *Herald* was a Republican paper in its political sympathies. Its principal competitor, the Democratic-leaning *LaPorte Argus*, published its first paper on November 5, 1836.

4. *Chicago Tribune*, May 7, 1908.

5. Letter from Torger Størseth of Selbu, Norway, to Bruce Johnson of the LaPorte County Historical Society, April 1, 2002. Størseth conducted independent genealogical research on the origins of the Belle Gunness family on behalf of the Historical Society and Anne Vestby, who produced a 2006 documentary for Norwegian television about the crimes of Belle. Størseth suggests that Sorensen and Gunness were acquainted with one another through the Sons of Norway lodge activities in Wicker Park, adjacent to the Logan Square community of Chicago, although contemporary newspaper accounts tell us that the Wicker Park Chapter No. 121 of the Independent Order of Mutual Aid was affiliated with the trade union that Mads paid dues to, not the Sons of Norway. It is probable that the Sorensens were also active in the Sons of Norway chapter, however. In the heyday of ethnic societies, membership was of paramount importance for immigrants navigating their way in the new country. Based in Minneapolis and founded in the 1870s by American-born Norwegians whose roots can be traced to a region near Trondheim, where Belle Gunness was born, the Sons of Norway—with more than 75,000 members and 420 local lodges—is the largest Norwegian organization outside of Europe. The organization is still active and viable today, with seven lodges in Chicago and the suburbs, although like other European ethnic fraternal societies, it has suffered a steady erosion of membership through the years due to the passing of older generations and assimilation of younger members into mainstream American life.

6. Alma Street was later renamed La Trobe Street. Chicago city streets were renumbered in 1909, and 620 Alma became 827 North La Trobe.

7. *Chicago American,* May 8, 1908.

8. *Chicago Tribune*, May 7, 1908.

9. *Chicago Daily News*, May 7, 1908.

10. Ibid.

11. Herman F. Schuettler (1861–1918) rose from the rank of patrolman to superintendent of the Chicago Police Department during a brilliant 35-year career spanning the unrest of the Haymarket riot era of the late 1880s up through the end of World War I. Born in Chicago near the old North Side German quarter of the city, Schuettler gained fame during the anarchist troubles of 1886. He arrested and took down bomb maker Louis Lingg after a violent struggle. He was promoted to the rank of captain in 1890 after helping solve the 1889 murder of Dr. Patrick Cronin, an Irish nationalist killed by members of the Clan na Gael, a violent splinter group of the Fenian brotherhood dedicated to the overthrow of British rule in Ireland. Schuettler, one of the finest detectives in the department, was involved in the investigation of nearly every famous Chicago murder of the day, including the 1898 arrest of Adolph Luetgert, the "sausage vat" killer who chopped up his wife and tossed her into a vat of boiling sausage in his factory. Promoted to assistant chief of police in 1904, Schuettler's famed "flying squad" of detectives, who roamed the city police districts, zealously closed down illegal poolrooms and gambling operations citywide during a 10-year period, 1900–1910. Schuettler was scrupulously honest, and there was never a hint of scandal attached to his name—a remarkable achievement given the unsavory reputation for corruption and brutality plaguing this department for so many decades. A large, rawboned man with a quiet disposition, he was named superintendent by Mayor William Hale Thompson on January 10, 1917, during a tumultuous period of scandal and strife and took it upon himself to initiate many internal reforms before suffering a nervous breakdown that sidelined him up until the moment of death on August 22, 1918. "Old Herm died in harness" it was said by the veteran rank and file at the time—a supreme compliment to an outstanding police professional and a man of high integrity.

12. *Chicago Tribune* May 8, 1908.

13. Ibid.

14. Ibid.

15. *LaPorte Daily Herald*, May 7, 1908.

16. *Chicago Record-Herald*, May 9, 1908.

17. Between 1865 and 1914, 500 Norwegian language newspapers were launched in the U.S. John Anderson, founder and publisher of the *Skandinaven,* published the paper for Norwegians, Swedes, and Danes from his Chicago plant as a weekly, then later as a tri-weekly edition. The newspaper was issued continuously from 1866 to 1941. The *Decorah-Posten,* founded in Iowa in 1874, and the *Minneapolis Tidende* were two other influential Norwegian news journals spanning the news of the Midwest and the Great Plains. The *Tidende* was launched in 1887 and ceased publication in 1937. Both the *Skandinaven* and the *Tidende* were absorbed by the *Decorah-Posten* by 1941. All of these publications scrupulously avoided politics, instead placing attention on local events, the serialization of popular literature, and items of current interests aimed at family tastes and interests. See Odd S. Lovoll, "The Decorah Posten: Story of an Immigrant Newspaper," *Norwegian-American Studies*, vol. 27, p.77. The James Simon and Patricia Finney Center for Research Libraries in Quebec, Canada, has archived a collection of 97 ethnic Scandinavian newspapers.

18. *Chicago American*, May 8, 1908.

19. Jasper Packard, *History of La Porte County, Indiana, and Its Townships, Towns and Cities* (LaPorte, IN: S. E. Taylor & Company, 1876).

20. Ibid.

21. From Josiah Cheney, "*The Story about Belle Gunness*" (unpublished, undated pamphlet, LaPorte County Historical Society), 3.

22. *Chicago Record-Herald*, May 10, 1908.

23. There are varying opinions among community historians concerning Walker's role in building the house and his daughter's ownership of the property. A *Chicago Daily News* reporter scoured the records of the LaPorte County Abstract Company, turning up the names of Adam Polke and August Drebing in a chain of ownership. See the *Daily News*, May 7, 1908. A curator at the LaPorte County Historical Society Museum told the author that Josiah Cheney, publisher of the *LaPorte Argus*, built the home, but that seems rather unlikely in light of the contemporary account in the *Daily News*.

24. *Chicago American*, May 8, 1908. Interview with an old-timer with first-hand recollections.

25. In her book *The Mistress of Murder Hill*, author Sylvia Shepherd states that Eddy returned to Chicago and committed suicide. See Sylvia Shepherd, *The Mistress of Murder Hill: The Serial Killings of Belle Gunness* (Indiana: First Books Library, 2001), 17.

26. *Chicago American*, May 8, 1908.

Chapter Three

1. *Chicago American,* February 23, 1906.

2. Johann Hoch, "How I Married 50 Wives and What Became of Them," *American Magazine: Supplement to the Chicago Sunday American,* July 23, 1905. The interview was granted to the *American* while Hoch was on death row at the Cook County Jail hoping for a reprieve from the governor and the state pardons board. It is the only extended interview given by the bigamist-murderer, and it is a remarkably revealing and candid confession. However, Hoch spun so many lies and half-truths that his reminiscences of his life must be viewed with the greatest skepticism.

3. Ibid.

4. *Chicago Tribune*, February 22, 1906.

5. Hoch, "How I Married 50 Wives."

6. Information concerning Hoch's family origins was supplied to the Rev. Herman C.A. Haas of Wheeling, West Virginia, by Herr Rung, prosecuting attorney of Mainz, in November 1898. His letter to Rev. Haas was reprinted in A.J. Schutzer's article, "The Lady Killer," *American Heritage Magazine*, October 1964.

7. *Chicago Tribune*, February 4, 1905.

8. Hoch, "How I Married 50 Wives."

9. Ibid.

10. Ibid.

11. Ibid.

12. *Chicago Journal*, February 16, 1905.

13. Hoch, "How I Married 50 Wives."

14. Ibid.

15. Hoch was the married name of Caroline Hoch of Wheeling, West Virginia, a widow he married and murdered in 1895.

16. *Chicago Tribune*, January 28, 1905.

17. *Chicago Tribune*, February 4, 1905.

18. *New York Herald*, February 3, 1905.

19. Hoch, "How I Married 50 Wives."

20. Ibid.

21. Ibid.

22. *Chicago Journal*, February 3, 1905; *Chicago Inter-Ocean*, February 22, 1906. A search of passenger lists of the North German line between 1888 and 1895 failed to turn up the name Jacob Schmidt or Johann Hoch. Newspaper reports concerning his arrival in the U.S. are contradictory: the *Inter-Ocean* and the *Tribune* assert that Hoch arrived on these shores in 1894–1895, and if that is true, it is hard to imagine anyone, let alone Hoch who always operated on the fringes, carrying out that many polygamous murder schemes in so many places in so short a period of time.

23. *Chicago Journal*, February 11, 1905.

Chapter Four

1. For a nineteenth-century woman, the addition of a baby into a prudish, closely knit community of high moral tone without the usual announcements accompanied by the period of normal maternal confinement struck everyone as anomalous and raised many disturbing questions that would eventually come back to haunt the West Side neighborhood for years to come. Belle's grandfather was Peder Paulsen Garberg, born 1784, and her grandmother Marit Johnsdatter Dyrdal was born a year later. Belle's oldest brother, Peder, born September 11, 1843, took the name Peder Moen after the small town of Moen in Nordland, a region of Norway. Many of the family descendents go by that name today. Genealogical information is courtesy of Torger Størseth.

2. "*The Story of the Belle Gunness Murder Farm*," unpublished document drawn from the 1908 volume *The Gunness Mystery* by Thompson & Thomas, published in Chicago (on file in the LaPorte County Historical Society, LaPorte, IN). Salzer and Tyler provided a historical footnote and added it to this document in 1982.

3. Janet Langlois, *Belle Gunness: The Lady Bluebeard* (Bloomington, IN: Indiana University Press, 1985), 2.

4. Ibid.

5. Betty Alt and Sandra Wells, *Wicked Women: Black Widows, Child Killers and Other Women in Crime* (Boulder, CO: Paladin Press, 2000), 8.

6. Brooklyn-born psychologist Abraham Harold Maslow (1908–1970) is considered to be the father of the humanistic psychology movement. Maslow was a professor at Brandeis University from 1951 to 1969 and later was a resident fellow of the Laughlin Institution in California. See Abraham Maslow, "A Theory of Human Motivation," *Psychological Review* (50: 4), 370–96.

7. Micki Pistorius, *Fatal Females: Women Who Kill* (New York: Penguin Global, 2005). The author discusses 50 documented cases of South African female killers according to the motives and natures of their crimes.

8. It seems curious that the two sisters should share the same name. In another account, the older sister in Chicago is listed as Olina; however, Torger Størseth maintains that Olina was an unmarried mother who never left Norway.

9. Built in 1852 by the Thomas Wingate Company in England, the *Tasso* was originally christened the *Scandinavian*. In 1886, the ship ran aground at the mouth of the Bømlofjord on the way to Hull and was scuttled.

10. *Chicago Journal*, June 1, 1908.

11. The Independent Evangelical Lutheran Bethania Congregation was organized in 1878 by Pastor John Z. Torgerson, who had previously been affiliated with the Trinity Lutheran Church and Eielsen Synod congregation, then located on the West Side at Grand Avenue and Peoria (387 W. Grand). Although catering to the large Norwegian immigrant community located along the Near Northwest Side Milwaukee Avenue corridor, the congregation conducted both English and Norwegian services. Rev. Torgerson was pastor from 1878 to 1905. See the Archives of the Evangelical Lutheran Church in America at <http://www2.elca.org/archives/chicagochurches/bethania.html>.

12. *Lakeside Annual Directories: 1895 and 1900* (Chicago, IL: The Chicago Directory Company). The 1895 directory lists Mad Sorensen at this address and his employment as a carpenter. In 1900, the *Directory* confirmed his address at 620 Alma Street. Unless a woman was a widow or single, the city directories only included the names of men in the A–Z listings.

13. *Chicago Daily News*, May 7, 1908.

14. *Chicago Journal*, May 11, 1908.

15. The *Lakeside Directory* lists the business as the Sorensen-Christensen Grocery at 119 N. Humboldt.

16. *Chicago Daily News*, May 11, 1908.

17. Ibid.

18. *Chicago American*, May 8, 1908.

19. *Chicago Daily News*, May 11, 1908.

Chapter Five

1. *Chicago Record*, August 21, 1895.

2. "Fired for a Purpose," *Chicago Tribune*, August 20, 1895.

3. Ibid.

4. In his 1975 book *Torture Doctor*, author David Franke cites Holmes's explanation of Hatch as a prospective suitor of Minnie Williams in Holmes's death row memoir titled *Holmes' Own Story*. See David Franke, *Torture Doctor* (New York: Hawthorn Books, 1975), 121.

5. *Chicago Tribune*, November 20, 1894.

6. The trafficking in human cadavers was so out of hand that by the 1870s, the families of the deceased were purchasing specially manufactured land mines to place in the ground near the headstone to maim or kill body snatchers.

7. *Chicago Tribune*, November 22, 1894.

8. Ibid.

9. *Chicago Record*, July 25, 1895.

10. *Chicago Tribune*, August 1, 1895.

11. Jeptha Howe was indicted for fraud but was eventually acquitted of wrongdoing in the Holmes insurance swindle. He went on to a long career in Republican politics in St. Louis, although his business affairs were dubious. He was the front man for a St. Louis company interested in establishing a 50-year streetcar monopoly that would utilize the bridges spanning the Mississippi River into Illinois. William Lorimer, Republican Party boss in Illinois who was censured and removed from his U.S. Senate seat for taking bribes, was a co-conspirator in this scheme. See the *Chicago Tribune*, June 13, 1914, and the *St. Louis Post Dispatch*, June 13, 1914.

12. Marion Hedgepeth had a long criminal record in Missouri, California, Nebraska, Iowa, and other Western states. He was shot and killed by a Chicago policeman on New Year's Eve 1910 while holding up a saloon on West Sixteenth Street. *Kansas City Times*, January 4, 1910.

13. Frank Cipriani, "Murder Castle!" *Chicago Tribune*, March 21, 1937.

14. "Autobiography of an Arch Murderer," *Chicago Tribune*, April 11, 1896.

15. *Chicago Tribune*, May 7, 1896.

16. Ibid.

17. *Chicago Tribune*, July 29, 1895.

18. *Chicago Tribune*, August 2, 1895.

19. *Chicago Record*, July 31, 1895.

Chapter Six

1. *New York DailyTribune*, May 10, 1908.

2. *Chicago Tribune*, May 8, 1908.

3. Langlois, *The Lady Bluebeard*, 61.

4. Ibid.

5. Often called the "American George Louis Du Maurier"(the famed illustrator for *London Punch* in the 1880s whose illustrations mirrored contemporary social mores), artist and illustrator Charles Dana Gibson (1867–1944) created the Gibson Girl in 1895, who was modeled after his wife, Irene Langhorne, and her sister Nancy Astor. The popular image appeared in nearly every leading American publication up through World War I.

6. Quoted in Langlois, *The Lady Bluebeard*, 56–57. The quotation is actually drawn from the 1955 published volume authored by Lillian de la Torre, titled *The Truth about Belle Gunness*.

7. Langlois, *The Lady Bluebeard*, 57.

8. *Chicago Journal*, May 13, 1908.

9. *Chicago Tribune*, May 10, 1908.

10. See the *LaPorte Argus-Bulletin*, May 8, 1908.

11. *Chicago American*, May 6, 1908.

12. *New York Daily Tribune*, May 10, 1908.

13. Deposition of witness Chris Christofferson as told to the coroner of LaPorte County, Indiana. Exhibit C, May 26, 1908. LaPorte County Historical Society Museum.

14. Ibid.

15. Deposition of witness Martin Gurholt as told to the coroner of LaPorte County, Indiana. Exhibit B, May 25, 1908. LaPorte County Historical Society Museum.

16. *Chicago American*, May 22, 1908. Also the *Chicago Tribune*, May 9, 1908.

17. *Chicago Tribune*, May 10, 1908.

Chapter Seven

1. *Chicago American,*February 1, 1905.

2. *Chicago Tribune*, January 25, 1905.

3. "Hoch Glories in Marital Record," *Chicago Tribune*, February 4, 1905.

4. Ibid.

5. *Chicago American*, January 23, 1905.

6. *Chicago Journal*, January 25, 1905.

7. Ibid.

8. *Chicago Tribune*, January 26, 1905.

9. Ibid.

10. Major abdominal surgery in West Virginia was first performed in April 1882 at Wheeling Hospital by Dr. Gregory Ackerman, a man of renown in the medical profession.

11. A.L. Schutzer, "The Lady Killer," *American Heritage Magazine* 15 (October 1964): 36–39, 91–94. The author of this article reviewed the known facts and essential case history of Johann Hoch, with particular focus on the West Virginia aspects of Hoch's career. Schutzer made several mistakes in his chronology of events and the precise dates of the numerous Hoch marriages, but that's understandable as newspaper reporters working on deadlines were left scratching their heads in wonderment as they attempted to sift through and sort out the bewildering maze of women coming forward who claimed to have married Hoch. See also the *Wheeling Register*, June 15, 1895; July 4, 1895.

12. Information about Caroline Miller Hoch-Huff is contained in an online report authored by Wheeling, West Virginia, genealogist Linda Cunningham Fluharty titled "Caroline Miller Hoch Huff: Victim of a Serial Killer," at <http://www.lindapages.com/wags-ohio/carolinehoch.htm> Fluharty contends that Caroline was born in Germany, and the correct spelling of her first name was Karoline.

13. The account was provided by Bellaire resident Conrad Fitschle and reported in the *Wheeling Register*, July 14, 1895. See also Schutzer, "The Lady Killer," 37.

Chapter Eight

1. *Chicago American*, May 28, 1908 and the *Chicago Tribune*, June 3, 1908. See also Shepherd, *The Mistress of Murder Hill*, 128–32. Julius Truelson told LaPorte County Sheriff Albert Smutzer that he had met up with Belle in Chicago's Sherman House Hotel in 1904 in response to one of her matrimonial ads. According to his account, he accompanied Belle back to LaPorte but was told that he was too young and too poor to be of interest to her. Truelson was married to Mae O'Reilly on August 4, 1904, at St. Peter's Church in Albany, New York, but abandoned his bride after a two-week honeymoon, ran off, and joined the navy. The military was not to his liking, so he deserted the navy but was arrested a short time later and incarcerated. Truelson said he traveled to the Gunness farm during Christmas 1906 and helped Lamphere bury Jennie Olsen, but Truelson's story fell apart after it was discovered that Lamphere did not begin his term of employment until 1907. While all agreed that Truelson's imagination was vivid, they were also intrigued by his remarkable knowledge of the crimes and details that were never published.

2. *Chicago Journal*, June 1, 1908.

3. *Chicago Tribune*, May 14, 1961.

4. *New York Times*, May 7, 1908.

5. *New York Daily Tribune*, May 8, 1908.

6. Deposition of witness Jens G. Render as told to the coroner of LaPorte County, Indiana. Exhibit C, May 19, 1908. LaPorte County Historical Society Museum.

7. *New York Daily Tribune*, May 8, 1908.

8. Deposition of witness Mat Budsberg as told to the coroner of LaPorte County, Indiana. Exhibit B, May 7, 1908. LaPorte County Historical Society Museum.

9. *Chicago Tribune*, May 8, 1908.

10. Ray Lamphere told investigators that Belle used chloroform, an organic, sweet tasting compound, to subdue her victims. Gunness had ordered Lamphere to go into town to purchase the substance, but he refused. According to Lamphere's sworn statements, victim Andrew Helgelein had told Belle that chloroform was the best way of killing a sick hog on the property.

11. *Chicago Journal*, May 8, 1908.

12. *Chicago Journal*, May 7, 1908.

13. *Chicago Journal*, November 12, 1908.

14. *Chicago Journal*, May 8, 1908.

Chapter Nine

1. Hoch, "How I Married 50 Wives." Gold was discovered in Cripple Creek in 1891 by Robert "Bob" Miller Womack, a cowboy and part-time prospector. The discovery of gold transformed a sleepy little ranching community into one of the world's richest gold camps. By 1893, the population of the town had swelled from 500 to 10,000 people. The veracity of Hoch's encounter with the cheating miners is impossible to verify.

2. Thomas Samuel Duke, *Celebrated Criminal Cases of America* (San Francisco: The James H. Barry Co., 1910), 435. This "authorized" memoir was written by a former captain of police in San Francisco.

3. Dr. Francis W. McNamara, "Drama in the Death House: The Crimes of Johann Hoch the Bluebeard," *Chicago Tribune*, December 13, 1936.

4. "Fowler after Luke Colleran," *Chicago Tribune*, February 14, 1901. Chief Colleran, a member of the department from 1883–1901, was removed from his duties and ousted from the force by the Civil Service Commission on November 20, 1901, for "conduct unbecoming"—destroying evidence and protecting a notorious confidence man named Harry Featherstone.

5. *Chicago Tribune*, January 21, 1899. At that time, embalming fluid typically contained arsenic—but there were exceptions, as Hoch soon found out.

6. *Duluth News-Tribune*, February 7, 1905.

7. *Chicago American*, February 9, 1905.

8. Hoch, "How I Married 50 Wives"; and "Murder: Will it Always Out?" (no by-line) *Chicago Tribune*, November 9, 1913.

9. Johann Hoch to Johanna Reichel, February 12, 1904. Reprinted in the *Chicago American*, July 23, 1905.

10. Supreme Court of Illinois, *Hoch vs. The People of Illinois*, October 1905 Term. Transcript of Appeal, 11–12.

11. Ibid., 15.

12. Ibid.

13. Ibid., 19.

14. Ibid., 53.

15. Ibid.

16. Ibid. This conversation is repeated verbatim from the Illinois Supreme Court transcript, *Hoch vs. The People of Illinois*.

17. "Enacts a Scene of Hoch's Life," *Chicago Tribune*, May 3, 1905.

18. *Chicago Tribune*, February 11, 1905.

Chapter Ten

1. *Chicago Journal*, May 12, 1908. The *Chicago Sunday Record-Herald* echoed that feeling. "In the palmist days of the Holmes investigation, the 'Castle' murderer never was accused of killing more than thirty-five people. Johann Hoch's victims were variously estimated up to the neighborhood of thirty but the actual killings laid at his door, all of which were done with a certain nicety that did not disturb the sensibilities of an aesthetic lady killer, numbered probably eight. It is safe to say however that in the light of the disclosures of the past few days, Mrs. Belle Gunness, the LaPorte widow has eclipsed the record of the prairie vixen of Kansas [Kate Bender] and that she undoubtedly holds the palm as the most extensive slayer, man or woman, of the age."

2. "Witnesses Tell of Ray Lamphere Threats," *LaPorte Daily Herald*, November 17, 1908.

3. *The Gunness Story*, LaPorte County Historical Society, 16.

4. Belle Gunness to Andrew Helgelein. Letters in the archives of the LaPorte County Historical Society.

5. Belle Gunness to Asle Helgelein, March 27, 1908. Letter in the archives of the LaPorte County Historical Society.

6. "Did the Woman Flee?" *Chicago Daily News*, May 8, 1908.

7. *Chicago Tribune*, May 7, 1908.

8. Belle Gunness to Asle Helgelein, April 24, 1908. Letter in the archives of the LaPorte County Historical Society.

9. *New York Daily Tribune*, May 9, 1908.

10. *The Gunness Story*, LaPorte County Historical Society, 8.

11. *Chicago Journal*, May 13, 1908.

12. The Norwegian Lutheran Children's Home Society refused to accept the terms of the will or any of Belle's money. Incorporated in September 1897, the children's home opened at Irving Park Road and North 58th Avenue in 1899. On December 28, 1907, a devastating fire swept through the upper floors of the building, driving sixty children into the street. No one was injured in the conflagration, but an urgent appeal went out to the Norwegian community to raise funds in order to relocate the youngsters to Canfield Road in the Edison Park community on Chicago's Far Northwest Side, where a new facility was planned. Undoubtedly this appeal reached Belle Gunness directly through the pages of the *Skandinaven* newspaper, which actively promoted the fund-raising campaign, a campaign that touched her conscience—what little conscience she had left. In the summer of 1910, the building was dedicated, and seventy children took occupancy. The Lutheran Social Services closed the institution in the 1990s after eight decades of service. The complex was torn down and replaced with a subdivision of private homes. See Millie Hendricksen, *History of the Norwegian Lutheran Children's Home Society, Edison Park, Chicago, Illinois, 1896–1936* (Chicago: Norwegian Lutheran Children's Home Society, 1936), 13–16.

13. "Lair of Woman a Slaughter House," *Chicago Tribune*, May 6, 1908.

14. Liz Smith, according to published accounts, was once the mistress of several professional LaPorte men before settling into a life of squalor in a run-down street known as Paradise Row or Clabber Alley; the latter refers to her Irish neighbors who clabbered cream and potatoes. In her later years, Smith was a recluse and the town eccentric whom some people believed to be a witch. See Langlois, *The Lady Bluebeard*, 41–44.

15. *Chicago Tribune*, April 29, 1908.

16. *LaPorte Argus-Bulletin*, April 29, 1908.

17. *New York Daily Tribune*, May 10, 1908.

18. *Chicago Tribune*, November 20, 1908.

19. *Chicago American*, May 6, 1908.

20. *Chicago Tribune*, May 6, 1908.

21. *Chicago American*, May 8, 1908.

22. Lemuel Darrow (1867–1935), was the Mayor of LaPorte from 1898 to 1914 and again in 1934 at the time of his death. Born in Byron, Indiana, six miles east of LaPorte, Darrow built an electric railway from LaPorte to Michigan City during his career in public life. Despite being convicted of subornation of perjury by a jury in the Elkhart Circuit Court and disbarred from practicing law in Indiana, he was elected mayor of LaPorte for the fourth time on November 2, 1912, defeating Republican Julius Travis by a scant 262 votes. Regarding the illegal Porter racetrack, Indiana Governor Thomas Marshall ordered in the state militia at South Bend to close it down in 1912. See the *Chicago Tribune*, October 22, 1912. A biographical sketch of Darrow appears in E.D. Daniels, ed., *The Twentieth Century History and Biographical Record of LaPorte County, Indiana* (New York: The Lewis Publishing Company, 1904), and Shepherd, *The Mistress of Murder Hill*, 96–100.

23. *Chicago Tribune*, May 7, 1908.

24. "Ex-Sheriff Smutzer Bares Inside of Gunness Case," *LaPorte Herald-Argus*, May 11, 1934.

25. *Chicago American*, May 6, 1908.

26. "Belle Gunness: Wholesale Murderer?" *The Sunday-Record Herald*, May 10, 1908.

Chapter Eleven

1. "Dunne Managers Tax the Police," *Chicago Tribune*, February 11, 1907.

2. *Chicago American*, January 21, 1905.

3. Peter Hoffman (1863–1948) began his career in politics in 1898 after toiling in the grocery business. He was later appointed chief clerk for Northwestern Railroad before entering public life. He served as Cook County Coroner from 1904 to 1922 and was elected Cook County Sheriff in 1922. In 1925 he was convicted of contempt of court and sentenced to serve 30 days in his own jail for allowing furloughs and other special considerations to two bootleggers, Terry Druggan and Frankie Lake. He served in his official capacity all the while he was incarcerated. *The Front Page* debuted on Broadway in August 1928 and ran for 281 performances before being made into a hit motion picture in 1931.

4. *Chicago American*, January 21, 1905.

5. "Hoch Slew 20 Wives Police Declare," *Chicago American*, January 23, 1905.

6. George Murray, *The Madhouse on Madison Street* (Chicago: The Follett Company, 1965), 4–9. This is an excellent account of the history of the Hearst enterprise in Chicago even though the author, a veteran reporter, did not join the editorial staff of the paper until 1933.

7. Promoted to the captaincy of the South Chicago Station in 1907 and given command of the Maxwell Street Station several years later, Storen and two sergeants under his command were indicted in January 1915 on a charge of conspiracy to obstruct justice by failing to arrest thieves. Specifically, he was accused of accepting protection money from the "million dollar burglar trust"—a gang of Jewish criminals preying on Hassidic shopkeepers and businessmen on the West Side. Storen was

discharged "for the good of the service," a euphemistic phrase commonly used by the department when an officer was let go for egregious acts of corruption. See the *Chicago Tribune*, January 27, 1915 for an overview of the case.

8. *Chicago American*, January 24, 1905.

9. Émile *Gaboriau* (1832–1873) was a French writer, novelist, journalist, and pioneer of modern detective fiction. He was the author of *Les Esclaves de Paris*, *L'Affaire Lerouge*, and other novels featuring Mounsier Lecoq, master of disguise and deduction whose character was based on the real-life thief-turned-policeman and master detective, the famed François Vidocq (1775–1857).

10. *Chicago American*, February 13, 1905. Transcript of interview with Slyter printed in its entirety

11. Ibid. See also the *Chicago Journal*, February 13, 1905.

12. *Chicago Journal*, February 14, 1905.

13. Lewis G. Thombs, a married man with a wife and child, was hanged inside the Cook County Jail on August 8, 1902, after asserting his innocence of the crime. Thombs was the caretaker of the vessel *Peerless*. Through an employment agency he had hired Carrie Larson, a young Swedish domestic, to work as a cook on board the ship. But when the girl refused his sexual advances the first night on the job, he strangled her to death in the kitchen. Robert Keissig, a roustabout, was working on the *Peerless* on the night of the murder. Thombs ordered him to burn the girl's clothing and help him toss the body into the ice choked river. Keissig complied with the directive, but, torn by a guilty conscience, he confessed what he had done to his sister and a passenger who was sleeping in his cabin when the crime was committed. Keissig's testimony sent Thombs to the gallows. however, there was no evidence that Thombs was ever a bigamist, but he had a prior arrest for abducting and molesting an 11-year-old girl not long after his marriage in 1899. See the *Chicago TTribune*, January 11, 1902; April 1, 1902; and August 9, 1902.

14. *Chicago Tribune*, January 30, 1905.

15. Professor Walter Stanley Haines (1850–1923) was the son of a former Chicago mayor, John C. Haines. In a busy 50-year career, Walter Haines was called upon to examine evidence in many noteworthy Chicago criminal trials, including one dating back to the 1880s when he compared and contrasted bomb fragments that killed seven Chicago police officers in the Haymarket riot of May 4, 1886, with devices manufactured by defendant Louis Lingg, one of seven men on trial for capital murder. In 1889, he was asked to evaluate dried blood samples from the remains of Dr. Patrick Cronin, who had been murdered by Irish nationalists during an internal power struggle between members of the Fenian brotherhood.

16. *Chicago Tribune*, January 31, 1905.

17. "Woman Tells Story of Betraying Hoch," *Chicago American*, January 31, 1905.

18. *New York Herald*, February 5, 1905.

19. *New York Post*, January 31, 1905; *New York Herald*, February 2, 1905.

20. *New York Herald*, February 2, 1905.

21. *Chicago American*, February 2, 1905.

22. *Chicago Tribune*, February 1, 1905.

23. "The Bluebeard of Chicago Dies at the End of a Rope," *Chicago Tribune*, January 7, 1954.

24. *Chicago American*, February 4, 1905.

25. *New York Times*, February 1, 1905.

26. *Chicago Tribune*, February 5, 1905.

27. *Chicago Tribune,* February 9, 1905.

28. *Chicago American,* February 10, 1905.

29. Francis O'Neill (1848–1936) was appointed Police Superintendent in August 1901 by Mayor Carter Harrison II, and he served until August 1905. Reappointed twice, he was the longest serving chief up until 1905. O'Neill was an authority on Irish folk music who rescued and preserved hundreds of songs that would have otherwise disappeared. His musical accomplishments were recognized in the U.S. and abroad. His collection of music was later donated to Notre Dame University. Harry Olson (1867–1936) was a towering figure in Chicago jurisprudence. Appointed to the state's attorney's office in 1896, he served as the first Chief Justice of the Municipal Court from 1906 to 1930. The system he helped put in place was copied by 40 other U.S. municipalities. Twice a mayoral candidate on the Republican ticket in 1915 and 1919, Olson was a veteran of many famous Chicago criminal trials of the early twentieth century.

30. *Chicago Journal,* February 13, 1905. Confrontation between Hoch and his accusers reprinted verbatim.

31. *Chicago American,* February 13, 1905.

32. *Chicago Journal,* February 13, 1905.

33. Ibid.

34. *Chicago Journal,* February 15, 1905.

35. *Chicago Tribune,* March 5, 1905.

36. Dr. Francis W. McNamara, "Drama in the Death House: The Crimes of Johann Hoch the Bluebeard," *Chicago Tribune,* December 13, 1936. Joe Weber and Lew Fields were a vaudeville duo popular at the turn of the twentieth century. They specialized in performing comedic "dialect" routines—satiric and exaggerated lampooning of ethnic customs and accents, most notably German and Yiddish.

37. "Police Make Hoch Happy," *Chicago Tribune,* February 12, 1905.

38. Ibid.

Chapter Twelve

1. *Chicago Tribune,* May 8, 1908. Canadian-born Edwin Sims (1870–1948) served as U.S. Attorney for the Northern District of Illinois from 1906 to 1911. Sims built a strong reputation as a resolute fighter against organized prostitution, segregated vice districts, and white slavery rings.

2. *Chicago Tribune,* May 9, 1908.

3. Langlois, *The Lady Bluebeard,* 31.

4. The jail, which opened in 1907, was built of Bedford limestone approximately where the Foster and DeGarmo livery barn had stood. The jail was demolished before the eight million dollar LaPorte County Annex and Security Complex was completed in 1977.

5. Herman "Wirt" Worden (1875–1943) was a prominent Indiana attorney and later a judge in the LaPorte Circuit Court.

6. Speech of Wirt Worden, December 7, 1938. Excerpted from *The Gunness Story* (LaPorte County Historical Society, undated pamphlet), 12.

7. *Chicago American,* November 7, 1908; *LaPorte Daily Herald,* November 5, 1908.

8. *LaPorte Daily Herald,* November 12, 1908.

9. *LaPorte Daily Herald,* November 12, 1908; *Chicago American,* November 12, 1908.

10. "Mrs. Gunness Plotted to End Life of Joseph Maxson," *LaPorte Argus-Bulletin*, November 18, 1908.

11. Ibid.

12. Ibid.

13. Ibid.

14. *Chicago Tribune*, November 26, 1908.

15. *LaPorte Daily Herald*, November 27, 1908.

16. Built in 1860, the Indiana State Penitentiary at Michigan City is best known for the four-year confinement of its most famous inmate—bank robber John Dillinger, who was paroled on May 22, 1933.

17. *LaPorte Argus-Bulletin*, November 20, 1908.

18. William H. Blodgett, "Gunness Story as Told by Blodgett," *LaPorte Daily Herald-Argus*, July 23, 1930. Blodgett, staff correspondent of the *Indianapolis Star*, covered the Lamphere trial in 1908. His 1924 retrospective was published six years later in the *Herald-Argus*, a title that reflected the merger of the two LaPorte newspapers.

19. *The Gunness Story* (LaPorte County Historical Society, undated pamphlet), 14.

20. Interview with Daniel Hutson and Frederick Lambright in the *Chicago American*, November 9, 1908.

21. Ibid.

Chapter Thirteen

1. "Hoch's Defense to be Insanity," *Chicago Tribune*, February 13, 1905.

2. With $30 in his pocket, Adolph Luetgert emigrated to the U.S. in 1865. He worked as a tanner in Chicago for a dozen years before starting his North Side sausage making business in 1879. Luetgert was married twice. His first wife, Caroline Roepke, passed away in 1877 unexpectedly while in confinement awaiting childbirth. But within a year he was married to Louisa Becknesse, a much younger woman who bore him four children. Rumors of violent quarrels, money problems, and Adolph's courting of Christine Feldt, a rich widow whom he counted on to help him pay off his creditors, made the rounds of the neighborhood. Louisa vanished on May 1, 1897. Luetgert told the children that their mother had gone to Wisconsin to visit her sister. Inspector Herman Schuettler's detective detail found four small human bones and two gold rings in the vat where the sausage was boiled. One of the rings bore the initials L.L., and both likely had belonged to Louisa. The fiend had thrown her body into a rendering vat, one of six furnaces in the basement containing powerful potash acid, and he completed the work by casting the body into an intense fire. Luetgert was prosecuted by Charles Deneen, a future Illinois governor who considered Hoch's appeal for commutation of his sentence. The first trial resulted in a hung jury on October 21, 1897. Luetgert was retried a month later on November 26. This time the jury was unanimous, and he was found guilty and sentenced to life in prison. Life in prison proved to be a short sentence. Luetgert died in the Joliet Penitentiary just two years later—protesting his guilt all the way to the end and swearing that Louisa would come back to clear his name. She never did. For the best account of the Luetgert case, see Robert Loerzel, *Alchemy of Bones: Chicago's Luetgert Murder Case of 1897* (Urbana: University of Illinois Press, 2007).

3. When George Kersten (1853–1934) retired from the bench in 1926, his career record disclosed that he had the fewest reversals of any sitting judge in Chicago at that

time. Appointed a justice of the peace in 1883 by Mayor Harrison, his close friend and political sponsor, Kersten served for a time as a police magistrate in the Chicago Avenue station, which was characterized by a carnival-like atmosphere in which prosecutors, bailiffs, and defense attorneys kept their snuffboxes close at hand and freely imbibed during proceedings. Kersten presided over some of the most famous criminal proceedings of his era, including the celebrated 1903 "Car Barn Bandits" case involving four young felons engaged in a robbery-murder spree. In 1914 Kerten was appointed chief justice of the criminal court. A year later he presided over Chicago's first divorce court. He was credited with simplifying the criminal statutes, which culminated in the passage of a new civil practice act and simplification of the criminal code. A product of the Chicago Public School system, Kersten studied at Standau and Wiedlinger's German-American Institute. A three-member panel was summoned to investigate the ailing jurist's mental condition. Kersten was declared legally insane after exhibiting irrational behavior in his courtroom, including driving a clerk from the building and berating Assistant State's Attorney William McSwiggin in an unprofessional manner. Forced to step down, he was confined to his home up until his death from pneumonia nine years later. See the *New York Times*, February 8, 1934, and the *Chicago Tribune* for August 4, 1925, and February 9, 1934.

4. *Chicago American*, April 18, 1905.

5. *Chicago American*, April 20, 1905.

6. Ibid.

7. Ibid.

8. *Chicago Journal*, May 10, 1906.

9. *Chicago Tribune*, May 10, 1905.

10. *Chicago Tribune*, May 4, 1905.

11. *Chicago Chronicle*, May 13, 1905.

12. Dr. Kolischer served as President of the American Congress of Rehabilitative Medicine (ACRM) from 1932 to 1933. He was on the staff at the Mt. Sinai and Michael Reese Hospitals in Chicago at the time of his appointment.

13. *Chicago Journal*, May 16, 1905.

14. *Chicago Journal*, May 17, 1905.

15. *Chicago Journal*, May 18, 1905.

16. John Henry Cardinal Newman (1801–1890) converted from the Anglican faith to Roman Catholicism and was the first rector of the Catholic University in Dublin. He was later made a cardinal by Pope Leo XIII in 1879. While on a trip to the Mediterranean in 1832, he wrote "Lead, Kindly Light" and other hymns.

17. *Chicago Journal*, May 18, 1905.

18. *Chicago Tribune*, May 18, 1905.

19. *Chicago Journal*, May 19, 1905.

20. *Chicago Post*, May 19, 1905.

21. *Chicago Tribune, Chicago Journal, Chicago Post, Chicago Chronicle, Chicago Inter-Ocean, Chicago Record-Herald*, May 19, 1905.

22. *Chicago Tribune*, May 19, 1905.

23. The Briggs murder conviction was overturned by the U.S. Supreme Court, and the second trial in April 1906 resulted in acquittal.

24. "The Hoch Verdict," *Chicago Tribune*, May 21, 1905.

25. *Chicago Tribune*, June 4, 1905.

26. Although Hoch engaged a literary agent to shepherd his memoir through publication, it was never published. It is not known whether the manuscript was

claimed by Amelia Fischer following Hoch's execution or filed away in a forgotten archive in Chicago's evidence warehouse, although the latter scenario seems unlikely given the lengthy passage of time.

27. *Chicago Post*, February 16, 1906.

28. *Chicago Tribune*, June 18, 1905.

29. *Chicago Tribune*, July 28, 1905.

30. *Chicago Tribune*, July 29, 1905.

31. McNamara, "Drama in the Death House."

32. Frank Comerford (1877–1929) doomed his budding political career at the age of twenty-eight when he boldly accused two downstate Illinois legislators of bribery during a lecture to students at the Illinois College of Law on January 27, 1905. Comerford said he had conclusive proof that Richard Kinsella, who represented the Democratic caucus, bribed Democratic legislator W.S. Lurton of Jacksonville, Illinois, with $250 to withhold his vote on a piece of legislation. Comerford was a freshman lawmaker who lacked allies and sufficient influence within his own party to present his evidence before the bar of the House with any degree of hope that these charges might be properly investigated. He was branded a publicity seeking opportunist and summarily expelled on a trumped-up charge of slandering the Illinois General Assembly in what amounted to a "star chamber" proceeding—named after a former English court that became notorious for its arbitrary methods and severe punishments. Fellow Democrats deemed it prudent for the sake of their own political futures to vote against this young upstart who had attended the public schools in Chicago and lived with his mother on the West Side. His eloquence as a public speaker early on in his career earned him the sobriquet "The Boy Orator." After the politically motivated expulsion, Chicago Mayor Edward Dunne named him police attorney. Comerford continued his attacks against entrenched legislators from the bully pulpit and was later returned to the Illinois House by his constituents in a special election held in 1906, only to be defeated in his reelection bid a year later. He ran for Lieutenant Governor in 1912, attacking the "boss" system of the Democratic Party, but was unsuccessful in his bid. At the time of his death in August 1929, Comerford was a sitting judge in the Cook County Criminal Court. For a fine overview of his career, see James Doherty's "Chicago's Boy Orator Who Whipped the Gangsters," *Chicago Tribune*, March 9, 1952. See also "Move to Expel Graft Accuser," *Chicago Tribune*, February 1, 1905; and the *Minneapolis Tribune*, February 9, 1905.

33. *Chicago Journal*, February 1, 1906.

34. Ibid.

35. Lochinvar was the hero of a ballad included in the narrative poem *Marmion* (1808) by Sir Walter Scott.

36. Supreme Court of Illinois, October 1905 Term. Transcript of Appeal, p.263. Copy on file at the Chicago History Museum Library.

37. Murray, *The Madhouse on Madison Street*, 7.

38. *Chicago Tribune*, December 16, 1905.

39. Bright's disease is the historical classification for kidney disease that would be described in modern terms as nephritis, or chronic inflammation of the blood vessels of the kidneys. It was named after Dr. Richard Bright (1789–1858), who described the condition in the mid-nineteenth century.

40. Decision of the Illinois State Board of Pardons, Illinois State Archives, Institutional Jackets, 1893–1965, 403.002, Springfield, IL. The three-member State Board of Pardons was created in 1897. Prior to this time, all parole activity was handled by

the commissioners of the penitentiary while applications for executive clemency went directly to the Office of the Governor. The State Board of Pardons was abolished in 1917, and its paroling and pardoning responsibilities were transferred to the Division of Pardons and Paroles in the Department of Public Welfare.

41. *Chicago Post*, February 21, 1906.

42. John L. Whitman was the head jailer at the Cook County lockup from 1895 to 1907. He later served as superintendent of Illinois State Prisons under Governor Frank Lowden, then later as warden of the Stateville Penitentiary in Joliet.

43. *Chicago American*, February 23, 1906. August Spies, Albert Parsons, Adolph Fischer, and George Engel, the four men convicted of complicity in the Haymarket riot of May 4, 1886, were executed in the county jail on November 11, 1887.

44. Kenesaw Mountain Landis (1866–1944) was appointed a federal judge for the Northern District of Illinois by President Theodore Roosevelt on March 18, 1905. In 1907 he presided over the anti-trust case against Standard Oil Company, assessing them a $29 million fine for accepting illegal freight rail rebates. This and many other draconian Landis verdicts were later overturned on appeal. Small of stature and never weighing more than 150 pounds, Landis was nevertheless a striking figure with a commanding presence. In November 1920 he accepted the appointment of Commissioner of Major League Baseball, a post he held continuously until his death from a heart attack at St. Luke's Hospital in Chicago at age 78.

45. *Chicago Tribune, Chicago Post*, February 23, 1906.

46. *Chicago Inter-Ocean*, February 24, 1906.

Chapter Fourteen

1. With a mixture of amusement and horror, "Bluebeard's Mansion" was the name given to the modest cottage at 6430 S. Union Avenue by the old-timers of Englewood who remembered Johann Hoch entertaining Marie Walcker, Amelia Fischer, and a bevy of other lady friends. On May 26, 1954, the *Southtown Economist* reported that the wrecking ball had leveled the sinister old relic to make way for a $1.5-million off-street parking facility. There was no truth to a popular neighborhood legend that skeletal remains of one of Johann Hoch's victims were found between the walls. *Chicago Journal*, February 23, 1906.

2. *Chicago Tribune*, February 26, 1906.

3. The *American* became a tabloid in 1969 and was rechristened *Chicago Today*. That paper folded in 1974.

4. "Women Are Easy Says Carlton," *Washington Times*, July 31, 1905; also, "No Case Against Carlton," *New York Times*, July 14, 1905.

5. "Bigamist Get's 19 Years," *Arizona Journal-Miner*, October 2, 1905. See also the *Chicago American*, July 24 and August 3, 1905.

6. "Bigamy His Business," *New York Times*, August 25, 1905; *New York Daily Tribune*, August 27, 1905; *The Bystander*, September 6, 1905, No. 92, Vol. 6, p. 469.

7. *Auburn (N.Y) Democrat*, February 14, 1908.

8. *Chicago Tribune*, June 20, 1908. Newswire special to the *Chicago Tribune*.

9. "Chicago Wife of Witzhoff Says Bigamist Robbed Her but is a Fine Gentleman," *Chicago Examiner*, February 15, 1908. In this account Witzhoff's first name is Arthur, not George.

10. Chief Shippy and City of Chicago Corporation Counsel Avery Brundage

refused to issue the permit, and Goldman was unable to find a landlord willing to rent her a hall following the slaying of the priest. According to information gleaned from informants, Goldman and her supporters had decided on a strategy of planned assassinations as a way to foment social unrest within the community. The police and city officials were cognizant of the murders of three police officers killed in a recent street melee in Philadelphia by avowed anarchists and the threat these people posed to the maintenance of civil order. The chief saw no good reason to tempt the fates by issuing them a permit.

11. The author rediscovered this long buried and forgotten episode from Chicago police history during research for his book *To Serve & Collect: Chicago Politics and Police Corruption from the Lager Beer Riot to the Summerdale Scandal, 1880–1960* (see pp. 104–5), originally published by Praeger of Westport, CT. in 1990, then later in paperback by Southern Illinois University Press in 1998. The story remained forgotten until 2008 when Aleksandar Heman authored his novel *The Lazarus Project*, which paints a sympathetic portrait of Averbuch while casting George Shippy into the stereotypical role of police oppressor and the murderer of an unarmed working class man.

In our modern-day culture of victimology, it is always the simpler solution to find the greater evil lurking in diabolical conspiracies and attach wrong-doing to the policing agency or the government by applying twenty-first century notions of political correctness to people and events occurring over 100 years earlier than dissecting the historical record in an impartial manner. In this view of the world there are no perpetrators, only victims. Because Averbuch was one of society's "down-and-outers"—ragged, poor, and presumably filled with strong political conviction—he emerges as a hero of the left. The author of the *Lazarus Project* presumes to believe that a vicious police state succeeded in covering up evidence of a wanton murder of a young and naive "idealist" by a powerful police official—but he ignores or simply chooses to overlook the historic backdrop and events that were fresh in the public mind in 1908.

First there was the murder of the Denver priest, then anarchist rioting in Philadelphia. The memory of the deaths of seven police officers slain by an anarchist bomb in the Haymarket Riot of 1886; the 1881 assassination of a Russian monarch by revolutionaries; the attack against Pittsburgh industrialist Henry Frick and the slaying of President William McKinley in 1901 (both committed by Emma Goldman fanatics); and a lengthy record of violent incidents carried out by the anarchist movement since the 1870s understandably contributed to a climate of fear and paranoia in Chicago and across the country.

Moreover, Shippy's life had been recently threatened by radical elements, and he was warned that a gunman would be out to get him. It seems not entirely believable to suggest that Averbuch rang Shippy's doorbell for innocent reasons or that Shippy's son was shot by his father in the struggle with Averbuch, resulting in a conspiracy of silence and the death of an innocent "martyr" on the political left.

12. Edward Baumann, *May God Have Mercy on Your Soul: The Story of the Rope and the Thunderbolt* (Chicago: Bonus Books, 1993). The number of Cook County Jail executions (97, 1873–1929) cited by Baumann in his appendices may or may not be accurate. According to the author, he relied on published newspaper accounts that provided the date of each previous execution, and he worked his way backward from the most recent.

13. *Southtown Economist*, May 26, 1954.

Chapter Fifteen

1. *Chicago Tribune*, May 8, 1931; *LaPorte Herald-Argus*, April 29, 1931.
2. Author interview with Dr. Stephen Nawrocki (board-certified forensic anthropologist and tenured professor of biology and anthropology at the University of Indianapolis), January 25, 2010.
3. Author interview with Andrea Simmons (historian, Indianapolis attorney, and native of LaPorte), January 26, 2010.
4. *LaPorte Daily Herald*, May 5, 1916.
5. *LaPorte Argus-Bulletin*, May 8, 1916.
6. Surprisingly, museums and museum displays profiling predatory criminals are not uncommon. In Cherryvale, Kansas, a Bender Family Museum with personal artifacts from their 1870s murder spree was open to the public and on display from 1961 to 1978. For several years Cherryvale sponsored an annual Bender Days event until adverse public opinion cancelled the affair. Joe Pinkston operated the John Dillinger Museum, a fixture in the bed-and-breakfast community of Nashville, Indiana, for two decades. He eventually relocated his exhibits to Hammond. The 40 Whacks Museum in Salem, Massachusetts, occupies 3,000 square feet of exhibit space dedicated to retelling the story of the August 4, 1892, Fall River slayings of Andrew Borden and his wife, Abby Durfee Borden, by the spinster Lizzie Borden (daughter of Andrew and stepdaughter of Abby), who, like Belle Gunness, also inspired a famous limerick and whose heinous crime eventually became a grisly part of American folklore.
7. The Davison Patton Cemetery was once known as Walker Cemetery after John Walker, one of the city's founders who set aside a plot of farmland on his property for the burial of family members. Walker began selling lots to the public in 1856 through a public consortium known as the Pine Lake Cemetery Association. For years the burial ground was alternately known as the Pine Lake Cemetery. See the *LaPorte Herald-Argus,* May 27, 1932.
8. Langlois, *The Lady Bluebeard*, 31.
9. Ibid., 81.
10. Simmons interview, January 26, 2010.
11. Author interview with Kay Henderson (Chicago writer and historian), January 26, 2010
12. *Chicago Daily News*, May 8, 1908. See also "Gold and More Gold! Goal of Hoch and Mrs. Bella Gunness," *The Chicago American,* May 9, 1908.

Bibliography

Books

Alt, Betty, and Sandra Wells. *Wicked Women: Black Widows, Child Killers and Other Women in Crime*. Boulder, CO: Paladin Press, 2000.

Bass, Arnold. *Up Close and Personal: A History of La Porte County*. Bloomington, IN: Author House, 2006.

Baumann, Edward. *May God Have Mercy on Your Soul: The Story of the Rope and the Thunderbolt*. Chicago: Bonus Books, 1993.

Boessenecker, John. *Lawman: The Life and Times of Harry Morse, 1835–1912*. Norman: University of Oklahoma Press, 1998.

Daniels, E.D., ed. *A Twentieth Century History & Biographical Record of La Porte County, Indiana*. New York: Lewis Publishing Co., 1904.

Duke, Thomas Samuel. *Celebrated Criminal Cases of America*. San Francisco: The James H. Barry Co., 1910.

Franke, David. *The Torture Doctor*. New York: Hawthorn Books, 1975.

Hendricksen, Millie. *History of the Norwegian Lutheran Children's Home Society, Edison Park, Chicago, Illinois, 1896–1936*. Chicago: Norwegian Lutheran Children's Home Society, 1936.

Lakeside Annual Directory of the City of Chicago: 1895. Chicago, IL: The Chicago Directory Company.

Lakeside Annual Directory of the City of Chicago: 1900. Chicago, IL: The Chicago Directory Company.

Langlois, Janet L. *Belle Gunness: The Lady Bluebeard*. Bloomington: Indiana University Press, 1985.

La Porte Now and Then: 1832–1982. The La Porte Sesquicentennial Commission, 1982.

Lindberg, Richard. *Chicago Ragtime: Another Look at Chicago 1880–1920*. South Bend, IN: Icarus Press, 1985.

———. *To Serve & Collect: Chicago Politics and Police Corruption from the Lager Beer Riot to the Summerdale Scandal, 1855–1960*. Carbondale: Southern Illinois University Press, 1998.

Lovoll, Odd S., *A Century of Urban Life: The Norwegians in Chicago before 1930*. Northfield, MN: The Norwegian-American Historical Association, 1988.

Lundberg, Ferdinand. *Imperial Hearst: A Social Biography*. New York: Equinox Cooperative Press, 1936.

The Mrs. Gunness Mystery: A Thrilling Tale of Love, Duplicity and Crime. Chicago: Thompson and Thomas, 1908.

Murray, George. *The Madhouse on Madison Street*. Chicago: Follett Publishing Co., 1965.

Nasaw, David. *The Chief: The Life of William Randolph Hearst*. Boston: Houghton Mifflin, 2000.

Packard, Jasper, *History of La Porte County, Indiana, and Its Townships, Towns and Cities*. La Porte, IN: S. E. Taylor & Company, 1876. Transcribed for La Porte County Gen Web by Christine Scott, February 27, 2006. Reprinted chapters in <http://www.dunelady.com/laporte/all_histories.htm>.

Pistorius, Micki. *Fatal Females: Women Who Kill*. Johannesburg: Penguin Books, 2004.

Shepherd, Sylvia Elizabeth. *The Mistress of Murder Hill: The Serial Killings of Belle Gunness*. Indiana: 1st Books Library, 2001.

Vronsky, Peter. *Female Serial Killers: How and Why Women Become Monsters*. New York: Berkley Books, 2007.

———. *Serial Killers: The Method and Madness of Monsters*. New York: Berkley Books, 2004.

Articles

Baumann, Edward, and John O'Brien. "Hell's Belle." *Chicago Tribune Magazine* (March 1, 1987).

"Belle Gunness: Wholesale Murderer?" *The Sunday-Record Herald* (May 10, 1908).

Blodgett, William H. "Gunness Story as Told By Blodgett." *LaPorte Daily Herald-Argus* (July 23, 1930).

Cipriani, Frank. "Madame Bluebeard! The Crimes of Belle Gunness of Indiana's Murder Farm." *Chicago Tribune* (April 12, 1936).

———. "Murder Castle!" *Chicago Tribune* (March 21, 1937).

Fluharty, Linda Cunningham. "Caroline Miller Hoch Huff: Victim of a Serial Killer." <http://www.lindapages.com/wags-ohio/carolinehoch.htm>

Henning, Arthur Sears. "A Newspaper Era Comes to Life." *Chicago Tribune* (September 8, 1953).

Hoch, Johann. "How I Married 50 Wives and What Became of Them." *American Magazine. Supplement to the Chicago Sunday American* (July 23, 1905).

Lovoll, Odd S. "*The Decorah Posten*: Story of an Immigrant Newspaper." *Norwegian-American Studies*, vol. 27, online resource at: www.naha.stolaf.edu/pubsnas/volume27_5.htm, pg. 77

Maslow, Abraham. "A Theory of Human Motivation." *Psychological Review*, vol.50, no. 4 (1943): 370–96.

McNamara, Dr. Francis W. "Drama in the Death House: The Crimes of Johann Hoch the Bluebeard." *Chicago Tribune* (December 13, 1936.)

"Murder—Will it Always Out as a General Rule?" *Chicago Tribune* (November 9, 1913).

Reynolds, Ruth. "Was Justice Done?" *Chicago American* (February 12, 1961).

Schutzer, A.L. "The Lady Killer." *American Heritage Magazine*, vol. 15, issue 6, (October 1964): 36–39, 91–94..

Smith, Gene. "The National Police Gazette: A Visit to the Lower Depths." *American Heritage Magazine* vol. 23, no. 6 (October 1972).

Pamphlets, Documents, Unpublished Materials

Archives of the Evangelical Lutheran Church in America <http://www2.elca.org/archives/chicagochurches/bethania.html>

Belle Gunness, Written Correspondence, 1906–1908. LaPorte County, Indiana, Historical Society.

Coffeen, Robert F. "The Gunness Murder Mystery: Back for the 25th Time—Gunness Anniversary." LaPorte County Public Library Collection, LaPorte, Indiana.

Deposition of Witnesses by the Coroner of LaPorte County, Indiana. Exhibit A–E, May 1908. LaPorte County Indiana Historical Society.

"The Gunness Story." Undated pamphlet. La Porte County, Indiana, Historical Society.

"In the Supreme Court of Illinois, October Term 1903. Brief and Argument for the Plaintiff." Chicago History Museum Collection, Chicago, Illinois.

Simmons, Andrea. "Transcription of La Porte County Coroner Charles Mack's May 1908 Inquisition." September 23, 2006. La Porte County, Indiana, Historical Society.

Newspapers

Auburn (N.Y) Democrat

The Bystander

Chicago American

Chicago Chronicle

Chicago Daily News

Chicago Examiner

Chicago Inter-Ocean

Chicago Journal

Chicago Evening Post

Chicago Record

Chicago Record-Herald

Chicago Tribune

Duluth News-Tribune

Kansas City Times

LaPorte Argus-Bulletin

LaPorte Daily Herald

LaPorte Daily Herald-Argus

New York Daily Tribune

New York Herald

New York Post

New York Times

Southtown Economist

Washington Times

Wheeling Register

Index

About the Author

Richard Lindberg is a noted Chicago historian and the author of fourteen books, including *The Gambler King of Clark Street: Michael C. McDonald and the Rise of Chicago's Democratic Machine*, winner of the 2010 Society of Midland Authors Award for the top biography of 2009, and recipient of a Certificate of Excellence from the Illinois State Historical Society. In addition he has authored *Chicago Yesterday & Today*; *Shattered Sense of Innocence: The 1955 Murders of Three Chicago Children*; *To Serve & Collect: Chicago Politics & Police Corruption from the Lager Beer Riot to the Summerdale Scandal*; *Return to the Scene of the Crime: A Guide to Infamous Places in Chicago*; *Passport's Guide to Ethnic Chicago*; *Total White Sox*; and *Chicago Ragtime: Another Look at Chicago, 1880–1920*. He has provided commentary and historical interpretation on numerous local and national radio and television programs, including *American Justice, Cities of the Underworld, History's Mysteries, Masterminds, Deadly Women, Mobsters,* and National Public Radio's *All Things Considered*. Lindberg is a past president of the Society of Midland Authors and a 2008 recipient of the Morris J. Wexler Award from the Illinois Academy of Criminology.